D1100634

Risk Management in Sport and Recreation

John O. Spengler, JD, PhD

University of Florida

Daniel P. Connaughton, EdD

University of Florida

Andrew T. Pittman, PhD

Baylor University

HUMAN KINETICS

Library of Congress Cataloging-in-Publication Data

Spengler, John O. (John Otto), 1962-
  Risk management in sport and recreation / John O. Spengler, Daniel P.
Connaughton, Andrew T. Pittman.
      p. cm.
  Includes bibliographical referencs and index.
  ISBN 0-7360-5619-X (soft cover : alk. paper)   1.   Sports--Safety measures. 2.
Sports injuries--Prevention. 3.   Sports medicine.   I. Connaughton, Daniel, 1963-
II. Pittman, Andrew T., 1945- III. Title.
  GV344.S64 2005
  796'.028'9--dc22

                                        2005022308

ISBN-10: 0-7360-5619-X
ISBN-13: 978-0-7360-5619-9

The Web addresses cited in this text were current as of December 1, 2005, unless otherwise noted.

Acquisitions Editor: Myles Schrag; **Developmental Editor:** Amanda S. Ewing; **Assistant Editor:** Bethany J. Bentley; **Copyeditor:** Andrew Smith; **Proofreader:** Julie Marx Goodreau; **Permission Manager:** Carly Breeding; **Graphic Designer:** Robert Reuther; **Graphic Artist:** Denise Lowry; **Photo Manager:** Sarah Ritz; **Cover Designer:** Keith Blomberg; **Photographer (interior):** Sarah Ritz, except where otherwise noted; photo on page 19 by Kelly J. Huff; **Art Manager:** Kelly Hendren; **Illustrator:** Tim Offenstein; **Printer:** Versa Press

Printed in the United States of America   10   9   8   7   6   5   4   3   2

Human Kinetics
Web site: www.HumanKinetics.com

United States: Human Kinetics, P.O. Box 5076, Champaign, IL 61825-5076
800-747-4457
e-mail: humank@hkusa.com

Canada: Human Kinetics, 475 Devonshire Road, Unit 100, Windsor, ON N8Y 2L5
800-465-7301 (in Canada only)
e-mail: orders@hkcanada.com

Europe: Human Kinetics, 107 Bradford Road, Stanningley
Leeds LS28 6AT, United Kingdom
+44 (0) 113 255 5665
e-mail: hk@hkeurope.com

Australia: Human Kinetics, 57A Price Avenue, Lower Mitcham, South Australia 5062
08 8372 0999
e-mail: info@hkaustralia.com

New Zealand: Human Kinetics, Division of Sports Distributors NZ Ltd.
P.O. Box 300 226 Albany, North Shore City, Auckland
0064 9 448 1207
e-mail: info@humankinetics.co.nz

*We dedicate this book
to sport and recreation professionals
and to those who aspire
to enter this important field.*

Contents

Foreword **ix** | Preface **xi** | Acknowledgments **xv**

chapter 1 *Decision Making and Managing Risk* *1*

Issues Involved With Managing Risk 2
Threshold Issue 1: Deciding Whether to Create and Implement
  a Risk Management Plan 3
Threshold Issue 2: Developing a Framework for Managing Risk 8
Summary 9

chapter 2 *Medical Emergency Action Plans* *11*

Guidelines and Recommendations 13
Threshold Issue 1: Deciding Whether to Develp and Implement
  a Medical Emergency Action Plan 14
Threshold Issue 2: Understanding Key Aspects of a Medical Emergency
  Action Plan 16
Summary 20

chapter 3 *Protecting Children* *21*

Prevention Strategies for Child Abuse and Neglect 22
Threshold Issue 1: Determining Whether to Develop
  and Implement a Safety Plan to Protect Children 23
Threshold Issue 2: Recognizing Key Issues in Protecting Children
  From Harm by Others 25
Summary 28

chapter 4 *Exertional Heat Illness in Sport and Recreation* *31*

How the Body Handles Heat During Exercise 32
Heat Index 33
Types of Heat Illnesses 33
Guidelines and Recommendations 35
Threshold Issue 1: Deciding Whether to Develop and Implement a Heat
  Illness Plan 37
Threshold Issue 2: Recognizing Key Issues in Developing a Heat
  Illness Plan 38
Summary 40

chapter 5 *Lightning Safety* *41*

Importance of Lightning Safety 42
Guidelines and Recommendations 42

Threshold Issue 1: Deciding Whether to Develop and Implement
a Lightning Safety Plan 43
Threshold Issue 2: Including Necessary Components in a Lightning
Safety Plan 46
Summary 49

chapter 6   **Bloodborne Pathogens** **51**

Definition of Bloodborne Pathogens 52
Threshold Issue 1: Understanding Compliance Issues Relevant to
OSHA's Bloodborne Pathogens Standard 52
Threshold Issue 2: Understanding Key Aspects of OSHA's Bloodborne
Pathogens Standard 53
Summary 55

chapter 7   **Sudden Cardiac Arrest and the Use of Automated
External Defibrillators** **57**

What Is an AED? 58
Guidelines and Recommendations 59
Threshold Issue 1: Understanding Issues Relevant to the Purchase and Use
of AEDs 59
Threshold Issue 2: Understanding What to Consider When Using AEDs 62
Summary 64

chapter 8   **Drug Testing** **67**

Threshold Issue 1: Understanding the Legality of Developing
and Implementing a Drug Testing Plan 69
Threshold Issue 2: Recognizing Effective Components of a Drug Testing Plan 73
Summary 76

chapter 9   **Equipment, Premises, Instruction, and Supervision** **79**

Threshold Issue 1: Understanding Issues Relevant to Maintaining and Providing
Proper Equipment and Premises 80
Threshold Issue 2: Recognizing Key Issues in Providing Adequate Instruction
and Supervision 85
Summary 88

chapter 10   **Playground Safety** **91**

Playground Injuries 92
Guidelines and Recommendations 92
Threshold Issue 1: Deciding Whether to Comply With CPSC and ASTM Guidelines
and Standards 92
Threshold Issue 2: Knowing the Key Issues of the CPSC and ASTM Guidelines
and Standards 95
Summary 98

chapter 11   **Aquatic Safety** **101**

Types of Aquatic Incidents 102
Guidelines and Recommendations 104
Threshold Issue 1: Understanding Compliance Issues Relevant to Local, State,
and Federal Laws and Codes 105
Threshold Issue 2: Recognizing Key Issues in Aquatic Program Safety 106
Summary 111

Appendix A   Additional Information for Sport and Recreation Managers 113

Appendix B   Safety Guidelines Finder 149

References **163**   About the Authors **167**

Foreword

I am honored to write the foreword to a textbook written by colleagues who are scholars in sport and recreation risk management and are truly professional in all of their activities in academia and the sport and recreation industry.

I compliment the authors for tackling the topic of risk management for sport and recreation and adding to the limited number of resources in this area. Most textbooks on sport and recreation law devote a segment of the text to the subject but do not give it the attention it undoubtedly deserves. By contrast, *Risk Management in Sport and Recreation* raises key issues while guiding the reader through problems associated with them and the development of risk management strategies and plans. The text takes a practical approach by introducing a topic, sharing the research on it, and providing a step-by-step approach to managing risk in that area. Helpful comparisons of various recommended practices are likewise provided. Topics include such diverse areas as planning for medical emergencies; dealing with lightning, heart ailments, heat exhaustion, exposure to bloodborne pathogens, and aquatic safety; implementing drug testing; protecting children; and playground safety. What is truly unique about *Risk Management in Sport and Recreation* is that it specifically focuses on the medical and technical knowledge required for effective management of risk in sport and recreation and it brings a variety of policies, guidelines, and standards together in one location.

The predominant goal in teaching sport law to students and practitioners of sport management is, in fact, to teach them to manage risk. As a professor of sport law in a department of sport management at the University of Massachusetts, my role is to teach students to manage risk when they enter the business of sport. My primary concern is to help them to apply the legal and managerial concepts they learn in order to prevent injuries and limit liability. This plays an instrumental part in creating a safe environment for sport and recreation. *Risk Management in Sport and Recreation* serves my educational needs. At the same time, the book meets the needs of practitioners who must determine their exposure to risk and respond with an action plan. Thus, it will make a useful desk copy for the practitioner.

I trust *Risk Management in Sport and Recreation* will be useful to your needs as a student or practitioner of sport or recreation management.

—Lisa Pike Masteralexis

Preface

Finally, there is a book that takes a multidisciplinary approach to risk management. *Risk Management in Sport and Recreation* bridges the gap between sport, recreation, medical, and technical sources. After reading this book, you will know where to look for safety guidelines and standards on topics as diverse as movable soccer goals and lightning safety. During our extensive experience in working with practitioners through consulting and outreach activities, and through our teaching and research, we became aware of a serious void. The problem we discovered was that the sources for standards for many important issues in sport and recreation are scattered and difficult for practitioners to find. For example, were you aware that lightning safety recommendations for *recreation* are put forth by the National Athletic Trainers' Association, or that safety guidelines for *sport and recreation* activities involving youth are provided by organizations such as the American Academy of Orthopaedic Surgeons and the American Academy of Pediatrics?

Risk Management in Sport and Recreation will show you where to find relevant guidelines and standards and will assist you in understanding the issues important to implementing safety procedures, if you choose to do so. It is an excellent resource for all organizations that provide opportunities to participate in sport, recreation, and physical activity. These include resort managers, physical educators, camp directors, park and recreation professionals, fitness managers, coaches, athletic directors, and sport supervisors. The book is also a great resource for students, either as a primary text in a risk management course or as a supplemental text in sport and recreation law courses.

Organization of the Text

If you are a practitioner of sport and recreation, *Risk Management in Sport and Recreation* is organized in a manner that allows you to access information relevant to you in an efficient way. Additionally, if you are a student, this text provides a vehicle for generating thought and discussion on key risk management issues. Each chapter focuses specifically on issues that are applicable in the field of sport and recreation, including risk management; emergency medical planning; protecting children; dealing with heat-related illness, lightning safety, and bloodborne pathogens; operating automated external defibrillators; implementing drug testing; and addressing matters regarding equipment and contact sports, the safety of play areas, and aquatic safety. Within each chapter, you will also find links to informative Web sites and information designed to aid the decision-making process of improving safety and managing risk.

All chapters are organized in an easy-to-follow format. First, chapter objectives outline the chapter's key issues. Introductory material is then presented that defines the topic and explains its importance to the field from the standpoint of safety and risk. This is followed by information that addresses how and under what situations to implement a management and safety plan. A short summary wraps up the key issues of the chapter. Finally, a hypothetical real-world scenario shows how practitioners in various fields would identify the need for a plan and outlines the issues they should consider when implementing a plan. A number of follow-up questions are also provided. The scenarios are designed to generate thought and assist you with viewing the topic in a practical way.

Unique Features

Risk Management in Sport and Recreation contains several unique features designed to move you easily through the text to the key concepts and information most useful to you. One important feature is the key points. Throughout the text, key points are highlighted in text boxes. As the name implies, these points provide the reader with information that stresses the importance of the topic and matters related to it. Key points may take the form of statistics or other information that demonstrates the relevance of the topic to the sport and recreation profession.

A second unique feature of each chapter is what we have termed "threshold issues." We chose this moniker because the text is focused on presenting issues and information that will assist you in making your *own* decisions regarding risk management. We are not providing templates for managing risk or giving a final word on whether or how plans should be implemented. These are decisions that each person must make given his or her own situation. The threshold issues are designed simply to help in the decision-making process. The first threshold issue in each chapter presents matters to consider when determining whether to implement safety plans and procedures. Threshold issues that are addressed include (but are not limited to) liability, ethical questions, and management concerns (such as administrative support and cost). The specifics of each issue will vary given the nature of the topic presented in each chapter. A second threshold issue in each chapter presents information that will assist you in developing a safety plan and procedures. This is where information relevant to the applicable guidelines and standards comes into play. You can access this information through the sources within each chapter and through the safety guidelines finder.

A third feature of *Risk Management in Sport and Recreation* is the real-world scenarios presented at the end of each chapter. These are hypothetical situations that place the topic covered in the chapter in a practical context. The scenarios do not describe circumstances in which, for example, a lawsuit results from an injury to a participant in a sport or recreation event. Instead, they are designed to elicit critical thought regarding the concerns discussed in the chapter. Therefore, they illustrate situations in which the potential for harm exists and a manager must make a decision about how he or she will face the particular safety issue presented. Each scenario is followed by questions that are designed to allow you to apply what has been learned in the chapter to your own situation.

This text also contains two appendixes. Appendix A, *Additional Information for Sport and Recreation Managers*, offers several examples of emergency action plans, checklists, and recommendations from organizations as varied as the Centers for Disease Control and Prevention, the National Lightning Safety Institute, and university aquatic centers. You may want to refer to this appendix for guidance as you create action plans for your organization. Appendix B, a safety guidelines finder, is outlined in more detail in the next section.

Finally, this book also has a companion Web site that provides links to the many Web sites listed in this text, as well as links to new or updated safety guidelines. More information on the companion Web site can be found on page xiii.

Using the Safety Guidelines Finder

The safety guidelines finder in appendix B is your source for locating and linking to safety guidelines, recommendations, and standards for programs and activities in sport and recreation. It is organized under two headings: water-based activities and land-based activities.

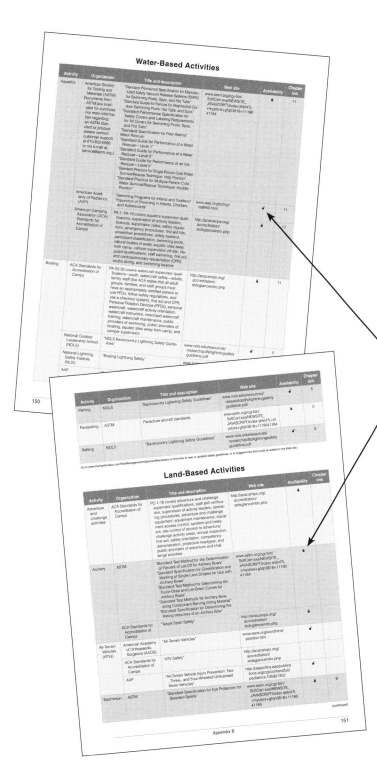

example, for baseball, the safety guidelines finder provides a reference to standards for bats, face guards, eye protection, and so on. The source of these standards is provided (by, for example, the American Society for Testing and Materials [ASTM]) along with a brief description or title of an applicable recommendation or guideline. For complete published guidelines, Web sites that contain the relevant materials or information regarding how to access them are provided. Please note that the tables within the chapters contain both home pages and more specific Web pages to direct you to the source. Much of this information is available for download free of charge. However, some information (such as that provided by the ASTM) is available for a fee.

- ⚙ = Available as a free download
- 🔒 = Information available for a fee or must be ordered

The table also identifies what chapters in this book contain additional information on safety issues relevant to the activity.

Using the Companion Web Site

The companion Web site will make it much easier for you to access the myriad Web sites used throughout the book. To access the companion Web site, go to the following address: www.HumanKinetics.com/RiskManagement InSportAndRecreation

To enter the Web site, please use the following password: riskmanagementwebsites

Once you've entered the site, you'll notice that it is broken down into several sections. They are the following:

- New and Updated Sites
- Chapter-by-Chapter Sites
- Safety Guidelines Finder

Each section is then further broken down to make it easier to find the Web site you wish to access.

Under each heading you will find activities listed alphabetically in the left-hand column. For each activity, you will then find a reference to guidelines, recommendations, and standards that apply to some aspect of that activity. For

Final Comments

Each chapter, as well as the appendixes, is of value from both a practical and an educational standpoint. The text points you toward relevant information while also providing considerable food for thought regarding how to approach key safety issues. These tools will help you to take the essential first step toward gathering information and addressing the basic issues related to managing risk. The material presented in *Risk Management in Sport and Recreation* is not intended as a substitute for appropriate training and certification, nor is it meant to provide specific medical or legal advice. Yet, armed with the information provided here, as well as with the advice of a competent lawyer or other source of authority, you will be better able to make informed decisions regarding the implementation of safety measures for your program and facility.

Disclaimer

This book, the tables, templates, and other information provided herein is intended to serve as a guide to the development of risk management practices. Legal, medical, and administrative issues relevant to managing risk can be complex and specific to individual agencies and organizations. In addition, state laws are subject to change by the legislature and by the courts of the United States and individual states. This book should not be used as a substitute for professional advice by qualified legal counsel, nor should it be used as a substitute for specific professional or medical training or certification. Managers should seek the advice of counsel concerning issues that have legal consequences.

Acknowledgments

I would like to thank my wife, Mariah, for her love and support throughout the time I worked on this book and my daughter, Caroline, who brings joy to my life every day. I also would like to thank my parents for their endless encouragement and support. Many thanks as well to Myles Schrag, Amy Tocco, and Amanda Ewing at Human Kinetics for their tireless efforts as we journeyed from concept development to the finished product.

—J.O. Spengler

I would like to recognize and thank my wife, Angela, and my parents for their love and support. It was a pleasure to work with my dedicated coauthors and the professional, hard-working staff at Human Kinetics.

—Dan Connaughton

I would like to thank J.O. and Dan for their friendship, support, and assistance during a challenging time that happened to coincide with the writing of this book. It is during those times when you really appreciate your colleagues. Also I would like to thank the staff at Human Kinetics for encouraging us and guiding us through to the finished product.

—Andy Pittman

Decision Making and Managing Risk

chapter objectives

After reading this chapter, you will have a thorough understanding of the following:

Threshold Issue 1: Deciding Whether to Create and Implement a Risk Management Plan
Threshold Issue 2: Developing a Framework for Managing Risk

The purpose of this text is to assist you in making decisions that will help you reduce both the risk of injury and death to participants, spectators, and staff, as well as the potential for lawsuits. This is the essence of risk management. When risk is managed well, everyone benefits. Developing an understanding of relevant guidelines and safety standards and learning how to access information and resources are part of the first step in managing risk. This chapter is intended to help you as you take this step. Table 1.1 provides a sample list of a number of organizations that play a prominent role in sport and recreation safety and whose standards and guidelines are provided throughout this book. Can you guess which of these organizations has recommendations relevant to soccer goals, playgrounds, heat illness, or lightning safety? Without prior knowledge, it is very difficult to tell. *Risk Management in Sport and Recreation* will show you how to access just this sort of information. Knowledge of safety standards and guidelines is an essential part of managing risk. The chapters that follow will help you use this knowledge both in determining whether to implement risk management plans and in determining how to do so. By the time you are finished with the book, you should have a good sense of the numerous issues to consider in managing risk.

> Knowledge of safety standards and guidelines is an essential part of effectively managing risk.

Table 1.1 Safety Standards and Guidelines From Selected Organizations

Organization	Abbreviation	Availability of publications	Home page
American Academy of Orthopaedic Surgeons	AAOS	Available online	www.aaos.org
American Academy of Pediatrics	AAP	Available online	www.aap.org
American Camping Association	ACA	Must order	www.acacamps.org
American College of Sports Medicine	ACSM	Available online	www.acsm.org
American Society for Testing and Materials	ASTM	Must order	www.astm.org
Consumer Product Safety Commission	CPSC	Available online	www.cpsc.gov
National Athletic Trainers' Association	NATA	Available online	www.nata.org
National Collegiate Athletic Association	NCAA	Available online	www2.ncaa.org
National Outdoor Leadership School	NOLS	Available online	www.nols.edu
U.S. Department of Education	USDOE	Available online	www.ed.gov

Issues Involved With Managing Risk

Most fundamentally, risk management entails reducing or eliminating the risk of injury and death and potential subsequent liability that comes about through involvement with sport and recreation programs and services. Carrying out an effective risk management plan requires making several important decisions. The first such decision to be made is whether to create and implement a risk management plan at all. This is discussed in Threshold Issue 1. It would be unwise to simply ignore potential risks given one's ethical and legal responsibilities to those under his or her care. However, practical issues do exist that must be addressed before implementing risk management plans or procedures. If an organization decides to implement a plan, then another series of decisions must be made. How best to do so is discussed later in Threshold Issue 2.

Threshold Issue 1: Deciding Whether to Create and Implement a Risk Management Plan

The first decision to make in managing risk is whether to take action. Some important considerations in determining whether to implement safety plans or procedures are listed here.

Statutory Requirements

In some states, it is required by law that sport and recreation organizations implement safety measures or comply with certain safety standards. For example, it may be the case that schools, park districts, and even health and fitness clubs have automated external defibrillators (AEDs) at their facilities. Or it is possible that compliance with playground safety standards must be met in order for organizations or programs to receive state funding. If required by state law, and compliance is mandatory, the decision regarding whether to implement a particular safety measure has been made for you. It is therefore important to be familiar with—or seek counsel from someone familiar with—laws relevant to your organization and program.

> If required by state law, and compliance is mandatory, the decision regarding whether to implement a particular safety measure has been made for you.

Cost

Many decisions, of necessity, are based on the amount of money available to an organization. For example, whether the organization is capable of having AEDs and planning for their use is dependent, in part, on whether it has the financial resources to purchase them. Where negligence lawsuits are brought against sport or recreation providers for the failure to provide a safe environment, cost and financial burden to the provider is often a factor in the case. Before deciding that safety equipment is not affordable, however, it is important to exhaust all potential funding options. Depending on the type and location of the organization, sometimes grant or subsidy programs are available that reduce or eliminate the cost of complying with safety standards. Some examples of alternative funding sources include donations from local civic organizations or local businesses, government and private grants, public charities, and traditional fund-raising events.

Liability Issues

The potential for being held liable for an injury or death is an important consideration when deciding whether to implement risk management plans or procedures. The issue is often twofold. First, will implementing a risk management plan increase your liability? Second, will it increase your liability if you decide not to implement a risk management plan? There is no definitive answer to either question, but there is information that can guide your decision. As to the first question, case law suggests that your potential liability is likely to increase if you have a safety plan but fail to follow it in an emergency situation and someone under your care is injured or killed. In chapter 5, for example, just this sort of situation is discussed with respect to lightning safety for golf courses. Regarding whether even having a safety plan will increase liability, an important consideration is whether state laws exist that offer protection to your organization in the event of a claim of negligence. Sport safety statutes may exist that shield providers of a variety of recreation and sport opportunities from specific kinds of lawsuits, as well as recreation land-use statutes that offer protection to land owners (public and private) for use of property for recreational purposes, Good Samaritan statutes, and laws addressed specifically to AED users and providers.

In the event that legal information is needed, there are numerous sources of legal information on the Web. The sources listed in table 1.2 provide a sample of selected sites. Most are free of charge but some do require a membership.

Be aware of both community and industry standards when trying to determine whether or not your liability will increase by failing to implement a risk management plan. In other words, you must know what sort of safety measures other

Table 1.2   Sources of Legal Information

Source	Home page	Information
American Bar Association	www.abanet.org	Full use of site restricted to those in legal profession
Courts.net	www.uscourts.gov	Site covers courts in the federal system
FedWorld.gov	www.fedworld.gov	Contains over 7,000 Supreme Court decisions
FindLaw	www.findlaw.com	Has a section available to the public containing information on many aspects of law
FirstGov.gov	www.first.gov/Topics/Reference_ShelfLaws.shtml	Has a section on laws and regulations that contains federal, state, and local laws and regulations
HeinOnline	www.heinonline.org	Source of legal publications
Legal Information Institute	www.law.cornell.edu	Operated by Cornell University; has many helpful links
LexisNexis	www.lexis-nexis.com	An excellent source of information for law and public records
TheLaw.net	www.thelaw.net	An online search service
Sport and Recreation Law Association	http://srlaweb.org	An excellent resource for information regarding legal aspects of sport and recreation
Sports Lawyers Association	www.sportslaw.org	Nonprofit international professional organization
The Library of Congress	www.loc.gov	Information on government legislation
VersusLaw	www.versuslaw.com	A subscription service that provides access to federal and state legislation.
Washburn Legal Research on the Web	www.washlaw.edu	Operated by the Washburn University School of Law; very comprehensive source of legal information
Westlaw	web2.westlaw.com	Excellent source of legal information (predominantly used by the legal profession)

similar organizations are putting into practice and whether these measures have themselves become community or industry standards. This is a primary factor that courts will consider in determining whether or not implementing a risk management plan counts as negligence and therefore whether you would be held liable.

An additional factor is the availability of standards, guidelines, and recommendations set forth by professional associations and recognized authorities in the field. These often have bearing on whether an organization breached its duty of care to its participants by failing to have a risk management plan or adequate safety measures in place.

Yet another factor is case law precedent, or the outcome of prior legal cases. Stay abreast of important case decisions that might have a bearing on your program or service and whether or not you should institute a particular safety measure.

One final factor to consider with respect to determining potential liability when deciding whether to implement a risk management plan is how well a given risk could be foreseen. Foreseeability is based, in part, on prior incidents resulting in injury or death. Ignorance of prior incidents is not a viable excuse if a decision not to address a particular safety measure is made when severe or numerous injuries have occurred before. Consultation with qualified legal counsel should be undertaken when considering all of these issues.

Ethics

In addition to attending to legal concerns, you likewise have an ethical responsibility to provide for the safety and well-being of participants and spectators. When determining whether to implement safety measures, emphasis is often placed on the bottom line—the impact that safety measures would have on financial resources. Yet, the cost of potential injury or death to participants or spectators in the absence of safety plans is obviously of great concern as well. Even in situations in which a plan would

> Even if the law does not specify that there is a need for risk management, you are ethically responsible for providing a reasonably safe environment.

cost an organization more to implement than it would save in terms of protection from lawsuits, there remains an ethical responsibility to provide for the safety and well-being of patrons.

Self-Evaluation

It is also wise for those responsible for safety to examine their personal motivations and consider the source of those motivations. For example, your decision regarding whether to implement a risk management plan for a particular risk category (for example, lightning safety) might be influenced by your perception of risk. Be aware of factors that might influence this perception. Some influences to consider are the following:

1. Your past experiences, such as having had a close encounter with lightning.
2. Your experience on the job, such as having had a child in your program injured on playground equipment.
3. The influence of the media on your perception of risk, such as having read news stories documenting the dangers of failing to have AEDs on hand.

4. The influence of a professional association of which you are a member, such as having participated in panel discussions or attended presentations on swimming pool safety.

5. The influence of friends and colleagues, such as having heard personal anecdotes about the importance of drug testing.

Other Management Concerns

Other management issues exist that shape our decisions as to whether we should implement risk management or safety plans. Consider the time and resources needed for creating and writing a plan, as well as the time and resources needed for training employees to carry out the plan. Other potential management concerns include the following:

- The availability of information necessary to develop a comprehensive plan
- The support from upper management in implementing a new safety measure

Table 1.3   Selected Issues and Information for Risk Management

Issue	Key considerations	Sources	Examples
Statutory requirements	Statutory mandates	Consultation* Publications Web sites	• *Journal of Legal Aspects of Sport,* law reviews • National Conference of State Legislatures: www.ncsl.org
Cost	Budgetary constraints	Manufacturers Grant or subsidy programs	• Information available at conferences (e.g., ACSM; American Alliance for Health, Physical Education, Recreation and Dance; National Recreation and Park Association [NRPA]; etc.), trade shows, Web sites, and literature • Local civic organizations, local businesses, government and private grants, public charities, and traditional fundraising events
Liability concerns	Standards, guidelines and recommendations	Consultation* Relevant agencies and professional associations Publications	• CPSC guidelines for public playground safety • NATA guidelines for lightning safety
	Community or industry standards	Consultation* Research	• Safety measures employed by others providing the same or similar sport and recreation opportunities
	Foreseeability	Consultation* Personal knowledge	• Accident and injury incident reports • Injury and death statistics
	Case law	Consultation* Publications	• *Journal of Legal Aspects of Sport, Parks and Recreation, Journal of Health, Physical Education, Recreation and Dance,* law reviews
	Statutory immunity	Consultation* Publications Web sites	• See selected publications previously listed • For AED immunity, see American Red Cross at www.redcross.org/ services/hss/courses/AEDGoodSamChart2004.pdf and consult state law
Other Management concerns	Knowledge, education, training	Professional association training and certification courses	• American Heart Association for AED training • NRPA playground safety certification
	Insurance	Insurance providers	• Web sites and literature
	Upper management support	Specific to organization	N/A

* Consult with an attorney or other competent professionals.

- Issues related to insurance coverage
- Whether the possibility of an injury or death is too remote to warrant the implementation of safety measures

These concerns should all be considered in relation to the issues mentioned previously. The decision regarding whether to develop and implement a plan is, of course, multifaceted and dependent on the type of hazards (risks) that the plan seeks to address. Table 1.3 provides an overview of issues mentioned in this chapter to assist you in making sound decisions about risk management. The threshold issue of whether to initiate a risk management plan is also illustrated in figure 1.1, which displays the conceptual framework that supports the matters we have been examining.

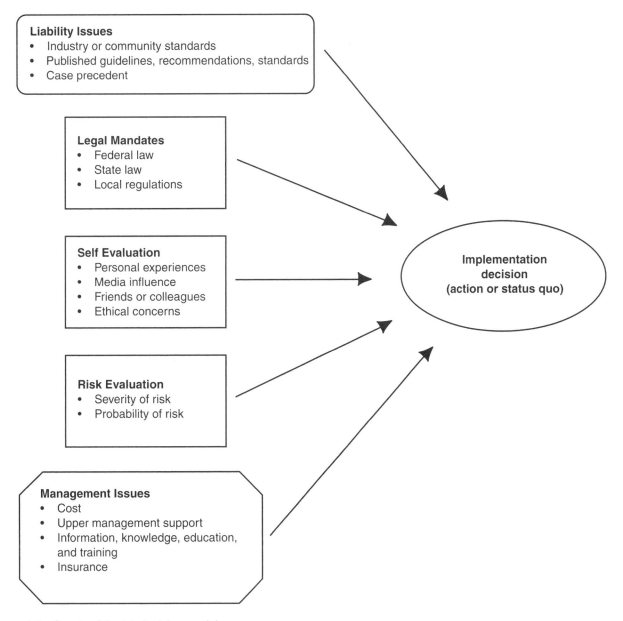

Figure 1.1 Sport safety risk decision model.

Threshold Issue 2: Developing a Framework for Managing Risk

If you have decided to develop and implement a comprehensive risk management plan, a new series of determinations must be made. The three main determinations are these:

- Identifying the general hazards for which a plan must account and specific hazards to which aspects of your program areas are susceptible
- Evaluating the potential severity and probability of harm produced by these hazards
- Developing methods to reduce the risk of injury or death to participants from these recognized hazards

The chapters that follow cover an array of pertinent issues and provide links to sources of information relevant to both general hazards and program areas that should address more specific hazards.

Identifying Hazard Categories

The first step in managing risk is to develop a plan for each major category of hazard that your organization may confront. Therefore, it is important to think about the categories of hazards that exist for your program or facility. Given the unique nature of each organization's programs and services, the sorts of hazards that need to be addressed will obviously vary. The most common hazards in sport and recreation include the following:

Bloodborne pathogens	Lightning
Cardiac arrest	Security issues
Child protection issues	Sport-related trauma
Heat-related illnesses	Vehicular accidents and injuries

In thinking about these hazards, it is often best to begin by hypothesizing worst-case scenarios for each. From this perspective, plans should then be developed that would result in the best possible outcomes.

Identifying Program Area Hazards

In addition to the general types of hazards mentioned previously, attention must next be directed to aspects of the program offered by your organization that carry the greatest potential for risk and are therefore the greatest potential for liability. Organizations that oversee contact sports, playgrounds, or aquatic activities, for instance, are certainly in need of focusing on risk management. Overseeing each of these involves particular hazards both with regard to the nature of the activities they promote and the equipment they use.

What categories of hazards exist in your program? You must identify those hazards before you can develop a risk management plan.

Evaluating Hazards

The next step in developing a risk management plan involves evaluating the hazards that you have identified. The level of risk of a given activity is generally measured by the frequency and severity of previous incidents that have caused injury or death. This measurement is based on incident reports, injury statistics, common knowledge, and experience. If a potential hazard is regarded as severe and quite likely to occur, the decision to address it is easy to make. If, however, the potential hazard is likely to occur but may well result only in a minor injury—or, on the other hand, is not likely to occur but could result in serious injury or death—how to deal with it becomes more difficult. In cases in which an injury can be quite severe, but the likelihood that it would occur is low (as with the risk of being struck by lightning, for instance), it is still wise to take a serious look at developing appropriate safety measures. The human cost of not having a plan in place in this sort of situation is just too great.

Sometimes you are readily given information that can help you evaluate how to respond to hazards. Safety instructions are often provided by manufacturers of sport and play equipment . For example, basic instructions for assembling and maintaining playground equipment are often readily available (see chapter 10). This provides excellent guidance for the person responsible for the playground as he or she works to assure that the equipment meets or exceeds the industry standard. These instructions will greatly help him or her manage the risk of potential injury.

> Where the risk of severe injury from a hazard is high but its likelihood is low, it is still wise to take a serious look at developing appropriate safety measures.

Reducing Risk From Hazards

Once a hazard has been evaluated and determined to pose a significant safety threat, methods by which to reduce the risk of harm must be considered. These methods can be as drastic as discontinuing a program or service or as simple as repairing or replacing a piece of equipment. A well-conceived risk management plan, documented and communicated to employees of your organization, should help significantly to reduce the risk posed by a hazard

Summary

Decisions pertaining to safety are the most important decisions that sport or recreation managers face. Therefore, it is vital that they understand the threshold issues relevant to the decision-making process. This chapter is intended to help the sport or recreation manager make informed decisions about risk and safety. Applied to key safety issues and program areas, the material provided here can guide them through the maze of issues that they are likely to confront in today's litigious society.

Medical Emergency Action Plans

chapter objectives

After reading this chapter, you will have a thorough understanding of the following:

Threshold Issue 1: Deciding Whether to Develop and Implement a Medical Emergency Action Plan

Threshold Issue 2: Understanding Key Aspects of a Medical Emergency Action Plan

Each year in the United States, an estimated 30 million children and adolescents participate in organized sports (National Institutes of Health 1992), and approximately 150 million adults participate in some type of physical activity unrelated to work (Centers for Disease Control and Prevention 2000). Engaging in these activities has numerous health benefits but also involves a risk for injury. For example, a youth sport athlete suddenly collapses and stops breathing. A set of bleachers collapses during a football game, injuring several spectators. A member of a health club suffers a sudden cardiac arrest. The Centers for Disease Control and Prevention (CDC) analyzed data from the National Electronic Injury Surveillance System All Injury Program (NEISS AIP) to characterize sports and recreation-related injuries among the U.S. population. Results of that analysis indicate that between July 2000 and June 2001 an estimated 4.3 million nonfatal sports and recreation-related injuries were treated in U.S. hospital emergency departments (Centers for Disease Control and Prevention 2002).

While the majority of injuries sustained during athletic or other physical activities are relatively minor, potential life-threatening emergencies often occur without warning (Andersen, Courson, Kleiner, and McLoda 2002). The short-term and long-term outcomes of a medical emergency will greatly depend on whether an adequate plan exists to handle the emergency. Those involved in organizing and overseeing physical activities must not only try to prevent medical emergencies but must also plan and practice for them.

A common mistake that many sport and recreation practitioners make is thinking that they will know exactly what to do when a medical emergency occurs. However, in many crisis situations, there is often no specific plan of action; and those involved may not know how to properly react in a calm and timely fashion. For example, a late 1990s survey of professional teams and college athletic programs revealed that only 56 percent of the responding professional teams and only 27 percent of college athletic departments had a formal crisis plan in place. More striking still, more than 70 percent of both professional and collegiate programs had experienced some sort of crisis the year prior to the survey (Hessert 1998).

Numerous problems, incidents, and issues confront a recreation and sport manager on a regular basis. They may range from minor situations to major catastrophic occurrences, such as fires; bomb threats; criminal activity; the collapse of bleachers; major power outages, serious medical emergencies; and even environmental emergencies like hurricanes, tornados, and floods. Additionally, serious medical emergencies, in particular, arise when a participant or spectator experiences acute illness or injury. Such situations can quickly escalate into a crisis if they are not brought under control, there is significant media coverage, or several resources for coping with the incident are required either from within or outside the organization.

Crises can involve one person (as with the death of an athlete, a student-athlete being charged with a serious crime, or the abduction of a young participant) but often involve many individuals (as with a bomb threat during a major athletic contest, a terrorist event, lightning striking a group of participants, or a situation in which a crowd gets out of control and riots occur during an event). A crisis situation is typically unforeseen and can be extensive in its scope of disruption and damage to the organization. Such damage can be extensive and cannot usually be corrected easily or quickly. Outside assistance is often necessary (Connaughton 2001). A comprehensive crisis management plan will address major catastrophic situations and will provide emergency action plans for several types of emergencies such as those mentioned above. This chapter, however, will only focus on planning for medical emergencies. For a list of organizations with emergency planning information, see table 2.1.

Table 2.1   Organizations With Information on Emergency Planning

Activity	Organization	Home page	Document	Web site
Health and fitness	American College of Sports Medicine (ACSM) and American Heart Association (AHA)	www.acsm.org and www.americanheart.org	"AHA/ACSM Joint Recommendations for Cardiovascular Screening, Staffing, and Emergency Policies at Health/ Fitness Facilities"	www.acsm.org/ publications/ positionStands.htm
General business and industry	Federal Emergency Management Agency	www.fema.gov	"Emergency Management Guide for Business and Industry"	www.fema.gov/library// bizindex.shtm
Schools	U.S. Department of Education AHA	www.ed.gov www.americanheart.org	"Practical Information on Crisis Planning: A Guide for Schools and Communities" "Emergency Planning for America's Schools" "Response to Cardiac Arrest and Selected Life-Threatening Medical Emergencies: The Medical Emergency Response Plan for Schools"	www.ed.gov/admins/lead/ safety/emergencyplan/ index.html www.ed.gov/news/ pressreleases/2003/03/ 0305-emergencyplan.pdf www.americanheart.org/ presenter.jhtml?identifier= 3017969
Sports	American Red Cross	www.redcross.org	Sport Safety Training course information	www.redcross.org/services/ hss/courses/sports.html
Athletics	National Athletic Trainers' Association	www.nata.org	"Emergency Planning in Athletics"	www.nata.org/ publicinformation/files/ emergencyplanning.pdf
Youth sports	U.S. Sports Academy	www.thesportjournal.org	"Creating an Emergency Action Plan for Youth Sports"	www.thesportjournal.org/ 2003Journal/Vol6-No4/ action-plan.asp
Workplace	Occupational Safety and Health Administration	www.osha.gov	"Emergency Preparedness and Response"	www.osha.gov/SLTC/ smallbusiness/sec10.html

Guidelines and Recommendations

Several national associations and governing bodies associated with sports, recreation, and physical activity programs recognize the need for emergency medical planning. For example, the National Collegiate Athletic Association (NCAA) and the National Federation of State High School Associations (NFSHSA) have recommended that all member institutions develop an emergency action plan (EAP) for their athletic programs. Other organizations recommending EAPs and links to their recommendations are listed in table 2.2.

Table 2.2 EAP Guidelines and Standards

Activity	Organization	Home page	Document	Web site
Football	USA Football	www.usafootball.com	"Emergency Action Plan"	www.usafootball.com/articles/17-health-safety/83-safety-tips/146-emergency-action-plan.php
College athletics	National Collegiate Athletic Association	www2.ncaa.org	"2003-2004 Sports Medicine Handbook" (see "Emergency Care and Coverage")	www.ncaa.org/library/sports_sciences/sports_med_handbook/2003-04/
High school athletics	National Federation of State High School Associations	www.nfhs.org	Sports Medicine Handbook (see information on emergency planning)	www.nfhs.org/scriptcontent/va_Custom/vimdisplays/contentpagedisplay.cfm?content_id=228
Sports for physically or mentally challenged participants	Special Olympics	www.specialolympics.org	"Coaching Guides: Medical Emergency Awareness"	www.specialolympics.org/Special+Olympics+Public+Website/English/Coach/Coaching_Guides/Sport+Safety+and+Risk+Management/Medical+Emergency+Awareness.htm#recommended
Schools	American Academy of Pediatrics	www.aap.org	"Guidelines for Emergency Medical Care in School"	http://aappolicy.aappublications.org/cgi/content/full/pediatrics;107/2/435
Adventure racing	United States Adventure Racing Association	www.usara.com	"Sanctioning Requirements" (see "Medical Plan")	www.usara.com/sanctioning.aspx
Youth sports	National Center for Sports Safety	www.sportssafety.org	"Developing an Emergency Action Plan"	www.sportssafety.org/articles/emergency-action-plan/
Sport and physical education	National Association for Sport and Physical Education	www.aahperd.org/naspe	"National Standards for Athletic Coaches" (see Domain: Injuries: Prevention, Care, and Management)	www.aahperd.org/naspe/template.cfm?template=domainsStandards.html

Threshold Issue 1: Deciding Whether to Develop and Implement a Medical Emergency Action Plan

In addition to having a professional responsibility for developing EAPs, a legal basis for doing so might also exist. The absence of an EAP, or an EAP that is not properly followed, may provide the basis for negligence claims.

The standards for providing adequate emergency care in the sport setting have been tested recently by the courts. These standards and the corresponding precedent have direct application to many sport and recreation activities. Physical educators, coaches, and recreational supervisors have a responsibility to those in their care to ensure that reasonable and prompt medical care is provided or secured in the event of a medical emergency. The following cases provide insight into the consequences of failing to have an appropriate medical emergency action plan.

The case of *Kleinknecht v. Gettysburg College* (1993) involved a 20-year-old college student, Drew, who was a lacrosse player for Gettysburg College. During a late-summer team practice Drew collapsed. His coach and teammates ran to his aid upon seeing him fall. They suspected that he had been hit, but instead he was in cardiac arrest.

No athletic trainers were present and no one in the vicinity was certified in cardiopulmonary resuscitation (CPR). In addition to not having an EAP, there were no communication devices at the practice field. The nearest phone was 250 yards (229 meters) away inside the training room at the stadium. A fence that surrounded the stadium and was 8 feet (2.4 meters) high had to be climbed in order to reach the training room.

Partly because there was no rehearsed EAP, there was much confusion. Players and staff ran to summon help. The coach ran toward the stadium. The team captain ran toward the training room. Another player ran toward the student union building. The team captain found a student trainer and notified others who called the head trainer and advised him of the situation. At the student union, an ambulance was called. The student trainer was the first person trained in CPR to reach Drew. She monitored his condition but did not perform CPR. Next, the head trainer and a band member who was trained as an emergency medical technician arrived at the scene at nearly the same time. They performed CPR on Drew until the ambulance arrived. Drew was then rushed to the hospital where he later died.

It is necessary for coaches and instructors to have a means of communication (such as a cell phone) to contact emergency medical personnel.

Drew's parents sued the college, claiming that it breached its duty when it failed to provide Drew with prompt and adequate medical care. The court agreed, reasoning that since lacrosse is a contact sport where life-threatening injury during participation is foreseeable, the college was responsible for taking reasonable precautions against the risk of death on the part of student-athletes while they are participating in their chosen sport. The court also ruled that reasonable measures must be in place to provide timely treatment in emergency situations.

A need for a properly executed EAP is likewise illustrated by *Cater v. City of Cleveland* (1998), in which a 12-year-old boy died from complications incurred as the result of nearly drowning at a municipal indoor swimming pool. On the day of the incident, four lifeguards were on duty, all certified by the American Red Cross. The boy was participating in a free swim. During the latter part of a free-swim period, swimmers in the deep end yelled to the lifeguards that someone was at the bottom of the pool. Two lifeguards pulled the boy from the water and began performing CPR. The pool manager was nearby when he heard a whistle blown by the guard and rushed over to assist with the resuscitation attempts. Several employees were told to call 911 but were unable to get through because they were unaware that they had to dial a 9 first to get an outside phone line. The paramedics arrived approximately 30 minutes after the boy was pulled from the water. He was taken to the hospital and later developed acute bronchial pneumonia and died.

The boy's parents brought a suit claiming that the municipality was negligent insofar as it provided inadequate supervision. The Supreme Court remanded the case to a jury to decide whether the municipality acted in a wanton or reckless manner in its use of personnel, facilities, or equipment. Among other issues in the case, the court found it appalling that the city had no policy or training regarding the making of emergency phone calls. The municipality admitted that it had failed to train their employees in the use of the phone to make emergency calls.

Both of these cases point out the need for a well-rehearsed EAP. As the cases demonstrate, time is critical when a medical emergency arises. It therefore would be prudent for those who organize and oversee physical activity programs to have communication devices available, such as hand-held radios or cell phones that allow for quick access to emergency medical personnel. At the very least, the nearest phones should be easy to locate, access, and operate. Additionally, staff should be trained in the proper use of the communication equipment.

> It is not enough simply to have an established emergency action plan; you have to properly implement it.

Having an established EAP that is understood and regularly practiced by all staff members can be of great help in the event of an actual emergency. Since it is impossible to operate a physical activity program that is 100 percent risk-free, all programs should consider developing and implementing EAPs that are appropriate for them.

Threshold Issue 2: Understanding Key Aspects of a Medical Emergency Action Plan

A medical EAP cannot be directly copied from an appendix in a book or from plans developed by other organizations. Instead, it must be specifically tailored to your organization and the programs you offer. Every program has unique aspects that must be carefully considered when developing an EAP. These include but are not limited to the nature and location of the program, the program participants and staff, the expected response time of local emergency medical services (EMS), and the facility and equipment that are used. Nonetheless, several general components are typically found in medical EAPs.

Creating a Planning Team

The initial step in developing and writing a medical EAP is to formulate a planning team whose members will initiate the process. The team may consist of coaches, parents, activity leaders, athletic directors, athletic trainers, team physicians, school nurses, organizational administrators and safety personnel, and local EMS personnel. The planning team's primary task is to identify medical emergencies that may arise within the organization. Several methods for identifying potential risks and emergencies exist. These methods include consultation with outside experts, reviewing sport or activity trends, and studying the organization's own accident and injury report forms. The locations in which prior incidents occurred, the nature of the incidents, and how they were handled are valuable information in developing an EAP.

Developing Plans for Medical Emergencies

While a medical EAP should be comprehensive and practical, it also should be flexible enough to adapt to any medical emergency. It should provide clear guidance for any individual who is confused or uncertain about the possible seriousness of a medical emergency. Hence, several crucial components must be considered when developing a medical EAP. Personnel issues should be addressed. The action plan should identify by job title those employees who will handle or assist with a medical emergency. Specific duties and responsibilities for each responder should be carefully outlined in a simple, concise format.

When creating a medical EAP, it is important to consult with qualified authorities and consider all possible contingencies.

Addressing Facility Issues

The location of emergency medical equipment, communication devices, emergency exits and shelters, elevators, alarm systems, and EMS meeting locations should be identified for each facility that is used. A specific medical EAP should be designed to meet the unique needs that may arise for participants at each venue. A map specific to each facility should clearly identify access roads, gates, stairs, elevators, ramps, phones, and the location of emergency equipment.

Assessing Equipment Issues

A medical EAP should list the emergency equipment that must be on hand to accomplish the tasks required in the event of a medical emergency. The type of equipment available should be identified (e.g., communication equipment, first aid kits, automated external defibrillators [AEDs], and backboards). Where the equipment is stored, who is to have access to it, and who is assigned to inspect and maintain it also should be specified.

Attending to Communication Issues

It is important to identify who makes what phone calls and in what order. Personnel should be given clear instructions regarding where to find communication equipment and how to make emergency communications. The exact location of telephones and other such devices should be specified and emergency phone numbers identified and posted. Staff should also be instructed on the following procedures when making an emergency phone call to the EMS:

- Dial the correct emergency number. The number is 911 in many communities. Dial 0 (for the operator) if the correct number is not known.
- Stay calm and provide the dispatcher with the necessary information. Most dispatchers will ask for specific information, including the exact location and address of the emergency (be sure to provide as many details as possible,

such as nearby intersections or landmarks, a building name, a floor and room number, and any further directions that are requested), the telephone number from which the call is originating, the nature of the emergency, how many people are injured; the condition of the victims, and what care is being provided.

• Do not hang up the phone until the dispatcher states that he or she has all necessary information (American Red Cross 2001).

To ensure that the communication system is functioning properly, it should be regularly checked. Likewise, a secondary communication system should be identified in case the primary system fails.

Handling Postemergency Issues

Once a medical emergency is over, conduct a thorough evaluation of how your medical EAP functioned. Consider including a determination of why the emergency occurred, if it could have been prevented, and how the situation was handled. An overall evaluation will assist in identifying flaws in the EAP and help lead to improvements. Updating and revising EAPs is an ongoing process.

Make certain that the medical EAP specifies exactly which sorts of documentation regarding the emergency must be created and kept. How, when, and who documents the event for the organization must likewise be established in advance. Specified personnel should know how to complete the necessary forms and to whom they should be sent. Policies for filing and retaining reports should be developed and follow-up procedures properly addressed.

See the Safety Guidelines Finder in appendix B for links to documents that provide safety information on various activities.

At the very least, all medical emergencies should be carefully documented with the use of an appropriate incident or injury report form that has been approved by the organization's legal counsel. Staff members must be very familiar with this form and the policies and procedures surrounding its use. For example, it is typical to fill out such a form and bring it to the attention of the organization's administration within 24 hours of an incident. These reports must be carefully retained for at least the length of the statute of limitations of the state in which the affected organization is located (Clement, 1998).

It is also necessary to have clear guidelines for whom to contact after an emergency (for instance, injured participants, parents, EMS, law enforcement, other pertinent risk management personnel, insurance companies, and so on) and when such contacts are to be made

Finally, it is important to determine when the EAP requires further evaluation and modification. It is a good idea to solicit input from all those both within and outside the organization who were involved in dealing with the incident. Both managerial and frontline staff should be consulted, as should the local EMS, fire and police departments, legal counsel, crisis planning and management consultants, and the organization's insurance company. These organizations should also be included in the testing, analysis, and rehearsal of the medical EAP. For example, EMS providers can predict the average response time to an emergency at a particular facility and assist in identifying strategic meeting locations. Perhaps there is an easy or obvious location at which to meet EMS personnel before directing them to the specific emergency location.

Testing the Medical EAP

Once an initial EAP is developed, your organization should simulate medical emergencies in an effort to evaluate it. After this simulation and subsequent evaluation, the EAP can be adjusted accordingly. Finally, develop and circulate the final plan to all affected parties.

Depending on the size and nature of the organization, all employees should be provided with a written copy, or easy access to a copy, of the medical EAP. In addition, all staff should be trained to properly follow the EAP at the beginning of their employment and periodically thereafter. Students and certain program participants can also be trained to assist in the event of an emergency. For example, they may be able to ensure that certain administrators have been notified, retrieve first aid supplies, or at least, behave in a manner that does not impede the EAP. In a school or recreational setting, the pertinent aspects of the EAP should be practiced with each new class or group.

Once an EAP has been established, training should be provided on a regular basis for all employees.

Regularly conduct announced and unannounced training sessions for implementing the EAP (Appenzeller and Seidler 1998). The American Heart Association/American College of Sports Medicine Recommendations for Cardiovascular Screening, Staffing, and Emergency Policies at Health/Fitness Facilities (1998) state that emergency action plans should be practiced at least once every three months and more often if there are changes in staff. Carefully retain documentation of all EAP rehearsals. Many administrators use standardized forms or videotape for evidence that their EAP was rehearsed.

Interacting With the Media

Organizations should train staff members to act as spokespersons to work with the news media following a medical emergency. Typically, one spokesperson should

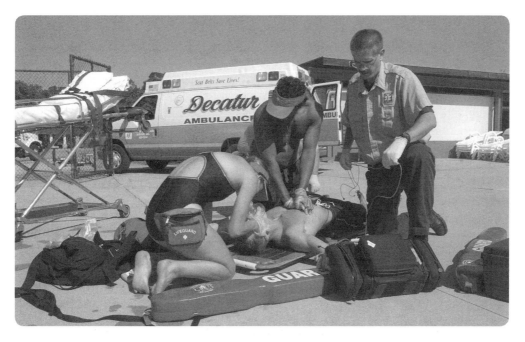

Practicing for a medical emergency is a good way to test your medical EAP.

For a sample injury report form that is part of a medical EAP, see page 115 in appendix A.

be designated. Centralized information minimizes miscommunication, so make certain that all personnel know that only this individual communicates with the media. The EAP should also identify the persons who decide what information is released.

Summary

Sport and recreational managers, physical educators, coaches, fitness instructors, and others involved in overseeing physical activities should establish a medical EAP prior to their next potential medical emergency. Knowing and practicing what to do in the event of a medical emergency should rank high on their priority list. Medical EAPs are an essential element of any effective risk management program. They should be carefully developed, regularly practiced and evaluated, and revised when necessary. If a medical emergency occurs, being prepared may mean the difference between life and death and the difference between a satisfied participant and a lawsuit.

Real-World Application

Scenario

While a physical education class is participating in a game of basketball, a student running toward the basket suddenly trips and hits the wall behind the basket with considerable force. As the physical education teacher runs to the scene, the student is quickly surrounded by her classmates who are all quite alarmed. The teacher, trained in first aid and CPR, quickly determines that the student has suffered a serious head injury and may have a spinal injury as well. The teacher realizes that EMS must be immediately summoned and screams out "someone call for an ambulance." Upon hearing this, several students run to the teacher's office at the far end of the gymnasium only to discover the door is locked. The students quickly return to the scene and advise the teacher that the door is locked. He throws the students the key and they run back, unlock the door, and attempt to call EMS. However, they are delayed in doing so because they do not know how to properly operate the new phone system. After several attempts they get through and the ambulance arrives several minutes later.

Practitioner Action

While the physical education teacher was trained in first aid and CPR, he had never developed a specific medical EAP. Since he had not planned and practiced for a medical emergency, he and his students were unprepared for this incident. This ultimately delayed the EMS's response. Afterwards, the physical educator discussed the issue of not having a medical EAP with his colleagues and administration. They worked together with the appropriate experts and developed one that they regularly practice.

Questions

1. How could the teacher have planned and rehearsed for such an emergency?
2. How could the teacher utilize students to assist in carrying out the medical EAP?
3. What equipment should be available for such an emergency?

Protecting Children

chapter objectives

After reading this chapter, you will have a thorough understanding of the following:

Threshold Issue 1: Determining Whether to Develop and Implement a Safety Plan to Protect Children

Threshold Issue 2: Recognizing Key Issues in Protecting Children From Harm by Others

For sport and recreation managers, the supervision of children is commonplace. Resorts often offer programs for the children of guests; children go to summer camps; and park and recreation departments offer many types of activities for children, such as organized sports, games, and learning activities. Youth sport leagues and teams are found in virtually every city and town in the United States. With so many opportunities to participate in such activities, however, children are put at an increasing risk of being subject to predatory practices by coaches, counselors, supervisors, and so on. In some states, protective measures have been established by the legislature to mandate, for instance, that employees or volunteers who work closely with children be subject to background checks. In others, it is up to the individual agencies and organizations to decide whether to implement procedures designed to protect children. Moreover, considerable attention has been paid to establishing clear and effective drop-off and pick-up procedures for children. Both issues are extremely important for child safety, and this chapter is designed to stimulate thought on these issues as well as to provide links to sources of pertinent information.

The protection of children in our society from those who desire to do them harm is of great importance both from an ethical and a legal standpoint.

Prevention Strategies for Child Abuse and Neglect

Harm to children can take any number of forms and is often described using the terms *abuse* and *neglect*. The Federal Child Abuse Prevention and Treatment Act (CAPTA), (42 U.S.C.A. §5106g), which has been amended by the Keeping Children and Families Safe Act of 2003, defines child abuse and neglect as at minimum,

- any recent act or failure to act on the part of a parent or caretaker, which results in death, serious physical or emotional harm, sexual abuse, or exploitation; or
- an act or failure to act that presents an imminent risk of serious harm (National Clearinghouse on Child Abuse and Neglect Information 2004).

Within the bounds of these minimal standards, each state defines child abuse and neglect somewhat differently. Most states, however, recognize four major types of harm:

Neglect

Physical abuse

Sexual abuse

Emotional abuse

These forms of ill treatment often occur in combination (National Clearinghouse on Child Abuse and Neglect Information 2004). In sport and recreation settings, sexual abuse and physical abuse are the most common forms of intentional harm done to children. Therefore, it is very important that background checks be performed to help identify those with prior convictions as sex offenders, who have committed other types of crimes, and who have otherwise abused or neglected children. Numerous organizations now conduct background checks for a reasonable fee. For example, Little League Baseball and Pop Warner Football use www.rapsheets.com to conduct background searches, while the Boy Scouts of America and the Boys and Girls Clubs of America use www.choicepoint.com. Information that can be obtained through a background check is also available through most states for free. You can search for data on sex offenders by state without paying a fee by using the following URL at the Web site for Little League Baseball: www.littleleague.org/common/childprotect/ states.asp.

Background checks are very important in protecting children from potential abusers.

Another key issue with regard to child protection is ensuring that children are safe after your program, practice, or game ends. The issue here is who picks up the child from your event. Procedures for ensuring that the proper person is picking up a child include the use of special code words, identification checks, and consent forms. Additional child protection issues that should be part of a comprehensive child protection plan include the proper training and certification of employees and volunteers and establishing strict guidelines for parental conduct at sport events. A good source for information for issues such as these is the Kids Sports Network (www.ksnusa.org). The information provided in Threshold Issue 1 raises the sorts of issues that must be addressed in evaluating whether to develop a safety plan for protecting children. Implementation issues specific to background checks and pick-up procedures are then examined.

Threshold Issue 1: Determining Whether to Develop and Implement a Safety Plan to Protect Children

In determining whether to develop and implement plans designed for the protection of children, the answer is clear. If your organization oversees any activities in which children participate, you have both an ethical and legal responsibility to take reasonable protective measures. The following describes this duty in greater detail.

See the Safety Guidelines Finder in appendix B for links to documents that provide safety information on various activities.

Ethical Responsibility

Our society places a high value on the safety and welfare of children. Just look at the effort and attention given to finding a missing child or aiding a child in need of rescue. Children need the help of adults to stay safe given that they often lack the physical, mental, and emotional maturity to provide for their own safety. Unfortunately, adult predators exist in our society, and they sometimes find their way into positions of authority and trust in camps, schools, and sport and recreation organizations that provide programs for children. It is the ethical responsibility of those in our field to develop and implement plans that will help to protect children in sport and recreation programs from those that mean to do them harm.

Background Checks Required by Statute

Not all states have laws that mandate criminal background checks, and both federal and state laws vary in terms of the organizations and parties covered in statutes that are designed to protect children. For example, Massachusetts requires camps to perform criminal background checks, while nearby Maine has no such requirement. New Hampshire requires background checks only if the state's Department for Youth, Children, and Families pays for children to attend camp. Obviously, it is important to seek counsel and become familiar with your state's law regarding background checks for those working with children.

Background Check Initiatives

Some sport and recreation associations and governing bodies now require local organizations providing programs and services to children to conduct background checks. The American Camping Association (ACA) requires, as a condition of accreditation, that camps conduct various forms of background checks on counselors and other camp personnel. Little League Baseball requires background checks for all those who work with children or who are otherwise responsible for the safety of children in their sanctioned programs. In addition, table 3.1 provides a list of selected youth sport and recreation professional organizations

Table 3.1   Selected Professional Associations With Initiatives on Background Checks

Activity	Organization	Home page	Protections	Document Web site
Camping	American Camping Association (ACA)	www.acacamps.org	The ACA's accreditation standard requires that camps conduct criminal background checks, reference checks, and employment checks.	www.acacamps.org/accreditation See recent standards revisions under "Human Resources" http://acacamps.org/accreditation/hr.pdf
Youth baseball	Little League Baseball	www.littleleague.org	In accordance with the Little League Child Protection Program, background checks are required for managers, coaches, members of the board of directors, and all others who work with children (including volunteers and hired workers).	www.littleleague.org/common/childprotect/index.asp and www.littleleague.org/common/childprotect/rapsheets.asp
Youth football	Pop Warner Football	www.popwarner.com	Background checks are required for coaches, members of the board of directors, and all others who work with children (including volunteers and hired workers).	www.popwarner.com/admin/check.asp?lable=check
Youth sports in general	National Alliance for Youth Sports (NAYS)	www.nays.org	The National Youth Sports Coaches Association (an affiliate of NAYS) has developed a volunteer coach screening program.	www.nays.org/IntMain.cfm?Page=12&Cat=3 and www.frpa.org/pdfs/articles/volunteerCoachScreening.pdf
	Kids Sports Network	www.ksnusa.org	Information for youth leagues on criminal background checks	www.ksnusa.org/cbc.htm
Scouting	Boy Scouts of America (BSA)	www.scouting.org	BSA has used Choicepoint for Internet-based criminal background checks on adult volunteers.	http://www.choicepoint.net/85256B350053E646/0/53FE66C04A963F7085256D19004A4701?Open
Youth organizations	Boys and Girls Clubs of America	www.bgca.org	Information is provided regarding the Choicepoint background screening service.	www.bgca.org/news/20020422.asp

that have background check initiatives. The Web sites provide useful information and examples of what the initiatives entail.

Background Checks Required by Contract

In addition to statutory requirements and mandates put forth by governing bodies, background checks might also be required as a condition of an agreement with another organization. For instance, background checks may be required by an insurance company as a condition of coverage for liability insurance or as a condition for a youth soccer program to use the facilities in a city park. Funding for a youth sport program also may be conditioned on whether background checks are performed for coaches and others working directly with children. Therefore, it is important to understand the agreements or contracts that your organization has with insurers and others who have authority over your funding and use of facilities.

For more information on background check applications, see page 116 in appendix A.

Legal Requirements

In determining liability should a child be harmed, not only the perpetrator but everyone in the chain of command above this person could be a potential target for a lawsuit. If someone in your organization intentionally harms a child, your liability as a manager—insofar as you are in a position of authority over that person—is likely to hinge on whether or not you have been negligent in your protective duties. The basic issue in determining negligence is whether a defendant met the required standard of care. If you are, say, the athletic director and a coach under your authority were to abuse a child, and the abuse is proven to have actually occurred, the coach could obviously be the target of legal action (criminal and possibly civil lawsuits). If you too were to become the target of a civil suit, an issue at trial would likely be whether a reasonable effort was made to uncover the criminal history of the coach through a background check. If a background check was not made, or was performed inadequately, you may well be held liable. You also might be liable if you had known of a pattern of abusive conduct on the part of the coach and either ignored it or, worse yet, covered it up. In addition, you might be questioned as to whether education and training was provided to coaches on the issue of child abuse. Was information provided on appropriate touching when instructing young athletes? The bottom line is that managers are potentially liable if they fail to provide adequate and reasonable measures to provide for the safety of children, even in the absence of legislation requiring them to do so.

As a manager, you must provide adequate and reasonable measures to ensure the safety of children.

Threshold Issue 2: Recognizing Key Issues in Protecting Children From Harm by Others

Given their ethical and legal responsibilities, it is very important for sport and recreation managers to provide for the protection of children. When implementing child protection policies and procedures, it is important to consider the following.

Cost

Cost is certainly a consideration in virtually every management decision with respect to which new procedures are implemented. In this chapter, we have focused on two specific measures of child protection: background checks and pick-up procedures. For the latter, the cost of implementing a system for identification of those who are picking up children from games or events is minimal in terms of dollars. Moreover, the cost of paperwork involved in implementing pick-up procedures is inconsequential when viewed in light of the potential consequences if no procedure is in place and a child is picked up by a predator. The greatest cost related to implementing and carrying out pick-up procedures is measured in terms of time and effort in training personnel and ensuring that the procedures are correctly followed. Again, however, the cost in terms of effort is well worth it.

There is a greater monetary cost to organizations that implement background checks. This financial burden varies in accordance with the type of search performed and the company chosen to conduct the search. The cost of a local or state search may be as low as $10, and national or more comprehensive searches can be as high as $60 (American Camping Association 2003). Yet, this price can be reduced when access to background checks is made possible through a professional association or organization that has an agreement with a provider of these services. For example, Little League Baseball, Pop Warner Football, and the Kids Sports Network (KSN) have an agreement with www.rapsheets.com that enables local sport and recreation providers to perform background checks for a lower fee. For a one-time setup fee of $25, local organizations working through KSN can conduct individual searches for $1.75 each. The searches allow access to more than 150 million conviction records in 44 states (Kids Sports Network 2004).

> Do not let the cost of background checks hinder your safety procedures. Many organizations offer background checks for a one-time fee or at reduced cost.

Resources

Before implementing child protection measures, you need to be knowledgeable about the issue of child abuse and neglect. It is also crucial to learn how you can help to protect children under your care from such harm. Table 3.2 provides a list of organizations and resources that can prove quite helpful in helping you to learn more about child protection issues.

Procedures

The procedures for conducting criminal background checks are somewhat tricky and should only be implemented after consultation with a competent authority on the subject in your state and community. Two universally available sources, however, provide an excellent synopsis of key issues and information relevant to background checks. These are the KSN and the Nonprofit Risk Management Center, listed in tables 3.1 and 3.2. The key issues they address include, but are not limited to, the following:

- Requirements for conducting criminal background checks
- Sources for conducting background checks

Table 3.2 Organizations and Resources: Background Checks and Child Protection

Organization	Home page	Information provided	Web site
Nonprofit Risk Management Center	www.nonprofitrisk.org	Criminal history background checks	www94311.temp.w1.com/csb_crim.htm
American Bar Association Center on Children and the Law	www.abanet.org/child/home.html	Laws and issues related to child protection	www.abanet.org/child/childpro.html
Sports Coach UK	www.sportscoachuk.org/home.htm	Sports Coach UK has information and resources on child protection issues relevant to abuse and neglect	www.sportscoachuk.org/home.htm
The Australian Sports Commission	www.ausport.gov.au	The Australian government provides information relevant to child abuse and protection issues in sport	www.ausport.gov.au/ethics/cpoverview.asp
U.S. Department of Health and Human Services Administration for Children and Families	www.acf.dhhs.gov	"What Is Child Abuse and Neglect?"	http://nccanch.acf.hhs.gov/pubs/factsheets/whatiscan.cfm

- Types of criminal background checks (for instance, name-based versus fingerprint as well as those that provide arrest versus conviction records)
- Preparing for conducting background checks (for example, knowing the requirements for notifying and getting permission from those being checked to do so, understanding the conditions under which results of a background check from a third party vendor can be distributed, being aware of when to notify those being checked of the results, and having a plan for who will have access to the background check information)
- Planning how to use the acquired information (including how your organization should proceed when incriminating information is uncovered, and what constitutes removal from, or denial to, a program)

As you can see from this list, it is important to understand the issues and carefully think through forming a plan for background checks before conducting them.

Regarding pick-up procedures, the means by which this is carried out varies greatly from organization to organization. Yet, in all cases the goal is to ensure that children are picked up by a parent or another designated individual who is responsible for the safety of the child. Be sure to consider the following when formulating a policy for child pick-up:

- Developing approved authorization forms
- Ensuring that written authorization to pick up a child has been received from a parent or another designated party
- Receiving approved photo identification from those responsible for picking up children
- Teaching children to use predetermined code words or numbers when being picked up
- Deciding whether only outgoing calls (calls from the organization) can be made to arrange for pick-ups
- Establishing the means never to leave a child unattended after an event

- Ensuring that a child never leaves an event unattended or with an unauthorized person
- Assessing penalty fees for late pick-up

For a sample child authorization pick-up form, see page 117 in appendix A.

As with background checks and other measures intended to protect children, pick-up procedures should be implemented only after consultation with a competent authority on the subject in your particular state and community. It is also important to become familiar with the pick-up procedures of other organizations similar to your own.

Summary

Keeping children reasonably safe in sport and recreation activities is always the right thing to do. It is also very important from a liability standpoint. Background checks and pick-up procedures are two key safety issues that sport and recreation managers must face today. When handled properly, the safety of children who participate in sport and recreation programs can be greatly improved, and parents can have better peace of mind when leaving their children in the hands of coaches, sport and recreation supervisors, and volunteers. Staying abreast of these and other key issues relevant to child safety is imperative given the world in which we live.

Real-World Application

Scenario

Jim recently has been placed in charge of a recreational youth football league. In this position, he is responsible for both volunteer and paid coaches and assistants. Jim is concerned about selecting and hiring good people, and he developed an application that is quite thorough. He would check references, but he does not know enough about background checks to perform them. Football practices are held each week; parents usually drop off their children and pick them up after practice. Jim is concerned about the safety of his young players and therefore requires the parent or person responsible for each player to sign a form both when dropping the player off and then again when picking them up. A photo ID is not required.

Larry is hired as a coach for one of the teams and coaches for several weeks without incident. Unknown to Jim, Larry is a convicted child molester. One day after practice, the parents are late to pick up one of the players. Larry asks the player if he needs a ride home. When the boy declines, Larry grabs him by the arm and tries to drag him to his van. The boy breaks free just as his parents arrive and come to his rescue. The parents are extremely upset and pull their son from the program. Jim realizes that he needs to have a plan to protect his young players from adult predators.

Practitioner Action

Jim is right. He does need a plan in place to help protect the children from harm. After visiting several Web sites, talking with child safety experts and representatives from professional associations, and studying the background check and child pick-up procedures of other coaches and leagues, he develops his own plan. Jim realizes that background checks are essential when children are under the supervision of adults and that there are readily accessible sources via the Internet to conduct them. He also realizes that there are better ways to ensure that his players are safe from predators after practice and that they are picked up by an appropriate responsible adult. This information is also readily available via the Internet.

Questions

1. What should a comprehensive background check include?
2. What types of background checks are available?
3. What are the key components of a procedure for ensuring the appropriate responsible adult picks up a child from an event, game, or practice?

Exertional Heat Illness in Sport and Recreation

chapter objectives

After reading this chapter, you will have a thorough understanding of the following:

Threshold Issue 1: Deciding Whether to Develop and Implement a Heat Illness Plan

Threshold Issue 2: Recognizing Key Issues in Developing a Heat Illness Plan

Many people succumb to heat-related deaths every year. From 1979 to 1999, excessive heat exposure resulted in 8,015 deaths in the United States. During that time, more people in the U.S. died from extreme heat than from hurricanes, tornadoes, floods, lightning, and earthquakes combined. In 2001, 300 people died of excessive heat exposure (Centers for Disease Control and Prevention 2004c). It is estimated that the average number of heat-related deaths in football alone is three players per year (Gatorade Sports Science Institute 2002). During 2002, for instance, a high school student in Indiana died of heat exhaustion, as did a college football player at the University of Florida and a professional football player with the Minnesota Vikings. The real tragedy with these cases is that heat-induced illnesses are entirely preventable. Teachers, coaches, fitness instructors, physical activity leaders, and others involved in sport and recreational activities need to be aware of the potential hazards associated with exercising in hot or humid climates and take appropriate measures to prevent heat-related illnesses.

How the Body Handles Heat During Exercise

The human body tries to remain within a relatively small temperature range. If the body temperature goes above or below this range, the body's physiological function is adversely affected. Regulation of temperature involves a delicate balance between heat gain and loss. The body gains heat in two primary ways: from exercise and from the environment. During exercise the body can generate a tremendous amount of heat. Also, if the environment is warmer than the body is, it will absorb heat from the environment. The human body typically thermoregulates very effectively. However, the combined stresses of exercise and heat exposure place extreme demands on it.

In an effort to counteract heat gain, the body has four main methods to dissipate heat. The first method is heat radiation, which requires that the surrounding environment be cooler than the body. This is the primary method of heat loss when humans are at rest, but it does not provide adequate cooling during exercise. A second method is convective cooling, which involves the motion of air or liquid over the skin. During bicycling, this type of cooling occurs as the body moves through the air. This may also occur from a cool breeze or from a fan blowing cooler air across a person's skin. Heat conduction is a third method, which requires a person to physically contact a cooler object and thereby transfer heat from the exerciser to the cooler object. Immersing oneself in a cool bath would provide a conductive medium for this type of transfer. Finally, the evaporation of sweat is the primary method by which an exerciser is cooled. It is estimated that 80 percent of heat loss during exercise is due to this method. As sweat evaporates from the skin it carries heat with it and cools the skin. With cooler skin, heat can move more rapidly from the body's core to the skin. Disrupting this method by limiting either the production or the evaporation of sweat quickly impairs thermoregulatory capabilities (Glass 1996).

Sweating and the perfusion of the skin with blood are necessary for maintaining a safe core temperature. However, sweating and increased blood flow to the

> The four ways by which heat is dissipated from the body are heat radiation, convective cooling, head conduction, and evaporation of sweat.

skin result in a loss of fluid from the central blood volume. In response, the body will attempt to protect its central blood volume and cardiovascular function. This comes at the expense of thermoregulation. The body's rates of sweat and blood flow to the skin will decrease in an effort to conserve body fluid, and dehydration will progress. As a result, core body temperature will rise, and unless exercise is reduced or stopped, heat illness is very likely to occur.

When exercise is performed in hot and humid conditions, it is much more difficult for the body to thermoregulate. Heat loss by convection, radiation, and evaporation is decreased even more in these conditions, which may cause a rapid rise in core temperature. When heat, humidity, and dehydration are combined, exercise becomes challenging and at times even dangerous.

When compared to adults and adolescents, children produce more heat relative to body mass during exercise. They also have a lower sweating capacity, and their core temperature rises at a higher rate when dehydrated (Bar-Or 1994). Additionally, thermoregulation in children exposed to heat occurs less efficiently because of their lower sweating capacity and a lower output from their heat-activated sweat glands (American College of Sports Medicine 2000). Therefore, children are more prone to heat illnesses than adults.

Certain other individuals are at a higher risk for developing heat illness. They include the elderly and those with bulimia, congenital heart disease, diabetes, high fever, obesity, vomiting, diarrhea, renal failure, and a history of heat-related illness; also those taking certain drugs or supplements with diuretic or stimulant properties are at higher risk for heat illness (Bar-Or 1994; Gatorade Sports Science Institute 2002). These individuals should be closely monitored during physical activity.

Heat Index

The National Weather Service has devised a more accurate measure of how hot it really feels when relative humidity (RH) is added to the actual air temperature. This is called the heat index (HI) and is sometimes referred to as the "apparent temperature." An HI chart is provided in figure 4.1. If the air temperature is 95 degrees Fahrenheit (35 degrees Celsius) (as shown on the left side of the chart) and the RH is 50 percent (as found at the top of the chart), the HI—or how hot it really feels—is 105 degrees Fahrenheit (41 degrees Celsius). This is the number at the intersection of the 95-degree row and the 50 percent column.

Types of Heat Illnesses

Heat illnesses are progressive conditions. If recognized in their early stages, they can usually be reversed. If not, they may progress to become a life-threatening condition. Three common types of heat illnesses are heat cramps, heat exhaustion, and heat stroke.

Heat cramps are painful, involuntary contractions of the exercising muscles and occur as a result of substantial fluid loss from sweating. Remove any person who has heat cramps from the heat source, and give him or her water to drink. Additional treatment includes rest from the exertional stress and passive stretching

Temperature (F) Versus Relative Humidity (%)

°F	90%	80%	70%	60%	50%	40%
80	85	84	82	81	80	79
85	101	96	92	90	86	84
90	121	113	105	99	94	90
95		133	122	113	105	98
100			142	129	118	109
105				148	133	121
110						135

HI	Possible Heat Disorder
80° F to 90° F	Fatigue possible with prolonged exposure and physical activity.
90° F to 105° F	Sunstroke, heat cramps, and heat exhaustion possible.
105° F to 130° F	Sunstroke, heat cramps, and heat exhaustion likely, and heat stroke possible.
130° F or greater	Heat stroke highly likely with continued exposure.

Figure 4.1 Heat index chart. Because of the nature of the HI calculation, the values in the chart have an error of plus or minus 1.3 degrees Fahrenheit (.7 degree Celsius). Since HI values assume that one is exposed to shady conditions and a light wind, exposure to full sunshine can increase HI by up to 15 degrees Fahrenheit (8.3 degrees Celsius). Also, strong winds—particularly with very hot, dry air—can be extremely hazardous.

Reprinted from the National Weather Service. www.crh.noaa.gov/pub/heat.htm

of the affected muscles. This is the least serious of the heat illnesses, and recovery usually occurs quickly. However, if left untreated or improperly treated, heat cramps will likely progress to heat exhaustion.

Heat exhaustion, also termed heat prostration, may elevate body temperature as high as 102 degrees Fahrenheit (39 degrees Celsius). Note that cramps are not always a precursor to this condition. Those who have heat exhaustion generally sweat profusely. Additional signs and symptoms may include cool, moist, pale, ashen, or flushed skin; a headache; nausea; dizziness; a rapid pulse; and weakness. This is a serious condition that must be immediately treated! Treatment should include moving the person who experiences heat exhaustion to a cool, and shaded area; elevating the lower limbs to prevent shock; replacing fluids if the person is conscious and able to drink; placing cool towels or ice packs on the wrists, ankles, groin, neck, and armpits; and seeking appropriate medical advice (American Academy of Orthopaedic Surgeons 1991). If heat exhaustion is not readily and properly treated, it may progress to heat stroke.

Heat stroke is a true medical emergency and a life-threatening condition. The skin may appear red, hot, and dry, although one may still be sweating profusely. Internal body temperature may rise to, or even above, 104 degrees Fahrenheit (40 degrees Celsius). Symptoms may include nausea, vomiting, extreme weakness, dizziness, confusion, and an altered level of consciousness. The victim may experience seizures and eventually a loss of consciousness. If there is any doubt regarding the level of heat illness a person is experiencing, he or she should be treated for heat stroke. Rapid cooling and medical attention are necessary. Emergency medical personnel should be called as soon as possible.

To help prevent heat illnesses, follow these recommendations (National Weather Service 2005):

> Heat illnesses can be treated by cooling the body and, in extreme situations, may require hospitalization.

- Slow down. Strenuous activities should be reduced, eliminated, or rescheduled to take place during the coolest time of the day. Individuals at risk should stay in the coolest available place, which is not necessarily indoors.

- Dress for summer. Lightweight, light-colored clothing reflects heat and sunlight and helps your body maintain normal temperatures.

- Put less fuel on your inner fires. Foods (like proteins) that increase metabolic heat production also increase water loss.

- Drink plenty of water or other nonalcoholic fluids. Your body needs water to keep cool. Drink plenty of fluids even if you don't feel thirsty. Persons who (1) have epilepsy or heart, kidney, or liver disease, (2) are on fluid-restrictive diets or (3) have a problem with fluid retention should consult a physician before increasing consumption of fluids.

- Do not drink alcoholic beverages.

- Do not take salt tablets unless specified by a physician.

- Spend more time in air-conditioned places. Air conditioning in homes and other buildings markedly reduces the risk of succumbing to heat illnesses. If you cannot afford an air conditioner, spending at least some time each day (during hot weather) in an air-conditioned environment affords some protection.

- Don't get too much sun. Sunburn makes the job of heat dissipation that much more difficult.

Hyponatremia in athletes is a rare medical condition that has claimed the lives of marathon runners and military recruits. This condition occurs when blood sodium concentration falls to a very low level. This results in a rapid swelling of the brain that can lead to seizures, coma, and death. While excessive fluid consumption is a major risk factor for hyponatremia, it is possible in the absence of excessive drinking. Ensuring that fluid intake does not exceed sweat loss and ingesting beverages or foods that contain sodium to counteract the sodium lost in sweat can reduce the risk of developing hyponatremia. For the vast majority of sport participants, dehydration remains the primary challenge, but hyponatremia should be acknowledged as a possible risk to those who drink more fluid than they lose in sweating (Murray, Eichner, & Stofan, 2003).

Guidelines and Recommendations

Several national associations and governing bodies associated with sport, recreation, and physical activity programs recognize the need for preventing heat illnesses. For example, the Inter-Association Task Force on Exertional Heat Illnesses has published *Preventing Exertional Heat Illness: A Consensus Statement*. The task force recommends that every athletic organization have a written plan for recognizing, preventing, and treating exertional heat illness. Further information and links to their recommendations and others are provided in table 4.1.

Table 4.1   Guidelines and Standards on Exertional Heat-Related Illness

Organization	Home page	Document	Web site
Inter-Association Task Force on Exertional Heat Illnesses	Not applicable	"Preventing Exertional Heat Illness: A Consensus Statement"	www.gssiweb.com/reflib/refs/625/ssn_exertioanlheatill.cfm?pid=38#figure1
National Collegiate Athletic Association (NCAA)	www2.ncaa.org	"NCAA 2004-2005 Sports Medicine Handbook" (see "Guideline 2c: Prevention of Heat Illness")	www2.ncaa.org/media_and_events/association_updates/2005/august/guideline2c.pdf
National Federation of State High School Associations	www.nfhs.org	"Sports Medicine: Recommendations for Hydration to Prevent Heat Illness" and "Heat Stress and Athletic Participation" (click on "Sports Medicine" and scroll down to "Heat and Hydration")	www.nfhs.org
National Athletic Trainers' Association (NATA)	www.nata.org	"Exertional Heat Illnesses" "Inter-Association Task Force on Exertional Heat Illnesses" "Youth Football and Heat Related Illness"	www.nata.org/publicinformation/position.htm
Centers for Disease Control and Prevention	www.cdc.gov	"Extreme Heat: A Prevention Guide to Promote Your Personal Health and Safety"	www.bt.cdc.gov/disasters/extremeheat/heat_guide.asp
National Weather Service	www.crh.noaa.gov/pub	"Heat Index"	www.crh.noaa.gov/pub/heat.htm
National Center for Sports Safety	www.sportssafety.org	"Preventing Heat Exhaustion and Dehydration"	www.sportssafety.org/articles/health-and-nutrition/
American Academy of Family Physicians	www.aafp.org	"How to Prevent Heat-Related Illnesses"	www.aafp.org/afp/20020601/2319ph.html
US Soccer Federation	www.ussoccer.com	"Hydration and Heat Illness Guidelines"	www.ussoccer.com/services/content.sps?iType=4036&icustompageid=6603
USA Football	www.usafootball.com	"Guide to Heat Illness"	www.usafootball.com/articles/17-health-safety/84-hydration/156-guide-to-heat-illness.php
American College of Sports Medicine	www.acsm.org	"New Youth Football Recommendations Emphasize Practice and Training Safety in the Heat"	www.acsm.org/publications/newsreleases2004/heat081704.htm
Gatorade Sports Science Institute	www.gssiweb.com	"Tackling the Heat: The Interactive Presentation" "Guidelines on Heat Safety in Football"	www.gssiweb.com/tackleheat/index.cfm www.gssiweb.com/reflib/refs/566/attackheatill.cfm?pf=1&CFID=965482&CFTOKEN=30127001
Defeat the Heat	www.defeattheheat.com	Public safety campaign designed to prevent dehydration and serious heat illness in active children.	www.gatorade.com/parents/

Threshold Issue 1: Deciding Whether to Develop and Implement a Heat Illness Plan

The following two cases demonstrate the need for a written plan for recognizing, preventing, and treating exertional heat illness.

Michael King, a 19-year-old sophomore and football player for the University of Indianapolis, suffered heat stroke during the first scheduled practice of the 2000 season. Later that day, Michael died from complications related to his heat illness.

Seeking compensatory and punitive damages for the wrongful death of her son, Michael's mother brought a negligence lawsuit against the university and several university officials. Mrs. King alleged that her son exhibited signs of heat stress that were negligently treated by university employees who were charged with a heightened duty of care toward student-athletes on the football team. The court allowed the plaintiff to recover compensatory damages but did not allow recovery for punitive damages (*King v. University of Indianapolis* 2002*)*.

Robert Mogabgab was on the football team at Benjamin Franklin Senior High School and was engaged in training exercises during the second day of training in August. Coaches O'Neil and Mondello were supervising the practice, which began at 3:45 p.m. at Audubon Park in New Orleans. Approximately two hours later, while performing wind sprints, Robert staggered and fell down and was assisted to the school bus by two of his teammates. The boys had difficulty getting him on the bus, and while on the bus Robert vomited.

> Every recreation and sport organization should have a policy and an emergency plan that addresses exertional heat illness. A sound plan includes key factors to identify its early stages.

The bus arrived at the school about 5:40 p.m., and Robert was helped into the school building where he was placed on the cafeteria floor on a blanket. He was undressed by his teammates, placed in a shower, taken out and placed on a blanket with another blanket covering him, and given an ammonia capsule by Coach Mondello. He was very clammy and pale and his breathing was heavy. His arms were massaged and an unsuccessful attempt was made to give him salt water. During this time, Coach O'Neil was in his office. At some point, a first-aid book was brought into the cafeteria and the coaches discussed what should be done. Around 6:40 p.m., parents of one of the players arrived and observed Robert lying on the cafeteria floor. The parents offered to call a physician. Coach Mondello refused the offer and said that Robert was his responsibility. Robert Mogabgab's mother was called at approximately 6:45 p.m., and a doctor arrived 30 minutes later. Almost two hours had passed since he originally became ill.

Robert was taken to the hospital, where his condition worsened. He died from complications related to heat stroke early the next morning. Robert's parents brought suit in the Civil District Court for the Parish of Orleans, which was dismissed. They appealed to the Fourth Circuit Court of Appeal, but it rendered a judgment in favor of the plaintiff (that is, the parents). A physician who examined Robert at the hospital the night he died stated that putting a blanket over a person with heat stroke is the wrong thing to do. He further explained that it is extremely important that a victim of heat stroke be brought to a physician and hospital immediately (*Mogabgab v. Orleans Parish School Board* 1970).

Threshold Issue 2: Recognizing Key Issues in Developing a Heat Illness Plan

If you decide to develop a written plan for recognizing, preventing, and treating exertional heat illness, the American Academy of Orthopaedic Surgeons (AAOS) (1991), the American College of Sports Medicine (ACSM) (1996 and 2000), Bar-Or (1994), the Gatorade Sports Science Institute (2002), Gisolfi (1996), Glass (1996), and Murray and Eichner (2003) recommend the following tips on risk management:

• All participants should be educated about the dangers of heat illness and the importance of proper hydration. When young children are involved, parents should also be educated.

• Acclimatization is very important when preparing to exercise in the heat. A few days of moderate physical activity, lasting up to 90 minutes, will provide some initial acclimatization. Most participants will begin to show improved acclimation within 4 or 5 days, with 10 to 14 days necessary for most physiological adaptations to occur. If participants have not been regularly exercising in the heat, start out with workouts that are shorter and lower in intensity. Glass (1996) recommends reducing exercise intensity by 10 percent to compensate for the elevated heart rate initially seen in unacclimated exercisers. Be particularly careful the first several times exercising outside. Also, be cautious of days that may be atypically hot or humid.

• If possible, exercise outside during the coolest parts of the day (early morning or evening) to minimize the impact of solar radiation.

• When to allow, modify, or prohibit physical activity should be based on existing guidelines, such as those available from the AAOS (1991), the ACSM (2000), and the Inter-Association Task Force on Exertional Heat Illnesses (2003). However, there is no absolute environmental measurement that can be applied to precisely predict possible heat illness. Therefore, it is important to be alert to the signs and symptoms of impending heat illness in all participants at all events.

Adequate rest periods and liquids are key components to keeping athletes safe during high temperatures.

• In hot conditions, the body temperature must not markedly increase during the warm-up phase before activity. Modifications to the warm-up phase and the subsequent activity can include exercising in the shade, reducing the intensity and duration of the warm-up and the activity, removing any unnecessary clothing or protective equipment, and drinking plenty of fluids. Rest periods should be longer and provided more frequently. Participants should be encouraged to cool down in the shade and take advantage of the cooling effect of fans.

• Fluids should be replaced as frequently as possible to prevent dehydration and heat illness. Participants must not rely on the sensation of thirst to indicate when it is time to drink! The thirst mechanism is inadequate for ensuring safe and proper hydration. Often, by the time a person feels thirsty, he or she is well on the way to becoming dehydrated. Drinking 12 to 20 ounces (.35 to .6 liter) of fluid (water or sports drink) before activity is recommended, but this cannot substitute for ingesting fluids during activity. Exercisers should drink at least 8 ounces (.24 liter) of fluid every 15 to 20 minutes during activity. The fluid should be mostly water with no more than 8 percent carbohydrate. Higher concentrations of carbohydrate take longer to be absorbed by the body.

• After activity ceases, participants should continue drinking proper fluids. Exercisers can weigh themselves before and after exercise. For every pound of body weight lost, one should consume approximately 24 ounces (.7 liter) of fluids. Exercisers should avoid diuretics such as alcohol and caffeinated beverages until adequate fluids have been replaced. Diuretics will cause an increase in urine production and rob the body of needed water.

• To assist in the evaporation of sweat and cooling of the body, exercisers should wear minimal loose-fitting clothing. Exercisers should not wear dark clothing that absorbs sunlight instead of reflecting it, as light colored clothing does. To assist with the evaporation of perspiration, exercisers should change out of saturated shirts or uniforms when possible. Special "breathable" clothing exists that also can assist with the evaporation of sweat. Athletes and participants should not wear rubber body suits. While a visor may help one stay cooler by warding off the sun, be aware that hats (and football helmets) may not allow heat to radiate from the head efficiently.

• While increasing sodium intake is important for preventing cramping, the use of salt tablets may lead to gastrointestinal discomfort and should be avoided. Ingesting sports drinks and slightly increasing the use of salt while eating meals and snacks is recommended.

• Pay special attention to larger participants, particularly those who are unfit, overweight, or not acclimated to the heat. These individuals are at a higher risk for heat illness.

• Those exercising should be encouraged to exercise with partners who can assist them in the event of heat illness.

Schedule plenty of breaks for your athletes and participants. Shade and plenty of liquids are recommended during these breaks.

• Advise athletes and other participants who take medication or supplements (either prescription or over-the-counter drugs) to consult with their physicians regarding the possible effects of exposure to heat.

• Be aware of where all activities are being conducted. Beware of any surface that radiates heat, such as asphalt basketball courts, running tracks, and concrete surfaces under artificial turf.

See the Safety Guidelines Finder in appendix B for links to documents that provide safety information on various activities.

• Learn to recognize the signs and symptoms of heat illness. Become certified in first aid and cardiopulmonary resuscitation. If someone suffers a heat illness, use extreme caution in allowing him or her to return to activity.

Summary

Heat-induced illnesses are preventable. Sport and recreation professionals, as well as others who supervise physical activity programs, need to be aware of the potential hazards associated with physical activity in hot or humid climates. They should take appropriate measures to prevent participants from succumbing to heat-related illnesses.

Real-World Application

Scenario

Since Coach Jones has several top runners returning, he is excited and eager to begin cross country practice early this fall. Although he lives and coaches in a northern state, the weather over the past two weeks has been unusually hot and humid. On the first day of practice, Coach Jones decides to do an easy, short workout. After the workout, several runners complain of the heat, others appear atypically flushed and are sweating profusely, and a couple of runners had to walk the last portion of the prescribed run. One of the parents asks Coach Jones what he plans to do regarding practice for the rest of the week, since the forecast predicts even hotter and more humid weather. The coach had not yet heard the forecast and responded by saying that he would think about it and call the athletes later that evening.

Practitioner Action

Coach Jones indeed verified that the forecast was predicting even hotter and more humid weather for the remainder of the week. Based on this knowledge, he decided to alter his plan. Accordingly, Coach Jones scheduled practices for early morning, a cooler part of the day. He also provided an extra fluid station along the training route and regularly stressed the importance of replacing fluids lost in sweat. Finally, Coach developed a handout on preventing exertional heat illnesses that he thoroughly discussed with his runners and provided to their parents.

Questions

1. What factors should Coach Jones consider when determining to modify practices, or even cancel them, because of the heat and humidity?

2. If the coach decides to conduct practice, what additional precautions should be taken?

3. What should the coach teach his athletes regarding exertional heat illnesses?

Lightning Safety

chapter objectives

After reading this chapter, you will have a thorough understanding of the following:

Threshold Issue 1: Deciding Whether to Develop and Implement a Lightning Safety Plan

Threshold Issue 2: Including Necessary Components in a Lightning Safety Plan

Lightning safety has become an important area of concern for sport and recreation providers. No longer considered strictly an unforeseeable "Act of God," lightning has become a more predictable force, hence a more foreseeable hazard with many outdoor activities. Advances in technology, a better understanding of the nature and potential occurrence of lightning strikes, and the existence of lightning safety guidelines and recommendations for outdoor activities have all increased the expectation that participants will be reasonably protected from lightning by those in charge of outdoor activities. Athletes on a practice field rely on their coaches to make sound judgments about when to leave the field and seek shelter; golfers often rely on course managers to sound a siren in the event of an imminent threat of lightning; and children at summer camp rely on camp directors to let them know when it is safe to go outside or when they must seek shelter if playing outside.

Importance of Lightning Safety

Lightning is one of the most underrated yet consistent causes of weather-related deaths and injuries. Every year in the United States, approximately 100 fatalities and hundreds of injuries that require medical attention are caused by lightning (Cherington 2001). Lightning-related deaths and injuries occurring during sport and recreational activities have risen dramatically over the past several decades. The majority of deaths and injuries occur between May and September, with the greatest risk period occurring between 10 a.m. and 7 p.m. Oftentimes, children are involved because they do not fully appreciate the risk of lightning. Without responsible supervision from leaders with knowledge of lightning safety, they are at increased risk. Moreover, outdoor activities such as organized sports or camping generally involve groups of participants. This puts more people at risk for injury in the event of a lightning strike.

Lightning strikes have killed and injured people at events ranging from festivals to soccer games to outdoor camping. A case example at a city park is *Bier v. City of New Philadelphia* (1984). In this situation that resulted in a lawsuit against the city, a group was enjoying a picnic at a city park when a thunderstorm approached. The group was under the cover of a metal-roofed picnic shelter packing up their supplies when a bolt of lightning stuck the shelter. This resulted in the death of Mr. Bier and injury to several of the remaining group members.

Guidelines and Recommendations

Several organizations provide recommendations for lightning safety. Table 5.1 contains information and links to these recommendations. Sport and recreation managers should be aware of these organizations and their recommendations for lightning safety. If your organization chooses to implement a lightning safety plan, the recommendations will prove valuable. The following section provides a summary of issues and recommendations from the groups listed in table 5.1 relevant to four categories of activities: organized recreation, organized sport, supervised nature-based recreation, and golf.

Table 5.1   Organizations With Information on Lightning Safety

Activity	Organization	Home page	Document	Web site
Supervised recreation and sport activities				
Organized recreation and sports	National Athletic Trainers' Association	www.nata.org	"Lightning Safety for Athletics and Recreation"	www.nata.org/publicinformation/files/lightning.pdf
	National Weather Service	www.noaa.gov	"Lightning Kills, Play It Safe"	www.lightningsafety.noaa.gov
	National Lightning Safety Institute (NLSI)	www.lightningsafety.com	"Lightning Safety for Organized Outdoor Athletic Events"	www.lightningsafety.com/nlsi_pls/ncaa.html
Collegiate sports	National Collegiate Athletic Association	www2.ncaa.org	NCAA administrative guidelines relevant to lightning safety	www.ncaa.org/library/sports_sciences/sports_med_handbook/2005-06/2005-06_sports_medicine_handbook.pdf
High school sports	National Federation of State High School Associations	www.nfhs.org	*Sports Medicine Handbook*	Available for a fee; call 800-776-3462
Swimming	NLSI	www.lightningsafety.com	"Indoor/Outdoor Swimming Pool Safety"	www.lightningsafety.com/nlsi_pls/swimming_pools.html
Nature-based recreational activities				
Outdoor recreation	National Outdoor Leadership School	www.nols.edu	"NOLS Backcountry Lightning Safety Guidelines"	www.nols.edu/resources/research/pdfs/lightningsafetyguideline.pdf
	NLSI	www.lightningsafety.com	"Lightning Safety for Campers and Hikers"	www.lightningsafety.com/nlsi_pls/ploutdoor.htm
Boating	NLSI	www.lightningsafety.com	"Boating Lightning Safety"	www.lightningsafety.com/nlsi_pls/boating.html
	Centers for Disease Control and Prevention	www.cdc.gov	National Agricultural Safety Database (NASD) "Boating-Lightning Protection"	www.cdc.gov/nasd/docs/d000001-d000100/d000007/d000007.html
Golf	NLSI	www.lightningsafety.com	"A Lightning Safety Mandate for the Game of Golf"	www.lightningsafety.com/nlsi_pls/golfsafetyrecommend.html

Threshold Issue 1: Deciding Whether to Develop and Implement a Lightning Safety Plan

The first decision to make regarding lightning safety is whether to have a comprehensive lightning safety plan. This is a threshold issue that should be decided based on consultation with a lightning safety expert or other competent authority. You can, however, also look to the recommendations provided in table 5.1 for guidance as well as case law and community and industry standards.

See the Safety Guidelines Finder in appendix B for links to documents that provide safety information on various activities.

Organized Recreation and Sport Activities

Those responsible for organized sport activities, such as recreational youth soccer or adult softball leagues and high school or collegiate athletics, must make the decision as to whether they should implement a lightning safety plan. For high school and college coaches, the National Athletic Trainer's Association (NATA), the National Federation of State High School Associations (NFHS) and the National Collegiate Athletic Association (NCAA) position statements are valuable resources to use in making this determination. For those responsible for organized recreational sports, the NATA position statement on lightning safety is worth examining. The NATA recommends creating and implementing a "comprehensive, proactive lightning safety policy or emergency action plan specific to lightning safety," and has identified the essential components of such a plan (Walsh et al. 2000, p. 472).

Supervised Nature-Based Recreational Activities

Outdoor activities such as boating, camping, and hiking in the backcountry pose a unique set of challenges for lightning safety. The National Outdoor Leadership School (NOLS) has published a position statement that is of value in making decisions regarding a lightning safety plan for those providing backcountry trips to areas outside the immediate reach of civilization. Additionally, the National Lightning Safety Institute (NLSI) and the Centers for Disease Control and Prevention (CDC) provide information relevant to boating and lightning safety. Both of these organizations' Web sites (listed in table 5.1) provide valuable information and links that will help you in formulating lightning safety plans if you deem it necessary to do so.

Different activities require different lightning safety plans. You should research these matters before creating your plan.

Golf

The NLSI is likewise a very valuable source of information for managers of golf courses. Golf presents unique challenges when it comes to lightning safety. It involves managing a course, but with the exception of lessons there is no direct supervision of individuals or groups of players—as is the case with youth soccer leagues and swimming pools, for example, where direct supervision occurs.

Case law provides some guidance regarding whether management would be held liable for the death of a golfer struck by lightning on its course. In the past, lightning was considered an unforeseeable act of God, and courts were reluctant to impose liability. For example, in *Hames v. State* (1991), a golfer was killed by a lightning strike that occurred during a round of golf at a course owned and operated by the state of Tennessee. When Phillip Hames and two other golfers began play the weather was overcast, but there were no signs of an imminent thunderstorm. There were no weather shelters on the course, nor were there any signs instructing players regarding what should be done in case of severe weather. After a thunderstorm had passed, the three players were found unconscious on the course about 800 yards (732 meters) from the clubhouse. Mr. Hames died as a result of a lightning strike. The course professional testified that it would have taken less than two minutes to reach the clubhouse by golf cart. The widow of Mr. Hames sued for wrongful death, arguing that there were no weather shelters, warning systems, or signs that indicated what to do in case of severe weather. At trial, experts testified that there were no recognized standards that stipulated whether golf courses must be equipped with shelters or warning devices. The court ruled that because lightning is so highly unpredictable, it is not reasonable to require management to anticipate when and where it will strike. The court did note, however, that it was significant that there were no industry standards regarding lightning detection and safety procedures.

In a later case, *Maussner v. Atlantic City Country Club, Inc.* (1997), the court also examined the issue of whether golf course owners owe a duty of care to protect players from lightning. The case was brought after Spencer Maussner was struck by lightning while playing golf at the Atlantic City Country Club, where he was a member. A snowstorm was predicted for that day, but after Spencer's group had played two holes it began instead to rain heavily. One of the players noticed a lightning bolt, and the players began making their way back to the clubhouse that was about one-half mile (.8 kilometer) away. There were no weather shelters along the way to the clubhouse for the players to use. While crossing one of the fairways on the way back to the clubhouse, Mr. Maussner was struck by lightning, resulting in substantial injuries.

Storm shelters can save lives and should be present in designated areas for the safety of golfers and other sport participants.

The staff at the country club generally monitored the weather by listening to the weather advisory channel and calling the National Aviation Facilities Experimental Center. That morning there were no warnings of lightning. The country club did not have any lightning detectors or a warning system but did have an evacuation plan whereby employees would remove golfers from the course when there were signs of lightning. The staff at the country club also encouraged golfers to take refuge in private homes along the course during severe weather. It claimed to have United States Golf Association posters on lightning safety in the locker room on the day of the incident, but Mr. Maussner claimed that they were posted after the incident. Mr. Maussner also stated that the management at the country club had not communicated that they would be able to seek shelter in private homes. The court recognized that new technology can allow golf course management to detect the existence of lightning. Although it did not rule that golf courses have an absolute duty to protect golfers from lightning strikes (one important factor being the cost involved), it did rule that when the proprietors of a golf course have procedures in place to protect golfers from lightning strikes, the proprietors owe the golfers a duty of reasonable care to implement those procedures properly. Therefore, if the choice is made to develop and implement a lightning safety plan for liability or ethical reasons, it is imperative that the plan be followed.

> When proprietors of a golf course have procedures in place to protect golfers from lightning strikes, the proprietors owe the golfers a duty of reasonable care to properly implement those procedures.

Threshold Issue 2: Including Necessary Components in a Lightning Safety Plan

If the choice is made to develop and implement a lightning safety plan, the next step is to understand the key elements that should be included in a plan and determine how it will be implemented. The following is a summary of components to be included in a lightning safety plan that are recommended by some or all of the organizations listed previously.

Supervised Recreation and Sport Activities

The NATA, the NLSI, and the National Weather Service all provide information that is broadly applicable to such supervised recreation and sport activities as softball, youth soccer, and so on. The NCAA has recommendations directed to collegiate athletics, while the NFHS directs its recommendations toward high school athletics. Each organization provides lightning safety information that contains similar themes. The following information is intended to provide a starting point for a better understanding of basic issues before going to those sources that would best suit your particular needs.

- **Decision maker.** As with any safety plan, it is important to have someone with knowledge of lightning safety in a position of authority to make lightning-related decisions. Key decisions involving lightning safety include (1) whether to suspend or cancel play, (2) determining where to move participants in the event of lightning danger, and (3) when to resume play, if possible. The NATA recommends establishing a chain of command that identifies who will make these decisions. All designated persons charged with this task should have formal training in lightning safety identification and emergency procedures.

- **Weather watcher.** A second key person in the chain of command looks for indications of threatening weather and notifies the decision maker when there is a danger of lightning. This person may be using anything from a handheld weather radio, a weather channel, the Internet, or sophisticated monitoring devices. In addition to monitoring weather detection or prediction equipment, he or she should also be watching the sky for lightning or threatening weather conditions.

- **Weather monitoring.** Technology designed to prevent lightning injuries and fatalities has progressed rapidly in recent years. Three types of technology include lightning detectors, lightning predictors, and lightning monitors. Lightning detectors are local devices that identify when there is lightning within a certain limited range. They can be handheld and are relatively easy to operate. Lightning predictors, unlike lightning detectors, measure atmospheric conditions that are most favorable for lightning strikes. Some systems available today will both predict lightning and warn of lightning danger using sirens. Lightning monitors use various weather networks to track storms. They range in sophistication from weather radios that sound alerts from the National Weather Service to online tracking systems. The most basic of these radios can cost as little as $20 and are portable (Kithil 2000). Even with the technology available today, simply watching the sky is an important part of the monitoring process.

- **Criteria for taking action.** It is important to have criteria for suspending and resuming activities that are communicated to those responsible for lightning safety and made a part of the lightning safety plan. It is recommended that a flash-to-bang count be used to determine when play should be stopped and safe shelter sought. The flash-to-bang count is the time between when a flash of lightning is seen and the associated thunder is heard. Watch the lightning flash and begin counting until you hear thunder. If there are 30 seconds or less between the flash and bang, it is recommended that participants be in a safe shelter or location, or immediately evacuated to one (Cooper, Holle, and Lopez 1999). To estimate out how far away the lightning is striking, you can divide the number of seconds counted between the flash and bang by five. For example, with a 30-second flash-to-bang count, the lightning is approximately 6 miles away. For resuming play, wait at least 30 minutes after the last lightning strike is seen or thunder heard (Schultz, Zinder, and Valovich 2001). This would put the storm and associated lightning approximately 10 miles away.

- **Safe structures.** It is important to designate safe shelters. Coaches, supervisors, and (of course) participants should know where they are located. The best plan and the most up-to-date monitoring systems are not of much use if there is no place for participants to go in a lightning storm. Identify or build structures that can quickly be accessed. Substantial structures and vehicles provide a degree of safety. Placing school buses in strategic locations—such as near playing fields—or moving children to the relative safety of a camp dining hall in a lightning storm are reasonable ideas. Dugouts and other buildings that are not grounded should not be used during lightning storms.

> A nontechnical way to monitor lightning is to use the flash-to-bang count. If there are 30 seconds or less between the flash of lightning and the bang of thunder, play should be suspended and participants should be in a safe shelter or location, or immediately seeking one.

- **Staff emergency training.** Most victims of lightning strikes die of cardiac arrest resulting from the trauma imposed by the electrical current. Therefore, it is very important for staff (first responders) to maintain current cardiopulmonary resuscitation (CPR) and first-aid certification.

Supervised Nature-Based Recreational Activities

Hiking and camping trips overseen by outdoor recreation providers as well as power boating, sailing, kayaking, and canoeing in a supervised environment all pose unique lightning safety risks. Since participants are often away from the safety of fixed structures and vehicles, and computers and sophisticated monitoring devices are not likely to be available, outdoor leaders should be aware of ways to minimize the risk of injury or death from lightning strikes. As with supervised sporting activities, it all starts with developing knowledge of lightning safety and formulating a plan. Here are some key recommendations:

- **Timing activities.** NOLS recommends timing activities to coincide with recognized weather patterns so that you are not caught in an unsafe area during a lightning storm. If you know that thunderstorms are likely in the late afternoon, time your trip so that you are off the water, off a mountaintop, or finished with a hike before a storm is likely to hit.

- **Safe terrain.** Avoid elevated areas such as peaks, ridges, and significantly higher ground during a lightning storm. When you hear thunder, move immediately to a lower area. Cave entrances and rock overhangs are *not* safe locations during a lightning storm. Also avoid wide-open ground and lone tall trees.

- **Camping.** Locate tents on safe terrain—away from lone trees and not exposed on high ground. Do not use metal tent stakes and poles, because they may conduct ground current. Knowledge of lightning safety is essential for outdoor leaders who are selecting tent sites.

- **Boating.** Lightning is particularly dangerous to boaters on rivers and lakes in flat terrain as well as on the ocean. Boaters should leave the water when they hear thunder and should avoid tall trees along the shoreline when leaving the boat for shore. Boats in the water should have lightning protection. The NLSI provides links to information regarding lightning protection for boats (see table 5.1).

Golf

The NLSI has published "A Lightning Safety Mandate for the Game of Golf," which can be found on their Web site as referenced in table 5.1. A summary of key components follows, but you should access the document for more complete information.

The United States Golf Association (USGA) makes available warning posters and stickers that provide golfers with tips on lightning safety (see figure 5.1). The NLSI recommends placing these in conspicuous places, such as at the door to the pro shop, beside cash registers, on employee bulletin boards, in golf carts, in locker rooms, on rest room mirrors, at the pump house, and on all operating machinery.

- **Weather monitoring.** The NLSI recommends monitoring changing weather conditions. Methods include using a weather radio, monitoring a weather-specific channel on television, logging on to an online weather service, getting notification from nearby commercial or government airfields, using a lightning detection and notification system, and looking out the window at the sky.

- **Notifying participants.** The NLSI recommends that if the management at your golf course chooses to implement lightning safety procedures, suggested ways to notify golfers of lightning danger are to post a daily weather advisory, blow an air horn or a siren, and put a safety notice on the scorecards.

For an example of the NLSI's lightning emergency plan, see page 118 in appendix A.

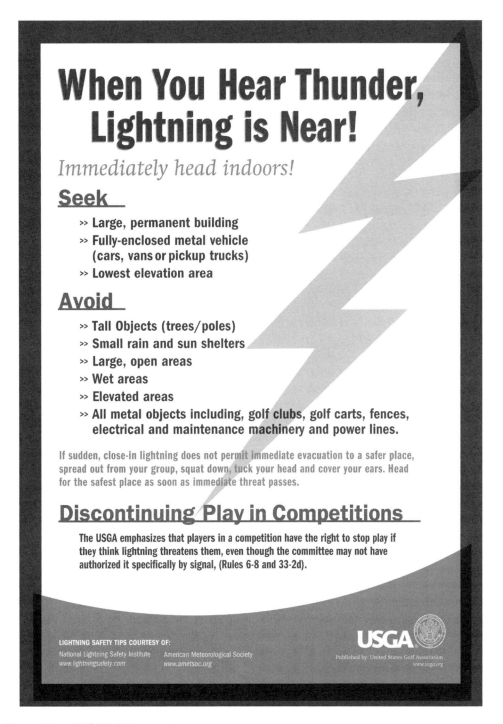

Figure 5.1   USGA lightning poster.

Summary

Lightning safety has become a key issue in risk management for those who provide opportunities in outdoor sport and recreation. For supervised outdoor activities such as camping and collegiate sports, the elements of a lightning safety plan can be broadly applied. For example, simple lightning safety components like waiting 30 minutes for a storm to pass before resuming activities can be applied equally to waiting to resume a baseball game and waiting to release children from the dining hall at camp. The information provided by professional associations provides valuable guidance on lightning safety that is applicable to a wide variety of supervised activities. The information provided in this chapter is designed to lead individuals and organizations responsible for the safety of participants, spectators, and staff to important information sources that will assist in making informed decisions regarding the development of safety measures for lightning.

Real-World Application

Scenario

Mark is the new coach of a youth baseball team. He played baseball throughout high school and was an umpire for intramural softball teams in college, but this is his first time coaching. At a recent practice an unexpected, fast-moving, lightning-producing thunderstorm comes upon his team. Mark interrupts practice, quickly moving his players off the field and into the dugout. He waits 10 minutes after the storm has passed and then resumes practice on the field. The rain has passed but he can still hear thunder and see lightning in the distance. Shortly after his team returns to the field, a bolt of lightning strikes one of the outfield lights. None of the players are injured, but it is way too close for comfort. After practice, several parents are upset after hearing about Mark's actions and the "near-miss." He realizes that he needs to have procedures in place to protect his players from lightning and to better detect when severe weather is on its way.

Practitioner Action

Mark is right. He does need a plan in place to protect his players from harm. After visiting several Web sites, talking with lightning safety experts and representatives from professional associations, and studying the lightning safety plans of other coaches, he created his own lightning safety plan. Mark realized that a dugout is not a safe place to seek shelter from lightning. He also learned that 10 minutes was too early after he believed the storm had passed to return to the field. He should have waited at least 30 minutes after the storm had passed to resume practice. Mark also investigated lightning detection systems and thought about additional ways to detect approaching lightning storms.

Questions

1. What do you think should be the elements of Mark's lightning safety plan?
2. How would you tailor a plan to other types of programs and activities such as golf, supervised recreational activities, or backcountry activities? What elements are similar? What is different?

Bloodborne Pathogens

chapter objectives

After reading this chapter, you will have a thorough understanding of the following:

Threshold Issue 1: Understanding Compliance Issues Relevant to OSHA's Bloodborne Pathogens Standard

Threshold Issue 2: Understanding Key Aspects of OSHA's Bloodborne Pathogens Standard

The purpose of this chapter is to introduce the Occupational Safety and Health Administration's (OSHA's) bloodborne pathogens (BBPs) standard. The information in this chapter is not a substitute for any provisions of the Occupational Safety and Health Act of 1970 or the requirements of 29 CFR 1910.1030, Occupational Exposure to Bloodborne Pathogens. Nor is this chapter intended to substitute for specific training and certification. Contact your local area or regional OSHA office to determine if compliance with this standard is required and, if so, how compliance can specifically be achieved.

OSHA's Office of Information and Consumer Affairs has developed fact sheets, brochures, and a videotape on the standard of bloodborne pathogens. You can obtain the brochure and fact sheets by writing OSHA Publications, 200 Constitution Avenue, NW, Room N3101, Washington, DC 20210 or by calling 202-219-8148. The videotape may be obtained through the National Audiovisual Center by calling 301-763-1896.

Definition of Bloodborne Pathogens

BBPs are microorganisms in human blood that can cause disease in humans. The BBPs of major concern include, but are not limited to, the hepatitis B virus (HBV) and the human immunodeficiency virus (HIV). The risk of infection with BBPs depends partly on the likelihood of exposure to blood or other potentially infectious materials wherever that exposure occurs. A single exposure incident could result in infection, subsequent illness, and in some cases death.

Threshold Issue 1: Understanding Compliance Issues Relevant to OSHA's Bloodborne Pathogens Standard

In 1991, with input from the Centers for Disease Control and Prevention (CDC), OSHA issued a standard entitled Occupational Exposure to Bloodborne Pathogens (29 CFR 1910.1030). The purpose of the BBP standard is to eliminate or reduce occupational exposure to blood and other potentially infectious materials in the work environment that could lead to disease or death. This hazard affects employees in many types of jobs and is not exclusive to the healthcare industry.

The BBP standard applies to all employers whose workers have "occupational exposure." This means that they (employees) may reasonably anticipate coming in contact with human blood or other potentially infectious bodily fluids while performing their job duties. If employees are trained and designated to be responsible for rendering first aid or medical assistance as part of their job responsibilities, they are covered by the protections of the standard.

For several examples of correspondence that provide further information regarding OSHA compliance, see page 119 in appendix A.

One of the central provisions of the BBP standard is that employers are responsible for identifying job classifications that entail occupational exposure. Who is subject to occupational exposure varies from program to program, but several groups may be particularly vulnerable. These include employees who are responsible for administering first aid and cardiopulmonary resuscitation (CPR); lifeguards and athletic trainers. Other such groups may include those responsible for childcare; custodial maintenance; or handling bloody laundry, razors, or other types of potentially infectious waste. Staff members, such as massage therapists, whose positions require close personal contact with clients are also potentially at risk of exposure to BBPs (Durkin 1998).

Threshold Issue 2: Understanding Key Aspects of OSHA's Bloodborne Pathogens Standard

The OSHA BBP standard requires employers to help minimize employee exposure to BBPs through proper planning, education, and record keeping. They must establish a written exposure control plan (ECP), which lists the tasks, procedures, and job classifications with which occupational exposure may occur. An ECP must also include procedures for evaluating the circumstances surrounding an exposure incident and communicating information regarding hazards to employees, as well as a schedule for implementing methods for compliance and information regarding postexposure follow-up (Zeigler 1997).

In terms of education, the standard requires that employers provide training at no cost to employees (during working hours) that alerts them to the risks posed by BBPs and informs them of steps they can take to eliminate or reduce possible exposure. Employers must provide this training to all employees who perform tasks where occupational exposure may take place. This training must be provided at the time of the initial assignment and at least annually thereafter. The standard specifies several elements that must be included in the training. These elements include, but are not limited to, information on how to obtain a copy of the BBP standard and an explanation of its requirements; information on bloodborne diseases and how they are transmitted; explanation of the ECP and how to obtain a copy; information on how to identify tasks that may result in occupational exposure; explanation of the use of engineering controls and personal protective equipment (such as gloves and face masks); information on HBV vaccination; information on the types, location, selection, proper use, removal, handling, and disposal of personal protective equipment; information on how to report an exposure incident and on postexposure follow-up; and a mandatory question and answer period that can cover any part of the training.

> Employers are required to establish a written exposure control plan (ECP) that lists the tasks, procedures, and job classifications with which occupational exposure may occur.

One of the most important elements of compliance is the implementation of *universal precautions*. As recommended by the CDC, both the employer and employees are required to assume that *all* blood and other potentially infectious materials are indeed infectious and must be handled accordingly. The employer must also provide at no cost to employees appropriate personal protective equipment, such as gloves and face masks.

Since gloves may not provide complete protection, basic hand washing remains a fundamental element of infection control. Facilities for proper hand washing need to be readily available in all areas where occupational exposure is anticipated. However, since running water and hand washing facilities are not

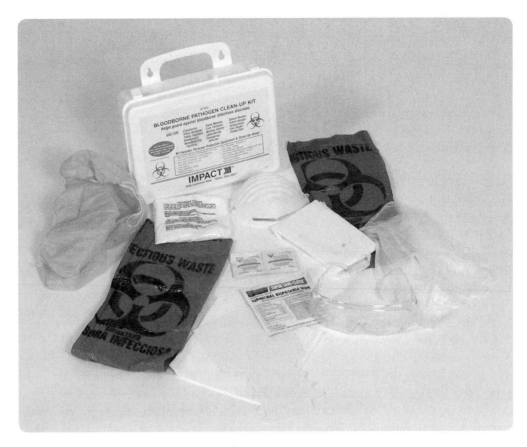

Certain items are imperative to have in a BBP clean-up kit. These kits can be ordered from various Web sites.

always available, the employer must provide appropriate antiseptic hand cleaner in conjunction with clean cloth or paper towels or antiseptic towelettes. When such alternatives are used, the hands should be washed with soap and running water as soon as possible.

In addition, the employer must offer, at its own expense, voluntary HBV vaccinations to all employees with occupational exposure. If an employee initially decides to decline the HBV vaccination but at a later date decides to accept it, the employer must make it available at that time. Employees who decline the HBV vaccination offered by the employer must sign a specific OSHA form of declination. Mandatory language for the declination is found in appendix A of the standard. A confidential postexposure medical evaluation and follow-up must also immediately be offered to employees who have had an exposure incident.

See the Safety Guidelines Finder in appendix B for links to documents that provide safety information on various activities.

The record-keeping element of the standard requires that employers maintain records related to vaccination status, training for all employees with occupational exposure, exposure incidents, and postexposure follow-up. Training records must be retained for three years, and medical records related to exposure incidents for each employee must be retained for the duration of his or her employment plus 30 years.

Summary

Bloodborne infections and diseases have the potential to produce catastrophic health consequences. It is absolutely crucial to have knowledge and awareness of related risk management strategies to protect those involved in the sport and recreation field. OSHA provides sound guidelines in dealing with BBPs, and their guidelines should be strictly followed.

Real-World Application

Scenario

During a recreational youth soccer game, two athletes collide at high speed. The impact results in one athlete's mouth, teeth, and jaw striking the other athlete's forehead. Both fall to the grass with considerable bleeding. The recreation supervisor grabs her first-aid kit and runs to the scene. As she begins to administer first aid, a parent approaches and identifies herself as an emergency-room nurse. The nurse quickly retrieves a pair of gloves from the first-aid kit and puts them on. After bandaging both athletes, there is a considerable amount of bloody medical waste (gauze, bandages, gloves, and so on). The nurse removes a red plastic bag, labeled "Biohazard," from the first-aid kit and proceeds to put all the wastes into it. Afterward, she informs the recreation supervisor that she is going to the restroom to wash her hands and suggests the same to the supervisor. While doing so, the nurse asks the supervisor if the recreation department has an ECP related to BBPs. The recreation supervisor is not sure.

Practitioner Action

The recreation supervisor reported the soccer injuries to her director and asked if the department had an ECP related to BBPs. The recently hired director inquired and found out that a plan did not exist. After viewing several Web sites, consulting with a state OSHA representative, and reviewing the ECPs of other recreation departments, he created one.

Questions

1. Which recreation department employees typically face exposure to BBPs?
2. How can a manager ensure that the appropriate employees are covered, educated, and trained in accordance with an ECP?

Sudden Cardiac Arrest and the Use of Automated External Defibrillators

chapter objectives

After reading this chapter, you will have a thorough understanding of the following:

Threshold Issue 1: Understanding Issues Relevant to the Purchase and Use of AEDs

Threshold Issue 2: Understanding What to Consider When Using AEDs

A critical management issue for sport and recreation practitioners is whether to purchase and use automated external defibrillators (AEDs). It is estimated that more than 100,000 lives can be saved each year if AEDs are available and used properly. Among these numbers are, to be sure, numerous persons engaged in sport or recreational activities such as golf, fitness training, aquatics, and team sports. The lives of spectators at sporting events undoubtedly can be saved with AEDs as well. In fact, studies show that sport stadiums, golf courses, and health and fitness facilities are among the top 10 public places with the highest incidence of sudden cardiac arrest (SCA) (Becker et al. 1998).

We often think of SCA happening to people who are in poor health, aged, or infirm. However, perfectly healthy individuals can also experience SCA by being victims of blunt trauma to the chest from the impact of a baseball or football, by being struck by lightning, or by nearly drowning. When SCA occurs, the time to defibrillation is a critical factor in determining whether the person will survive and fully recover. In general, for every minute that passes between the event and defibrillation, the probability of survival decreases by 7 to 10 percent. After 10 minutes, the probability of survival is extremely low (Department of Health and Human Services and General Services Administration 2001, p. 28496). At recreational or sport facilities in small towns, or in hard-to-reach areas like golf courses where emergency medical service (EMS) is many minutes away, the AED may be the only means available to accomplish early defibrillation.

> Studies show that sport stadiums, golf courses, and health and fitness facilities are among the top 10 public places with the highest incidence of sudden cardiac arrest (SCA).

What Is an AED?

An AED is a battery-operated device that has been developed to save the lives of victims of SCA (see figure 7.1). It determines whether the heart has stopped beating or is experiencing arrhythmia, and (if needed) it delivers an electric shock to restore normal heart rhythm. It has both audio and visual prompts that walk the user through the entire treatment process. The user simply has to attach pads to a victim's chest, turn the device on, and follow audio instructions. It will also prompt the responder to begin cardiopulmonary (CPR) if it is required. AEDs use a computer to analyze a person's heart rhythm and will not allow someone to be

Figure 7.1   An automated external defibrillator (AED).

shocked if the conditions are not appropriate (Spengler and Connaughton, 2001). A single unit currently costs approximately two thousand dollars, and price variations depend on make and model.

Guidelines and Recommendations

Several organizations provide recommendations for AED usage. Information and Web sites of these recommendations are provided in table 7.1. Sport and recreation managers should be aware of these organizations and their recommendations relevant to AEDs. As you can see, the applicability of the various recommendations is specific to the activity or organization. However, even if the recommendations do not address your particular situation, they provide a wealth of information on AEDs and may be useful in helping you make the threshold decision about whether to purchase and use AEDs.

Table 7.1   Recommendations Relevant to AED Usage

Activity	Organizations	Home page	Document	Web site
Health and fitness	American College of Sports Medicine and American Heart Association	www.acsm.org and www.americanheart.org	Joint position statement regarding AEDs in health and fitness facilities	www.acsm.org/publications/ positionStands.htm See also www.americanheart.org/prese nter.jhtml?identifier=3013236
	International Health, Racquet and Sports-club Association	http://cms.ihrsa.org	Position statement regarding AEDs	http://cms.ihrsa.org/IHRSA/ viewPage.cfm?pageId=593
Aquatics	International Life Saving Federation	www.ilsf.org	"Statements on Automatic External Defibrillation Use"	www.ilsf.org/medical/policy_03.htm
	Ellis & Associates: International Aquatic Safety and Risk Management Consultants	www.jellis.com	"Automatic External Defibrillator (AED) Policy"	www.jellis.com/news/aed/index.htm
Organized sports	National Athletic Trainers' Association	www.nata.org	"Official Statement: Automated External Defibrillators"	www.nata.org/publicinformation/docs/ aedofficialstatement.pdf
Golf	Golf Digest	www.golfdigest.com	"Links for Life"	www.golfdigest.com/features/index.ssf?/ features/linksforlife.html
General workplace	American College of Occupational and Environmental Medicine (ACOEM)	www.acoem.org	"ACOEM Guideline: Automated External Defibrillation"	www.acoem.org/guidelines/ article.asp?ID=41

Threshold Issue 1: Understanding Issues Relevant to the Purchase and Use of AEDs

The first decision to make is whether to purchase and use AEDs or to rely solely on EMS, patrons, or staff to render care without them. This decision must be based on consultation with a competent authority in your community or state.

To better prepare you for making this important decision, you should also consider the following.

Legal Mandate

The law requires some organizations to have AEDs. This is the case with schools, park districts, and even health and fitness clubs in certain parts of the United States. If this applies to your organization, your decision involves only issues of implementation, which are covered in the next section of this chapter.

Community Standards

You should know what other similar organizations are doing with regard to AEDs. If it looks as though the majority of others in your profession have AEDs, you should be concerned about whether this has become a community or industry standard that could possibly increase your liability if someone has SCA in your facility or program and dies or has medical complications as a result.

Laws

Consider the potential for liability when deciding whether to implement new plans or programs. With AEDs, the issues are twofold. First, will it increase your liability if you decide to have AEDs on-site? Second, will it increase your liability if you decide not to have them? There is no definitive answer to either question, only information that can help guide your decision. As to whether having an AED will increase your liability, you should know that statutes in every state offer some level of protection from liability for the user. In the sport setting, potential AED users may include lifeguards, fitness instructors, golf course attendants, members of ski patrols, stadium personnel, outdoor guides, and coaches and athletic trainers. Other states (they all differ) also offer protection to those who provide training in their use, medical oversight, and so on. The protection offered to those who use or are otherwise responsible for an AED is limited to conduct that does not amount to gross negligence or willful misconduct (something that goes above and beyond what is considered ordinary negligence). Information regarding AED legislation can be obtained from state legislative sources and consultation with legal experts. Also, the National Conference of State Legislatures and other sources (see table 7.2), have Web sites that provide a good starting point for learning about state-specific AED legislation.

As to whether or not having an AED will increase your liability, part of the answer depends on community or industry standards, as mentioned previously. Knowing what others are doing in the community or in your industry is very important for the purpose of understanding your potential liability. Understanding case law is also important when it comes to developing a sense of your potential liability for not having AEDs at your facility. For example, in 1996, a tennis player suffered SCA while playing at a tennis club in Pennsylvania. He survived but was permanently injured as a result. The tennis club did not have an AED on the premises at the time of the incident. It also did not have anyone on the staff trained in the use of an AED. A lawsuit was subsequently brought against the tennis club by the club member and his wife, who claimed that the club had been negligent with regard to its responsibilities to them as patrons. They claimed the facility should have had an AED available on the premises. The court initially

Table 7.2   Source for AED Laws and Regulations

Organization	Home page	Document	Web site
National Conference of State Legislatures	www.ncsl.org	"State Laws on Heart Attacks, Cardiac Arrest and Defibrillators"	www.ncsl.org/programs/health/aed.htm
National Center for Early Defibrillation	www.early-defib.org	"Understanding Legal Issues"	www.early-defib.org/03_06_02.html#manage_risk
American Red Cross (ARC)	www.redcross.org	"AED Legislation Update Fall 2004"	www.redcross.org/services/hss/courses/ AEDGoodSamChart2004.pdf
American Heart Association (AHA)	www.americanheart.org	"AED Legislation Update State Requirements"	www.americanheart.org/presenter.jhtml?identifier =3024006
Medtronic	www.aedhelp.com	AED Legislation by State	www.aedhelp.com/legal/legislation_states.cfm

found in favor of the club, but on appeal the decision was reversed and remanded to determine whether the tennis club had a duty to provide an AED (*Atcovitz v. Gulph Mills Tennis Club, Inc.* 2001). Note that even in 1996, there was a question as to whether a club had a duty to have an AED on its premises. Because AEDs have become more readily accepted, the duty to have an AED might well be more strongly solidified if there is a reasonable expectation among the public that AEDs are both easy to obtain and operate for trained individuals.

> Knowing community and industry standards, as well as understanding case law, are important to understanding your potential liability.

Recommendations

Given the importance of AEDs, various organizations and professional associations have put forth recommendations regarding whether certain industries should implement their use. The following section presents recommendations by type of activity, from the organizations listed in table 7.1.

• **Health and fitness.** The American Heart Association (AHA) and the American College of Sports Medicine (ACSM) jointly recommend the placement of AEDs in health and fitness facilities under certain conditions. Their recommendation reads as follows:

> Until further definitive data are available, AED placement is strongly encouraged in those health/fitness facilities with a large number of members...; those that offer special programs to clinical populations (i.e., programs for the elderly or those with medical conditions...); and those health/fitness facilities in which the time from the recognition of cardiac arrest until the first shock is delivered by the EMS is anticipated to be >5 minutes. In unsupervised exercise rooms... such as those that might be located in hotels, apartments complexes, or office buildings, the AED should be part of the overall Public Access Defibrillation (PAD) plan for the host facility" (Balady et al, 2002. p.562; PAD refers to making AEDs available in public or private places where large numbers of people, or people who at are high risk of cardiac arrest, gather).

Additionally, the International Health, Racquet and Sportsclub Association (IHRSA) takes the position that "although there is not a legal standard of care that requires that automated external defibrillators (AEDs) be in all fitness centers.

However, the association encourages health club operators to consider the advantages of installing AEDs in their facilities (International Health, Racquet and Sportsclub Association 2003).

- **Aquatics.** The International Life Saving Federation (ILSF) provides recommendations for lifeguards and the use of AEDs. The ILSF recommends that some lifesaving and lifeguard services undertake a comprehensive investigation of AED use to include, but not be limited to, such issues as AED response times, frequency of cardiac arrests, supervision and management issues, license requirements, and cost-benefit analysis. The ILSF recommends that decisions be community-level decisions. They further recognize that lifesavers and lifeguards may play a role in the delivery of AEDs under certain conditions but must receive appropriate training. The United States Lifesaving Association (USLA) recommendations mirror those of the ILSF. You can learn more about the USLA and their recommendations by visiting their Web site at www.usla.org.

Ellis and Associates (2004) mandate the implementation of AEDs at their aquatic facilities and use of a comprehensive aquatic risk management program. Ellis and Associates further require that its clients demonstrate that they are able to initiate the use of an AED "within two minutes from the time of victim water extrication" (Ellis and Associates 2004).

- **Golf.** Since cardiac arrest is the leading cause of death on golf courses, the AHA and *Golf Digest* began a public education and awareness program titled "Links for Life." This initiative is designed to encourage proprietors of golf courses to acquire AEDs and train staff in CPR and AED use. Other organizations participating in this project are the National Safety Council, the National Golf Course Owners Association, Club Managers Association, and the Golf Course Superintendents Association (Spengler and Connaughton 2001). More information on the Links for Life program is available at www.golfdigest.com (see table 7.1).

- **Organized athletic events.** The National Athletic Trainers' Association (NATA) recommends that each organization or institution that sponsors athletic activities or events develops and implements a written emergency plan. As a part of the plan, NATA recommends that administrators note that the AHA has established guidelines that call for making AEDs readily available and recognizing that defibrillation is necessary for life support in cases of SCA (Andersen et al 2002, p.103).

See the Safety Guidelines Finder in appendix B for links to documents that provide safety information on various activities.

Threshold Issue 2: Understanding What to Consider When Using AEDs

If the choice is made to purchase and use AEDs, the next step is to understand the key issues to address with regard to their use. The following is a summary of practical matters to consider that are recommended by professional associations or required by law. The laws of each state differ, so familiarize yourself with your state's laws and consult with someone with the requisite legal knowledge and authority before implementing a policy for the use of AEDs.

Cost

The cost of an AED can range from about $1,500 to $3,000 and varies according to the make and model chosen. Depending on the type and location of the agency or organization, grant or subsidy programs are sometimes available that help to reduce or eliminate the cost. Some examples of alternative funding sources are local civic organizations, local businesses, government and private grants, public charities, and traditional fundraising events. Information regarding funding options and suggestions for writing an AED program proposal can be obtained from the National Center for Early Defibrillation Web site at www.early-defib.org/03_06_05.html.

Training and Certification

State law often requires that organizations that use AEDs train staff accordingly. Consulting a Web site that covers the applicable state legislation (see table 7.2) and retaining counsel from a knowledgeable lawyer are good ways to find out if training and certification are required. Even if it is not required by law, those who intend to use AEDs should receive formal training. An AED user must know how to recognize the signs of SCA, when to contact EMS, how to perform CPR and use an AED. AED training courses and related resources are provided through local chapters of the AHA, the American Red Cross, and the National Safety Council, among others (see table 7.3). As an alternative to hands-on review sessions in the classroom, computer-based interactive training is available from some AED manufacturers.

Table 7.3 Selected AED Training Courses

Organization	Home page	To find local agency
American Heart Association	www.americanheart.org	Enter your zip code under Get Local Info in upper right-hand corner of Web page
American Red Cross	www.redcross.org	www.redcross.org/where/where.html
National Safety Council	www.nsc.org	www.nsc.org/training/selectagency.cfm

Medical Oversight

As with training, medical oversight is sometimes required by state law. Therefore, you should determine whether it is required by your state if you choose to acquire and use AEDs. Again, checking your state law and retaining counsel from a knowledgeable lawyer are good ways to find out if medical oversight is required. Oversight by medical directors (often licensed physicians) consists of many functions, such as providing program leadership, coordinating with local EMS, assisting in selection of AEDs, overseeing maintenance of the devices, developing an AED emergency action plan, assisting with or supervising initial

For an example of a state law relevant to the use of AEDs, see page 122 in appendix A.

AED training and continuing education, and keeping postuse data (National Center for Early Defibrillation, 2004). Note that states often place responsibility with the AED owners, similar in nature to the responsibility placed on medical directors. For example, AED owners may also be required to notify the local EMS of the type and location of the AEDs and ensure that each such device is properly maintained.

Summary

AEDs are certainly becoming more commonplace in our society. We now see them in many public places, including shopping malls and airports, and they are now found more regularly at sport and recreation facilities. It has been shown that AEDs save lives, so it is clear that they are important from both an ethical and medical standpoint. Additionally, as they become more commonplace, the bar will continue to be raised regarding the standard of care that organizations and facilities are expected to provide. Sport and recreation providers should therefore stay abreast of what industries and sectors of the sport and recreation profession are doing in terms of implementing the use of AEDs and whether there are local or state legal mandates for their use. The use of AEDs is a safety issue currently of great importance to the profession and one that will surely continue to grow in significance in future years.

Real-World Application

Scenario

Jennifer has recently taken a position as the manager of a health and fitness club. About half of its members are seniors over the age of 65. Jennifer learns that there have been three heart attacks at the facility in the past two years. In fact, the former manager lost his job a year earlier after a 70-year-old man died after suffering a SCA at the facility. Given this background information and the potential for such an event to occur again, Jennifer considers purchasing AEDs for the club. On her second day as manager, a 68-year-old woman collapses during her workout. She experiences SCA. Fortunately, an EMS crew is eating lunch at a restaurant just two doors down from the club. They are summoned by one of the employees at the club and are able to come to her aid quickly and save her life. Although greatly shaken by the experience, Jennifer still is not sure what to do next. Does she have a legal or ethical obligation to purchase AEDs, and are they even necessary? Also, if she does purchase AEDs, what training do she and her staff require? Jennifer decides that she needs advice and needs it quickly before facing another potential tragedy.

Practitioner Action

Jennifer is right to seek advice about the purchase of AEDs and the training required to use them. Even in the absence of previous incidents at the club, she needs to give serious thought to acquiring them. After visiting several Web sites; talking with legal counsel, industry experts, and representatives from professional associations; and learning what other fitness clubs are doing, she takes action. Jennifer learns just how important it is that she and her staff undergo AED training even though the devices are relatively simple to use. She also recognizes that they need CPR training as well. She gains an understanding of relevant state laws, including mandates for the use of AEDs and immunity provisions that apply to her and the health and fitness club should the AED actually be used. She also learns what the response time would be for EMS to reach her facility. She is lucky that emergency medical technicians were close by during the latest incident but certainly cannot rely on luck again. Finally, she learns what AEDs cost, how to maintain them, how many are needed, and where they should be placed in her facility. With this knowledge, she is able to make an informed decision.

Questions

1. What does the law in your state say with regard to requirements for training staff to use AEDs?

2. What are the immunity provisions in your state law for AED users or those otherwise responsible for their use? How has this law been interpreted (this requires consulting with an expert)?

3. How many AEDs are needed for facilities such as a health and fitness center, an aquatics center, a resort property, a city park, a playing field, and so on? Where should they be placed?

4. How do you tailor a plan to meet the needs of various types of programs and activities such as golf, recreational sports, and aquatics? What elements are similar? What is different?

5. How much would it cost a facility to purchase AEDs?

6. What is the response time for EMS to reach your property?

Drug Testing

chapter objectives

After reading this chapter, you will have a thorough understanding of the following:

Threshold Issue 1: Understanding the Legality of Developing and Implementing a Drug Testing
Plan

Threshold Issue 2: Recognizing Effective Components of a Drug Testing Plan

Today, athletes continue experimenting with newly discovered drug compounds to help improve their performance, and the use of recreational drugs, though illegal, continues to rise. According to several studies cited by Kucharson (2004), Mawdsley and Russo (2003), and Superville (2003), drug use has reached epidemic proportions. A recent study conducted by the University of Michigan indicated that in 2000, more than 50 percent of high school seniors reported they had used drugs.

Curbing drug use and implementing drug testing policies are concerns parents, coaches, and administrators must deal with. The adverse side effects of performance-enhancing drugs have been known for years, and the dangers of recreational drug use are well documented as well (see table 8.1).

Table 8.1   Performance Enhancers, Their Effects, and Their Adverse Side Effects

Performance enhancer	Performance effect	Adverse side effects
Beta blockers	Calms nerves	May constrict blood vessels
Blood doping	Increases oxygen supply to muscles and improves aerobic performance	Thickens blood and may cause heart attacks
Central nervous system stimulants	Stimulates the nervous system by causing the nervous system to over react	May cause performance-related injury by stimulating a physical reaction that causes an injury to the muscular or skeletal systems
Diuretics	Reduces weight and masks presence of drugs in system	Can cause dehydration
Erythropoietin	Increases production of red blood cells, which improves overall performance	Can thicken blood, which causes heart attacks
Heroin, marijuana	Masks pain	Can cause greater injuries by allowing the athlete to perform when they should not be
Human and animal growth hormones	Builds muscle mass and strength	Can cause a fatal neurological disorder
Insulin-like growth factor	Increases muscle mass and reduces body fat	May cause heart enlargement
Steroids	Accelerates muscle growth	Increases risks of cancer, liver dysfunction, kidney disorders, and heart disease

For the purposes of this chapter, we will focus on drug testing as it relates to athletes in park and recreation programs and schools (i.e., the K-12 age range) and in private institutions such as private schools and fitness clubs. Drug testing polices at the college and professional levels of athletics typically deal with athletes who have reached the age of majority, and therefore, have obtained different legal status than younger athletes. In addition, drug testing policies at these levels are often dictated by the institutions' governing body, such as the NCAA for some college-level athletes, or are dictated by the collective bargaining relationship between players and management. These situations are beyond the scope of this chapter. Information on drug testing policies for professional sports can be found on the Web.

We also will focus on recreational drug use rather than performance-enhancing drugs. This is because most tests for detecting performance-enhancing drugs are too expensive for schools and park districts to afford and because the majority of cases cited involve recreational drug use and its effects. Table 8.2 provides links to excellent information sources regarding drug testing and other relevant information.

Table 8.2 Web Sites on Drug Testing Information

Organization	Home page	Document	Web site
Drug and Alcohol Testing Industry Association	www.datia.org	Information on drug and alcohol industry	www.datia.org
Drug Testing News	www.drugtestingnews.com	Drug testing legislation, legal issues, business and technology	www.drugtestingnews.com
International Journal of Drug Testing	www.criminology.fsu.edu/journal	Drug testing journal	www.criminology.fsu.edu/journal
NBA Players Association	www.nbpa.com	Drug policy for testing professional basketball players	www.nbpa.com/cba_articles/article-XXXIII.php
The National Center for Drug Free Sport	www.drugfreesport.com/home.asp	Information on drug testing	www.drugfreesport.com/home.asp
National Collegiate Athletic Association Drug Testing Program	www2.ncaa.org	College drug testing	www2.ncaa.org/legislation_and_governance/eligibility_and_conduct/drug_testing.html
National Council on Alcoholism and Drug Dependence	www.ncadd.org	Policy statement on drug testing	www.ncadd.org/programs/advocacy/policytest.html
National Federation of State High School Associations	www.nfhs.org	Sports medicine: Drug testing in high school activities	www.nfhs.org/ScriptContent/VA_Custom/vimdisplays/contentpagedisplay.cfm?Content_ID=233&SearchWord=drug%20testing
National Institute on Drug Abuse	www.drugabuse.gov	Information on drug testing and workplace issues	www.drugabuse.gov/DrugPages/testing.html/
Office of National Drug Control Policy	www.whitehousedrugpolicy.gov	Government policy on drug testing in schools	www.whitehousedrugpolicy.gov/publications/drug%5Ftesting/
OHS Health and Safety Services, Inc.	www.ohsinc.com	Information on drug testing laws	www.ohsinc.com/laws_state_drug_testing_laws_SAID.htm
U.S. Department of Health and Human Services and National Clearinghouse for Alcohol and Drug Information	www.health.org	Publications on drug testing	www.health.org/govpubs/workit/ts9.aspx

Threshold Issue 1: Understanding the Legality of Developing and Implementing a Drug Testing Plan

It is important to understand the legality of creating and implementing a drug testing plan. What precedent exists for balancing a person's right to privacy against an institution's concern with the possible negative affects associated with drug use?

Public Institutions

Public institutions, such as park and recreation departments and public schools, are considered to be state actors, so they must follow the dictates of the Fourth Amendment to the U.S. Constitution as well as any particular provisions from the state constitutions that apply to them . In essence, the Fourth Amendment protects people and their houses, papers, and effects against unreasonable searches and seizures. Similar guidelines laid out in state constitutions may be even stricter than those in the Fourth Amendment.

The right of the people to be secure in their persons, houses, papers, and effects, against unreasonable searches and seizures, shall not be violated, and no Warrants shall issue, but upon probable cause, supported by Oath or affirmation, and particularly describing the place to be searched, and the persons or things to be seized (U.S. Constitution, Amendment IV).

If a search is conducted, and a drug test is considered a search, the search must be reasonable and the intrusion of the test on an individual's privacy must be weighed against the government's interest in conducting the test. Reasonableness will depend on the circumstances.

In most instances, suspicion is not required in order to perform a test.

Because the use of certain recreational and performance-enhancing drugs is illegal according to federal statutes, many institutions have attempted to implement drug testing policies in order to deter their students, participants, or members from using drugs, and also to detect drug use in order to either provide assistance to those who do not understand the dangers involved in drug use or to provide information to law enforcement officials in order that they may become involved to rid the institution of drug users. At the recreational or high school sport level, officials also know that drug use can be very dangerous to young participants.

However, many times the athletes forced to submit to a drug testing program do not do so willingly. They feel that the drug test infringes on their privacy rights as protected by the federal constitution and that they should not have to submit to the test. These individuals are typically not drug users; instead they are participants who find that if they do not submit to the testing, they will not be able to continue participating in the sport or activity of their choice. Beginning in the 1980s, these individuals sued the institutions who developed the drug testing policies so that they could avoid being tested as a requirement of participation. Until 1995, institutions who attempted to implement drug testing policies were often unsure as to whether their policies would be upheld in a court of law. However, in 1995 the U.S. Supreme Court finally dealt with the issue.

In *Vernonia School District 47J v. Acton,* the Supreme Court reviewed the constitutionality of a drug testing program applied to student-athletes at the high school level. In the mid 1980s, teachers and administrators in the Vernonia School District noticed a sharp increase in student drug use and an increase in disciplinary problems at the school. The school district also found that student-athletes were both users and leaders of the drug culture. The district implemented a drug testing policy that applied to all students participating in athletics, requiring each student to sign a form consenting to the random urinalysis testing policy before being allowed to participate in sports. During the test, the student would enter a locker room with an adult monitor who would check the sample produced for temperature and tampering. Seventh grader James Acton refused to sign the consent form and was not allowed to play football. His family sued claiming that the drug testing policy violated the Fourth Amendment.

The Supreme Court noted that any search, like the drug test, must be judged by its reasonableness. This reasonableness "is judged by balancing its intrusion on the individual's Fourth Amendment interests against its promotion of legitimate governmental interests" (pp. 652-653).

The focus of the case was on the balancing of the interests involved. Initially, the Court found that while in public school, students maintain diminished privacy rights because they are under the temporary custody of the state and are subject to vaccinations and medical exams due to the school's custodial relationship over them. Student-athletes have an even lesser expectation of privacy because there is an element of communal undress to athletics and they voluntarily subject themselves to more regulations (such as preseason physical exams, acquisition of insurance coverage, maintenance of minimum grade point averages), than other students (p. 657). The Court also found that the way the test was conducted was similar to situations encountered in public restrooms, so the privacy interests compromised by the testing were negligible.

The Court then turned to the school district's reasons for implementing the testing plan. It found that the school district was faced with an important governmental interest because drug use at school was a serious problem, disrupting the educational process and harming children. The Court agreed that there was an immediate crisis in the district and that the drug testing program attempted to effectively combat this problem.

Balancing this government interest against the students' diminished privacy rights, the Court held that the drug testing policy was reasonable. After this case, many school districts implemented drug testing programs aimed at student-athletes. However, the question soon shifted to whether drug testing programs could be implemented as a prerequisite to participation in any extracurricular activity. This question was addressed by the Supreme Court in 2002.

In the fall of 1998, the school district of Tecumseh, Oklahoma, adopted the Student Activities Testing Policy, which required all middle and high school students to consent to drug testing in order to participate in any extracurricular activity. Teachers testified they had seen students who appeared to be under the influence of drugs and that they had heard students speaking openly about using drugs. A drug dog found marijuana cigarettes near the school parking lot, and police officers found drugs or drug paraphernalia in a student's car.

Under the policy, students were required to take a drug test before participating in an extracurricular activity, to submit to random drug testing while participating in that activity, and to agree to be tested at any time upon reasonable suspicion. The medical tests were designed to detect only the use of illegal drugs, including amphetamines, marijuana, cocaine, opiates, and barbiturates, not medical conditions or the presence of authorized prescription medications. Similar to the situation in Vernonia, the school district did have evidence of drug use at Tecumseh schools.

Two students filed suit alleging that the policy violated the Fourth Amendment. The district court held that the policy was constitutional and granted a summary judgment to the school district, allowing the program to be implemented. This decision was reversed by the Tenth Circuit Court of Appeals, which held that the policy violated the Fourth Amendment. The case was subsequently appealed to the U.S. Supreme Court.

Following the reasonableness test laid out in Vernonia, the Supreme Court considered three issues:

- The nature of the privacy interest allegedly compromised by the drug testing program
- The character of the intrusion imposed by the policy

- The nature and immediacy of the government's concerns and the efficacy of the policy in meeting them

All students participating in extracurricular activities were required to abide by the rules of the Oklahoma Secondary Schools Activities Association. These rules held that students had to be monitored by a faculty sponsor. Thus, along with the element of communal undress in some of the activities, those students affected by the policy had a diminished expectation of privacy. After a review of the procedures for collecting a specimen and maintaining a chain of custody over the specimen, the court ruled that they were not intrusive enough to violate students' privacy rights. Finally, the court affirmed the right of the school district to conduct testing even if evidence of drug use was not based on an individualized suspicion of wrongdoing (*Board v. Earls* 2002).

After Earls and Vernonia, it is now clear that public schools can test all students involved in extracurricular activities and not merely student-athletes. However, this does not mean that schools or other public institutions can somehow ignore federal constitutional requirements. Instead, the Supreme Court has only recognized that children possess lesser privacy interests than others while they are under the supervision of the public institution. In addition, a drug testing plan implemented by a public institution must be similar to those described in these two cases. Finally, some individual state constitutions have actually strengthened the privacy rights of their citizens within the particular state constitution. Therefore, any organization attempting to implement a drug testing plan must be aware of both federal and state constitutional requirements.

In summary, any drug-testing plan must comply with applicable federal and state provisions. It is imperative that those responsible for creating drug-testing policies become familiar with those laws. In addition, any administrative rules and regulations of the organization must be followed, although these must also comply with federal and state constitutional requirements. These rules and regulations must be reviewed by legal counsel to ensure compliance with federal and state laws. In the absence of administrative rules and regulations, legal counsel must be consulted to draft a drug testing plan.

Private Institutions

If your organization is a private institution (such as a private school or a private sport club), federal constitutional protections do not apply, and state constitutional provisions may not apply. However, some private institutions make an attempt to comply with these constitutional provisions, because otherwise their members or participants may realize that they are not being provided with the same privileges as those in public organizations. Others make certain conditions, such as submission to a drug testing program, a requirement of membership in the private organization, so the issue is dealt with immediately. Regardless, if an individual voluntarily joins a private organization, or voluntarily participates in a private activity, and the private organization requires them to submit to a drug test, it is not likely that they will be able to avoid the test by claiming that it violates their rights.

Sometimes, however, the distinction between a public and a private institution is not so easy to determine. For example, if a private management company manages a public golf course, that private management company might be deemed to be a state actor, thus coming under the umbrella of the constitution because of its close connection with the governmental entity. This is especially true if the governmental entity in any way influences the management of the facility. This influence may come in the form of funds provided by the government, hiring of the management staff influenced by the government, or other types of support.

Threshold Issue 2: Recognizing Effective Components of a Drug Testing Plan

To ensure that your drug testing plan withstands judicial scrutiny, your organization should try to incorporate as many of these characteristics into the plan as possible.

Gather Input From Parents and Law Enforcement Officials

Before implementing a drug testing program, especially in a public school setting, input from parents and local law enforcement officials should be solicited. This should result in lessened opposition if a program is subsequently started.

Questions to local law enforcement officials might include the following:

- What is the rate of drug use among local youth?
- What types of drugs are being used?
- How many incidences have been reported or investigated?
- Do you perceive this rate as being a problem?

Questions to parents might include the following:

- Are you aware of any drug use by local youth?
- Is your child using drugs?
- Do you perceive drug use among local youth as a problem?

Town-hall type meetings should be scheduled to give parents the opportunity to voice their concerns to the officials contemplating the establishment of a drug testing plan. Legal counsel, local law enforcement officials, parents, and youth should be invited to those meetings. Phone hot lines and Web sites might be used to gather information from those who cannot attend meetings. The more input that is gathered, the less chance that the drug testing plan, if one is implemented, will be challenged.

Provide Advance Notification by Written Policy

Groups to be tested should be given advanced written notice of the drug testing plan and should be required to sign a document indicating their consent to being tested. This written notification should be given as far in advance of the testing date as possible. If someone refuses to sign, they should be denied the benefits of participation or employment in the organization.

Identify Substances for Which to Test

The substances for which you plan to test should be listed in the written plan that you distribute. Drugs stay in the body for differing time periods. Cocaine will only last about four days, whereas oil-based steroids that are taken by injection may be detected up to nine months after administration. This is one reason why random, year-round testing is preferred as opposed to an annual test. Cost is another factor in deciding which drugs to test for. Each test could cost from $30 to several hundred dollars, depending on what substances are being sought with the test.

Test Targeted Groups

Testing a targeted group has been upheld many times by the courts, and those who are involved in extracurricular activities (see *Board v. Earls 2002*) or have driving privileges have been the most frequently targeted groups. Random selection within targeted groups also has been upheld by the courts many times. Some commentators have argued that the entire student body should be tested, because recreational drug abuse is more prevalent in the student body as a whole. However, courts have been reluctant to allow testing of all students.

Limit Access to Results

A strict chain of custody regarding both samples and information has to be established to ensure privacy. A chain-of-custody form should be used for tracking who has access to information about the tests. Preferably, the testing should be conducted in an approved drug testing lab. For instance, the federal government has a number of approved labs depending on the type of drugs to be tested. If urinalysis is used, the sample should be placed in two vials, which are sealed and coded. Only the person being tested and the monitor should know the individual's code. Reveal the results of the test only to those persons who need to know them, such as the principal, the appropriate supervisor, and the person who was tested. Federal law prohibits the results being revealed to law enforcement officials unless requested by a court order.

Use an Adult Monitor

Anecdotal evidence indicates that individuals being tested will use a variety of illicit means to pass drug tests. It may be appropriate to use a same-sex adult monitor. The adult monitor should be an employee of the lab at which the testing is being conducted. School health officials may be used if the testing is being conducted on school grounds.

Direct observation is not always necessary and in some instances may be inappropriate. Listening to the sounds of urination may be all that is needed. In any event, the testing site should be checked to ensure that the site has been properly prepared and no tampering of the site has occurred.

Provide Medical Information

If a test is positive, an individual should be given an opportunity to explain the results. At this point, the individual should be asked to provide medical information that may have resulted in a positive test.

Use Accurate Techniques

The gas chromatography/mass spectrometry (GC/MS) test is considered one of the more accurate tests currently available, but because of how much it costs, may not be practical to some organizations. Consider using a laboratory that first uses the enzyme multiplied immunoassay technique (EMIT), and then confirm any positive result by using the GC/MS test. Some organizations and schools are testing by taking a hair sample. A hair sample of 1.5 inches (or roughly 4 centimeters) will reveal drug use over the previous 90 days. Regardless of which technique is used, if the first sample is positive and the second sample is negative, the results of the second sample should be accepted as the final outcome. Testing a second sample will offset the effect of a false-positive: a positive result when the result should be negative. False-negatives may also occur. False tests occur largely in one of three ways:

- Chain-of-custody error: the process is not supervised.
- Clerical error: the test is performed properly, but the results are incorrectly reported.
- Technical error: the test is performed incorrectly.

Emphasize the Benefits of the Program

In all settings, a primary emphasis of the program should be educational. If a person produces a positive result, he or she should be required to attend a drug education and prevention program. In a school setting, students may be precluded from participating in extracurricular programs but should not be suspended from school unless required by law. In an employment setting, individuals may be suspended, not hired, or fired, depending on the circumstances.

Prevention programs may vary widely but generally contain several elements: alternative programs; a community-based process; early intervention; education; environmental, informational, and problem identification; and referral (Office of National Drug Control Policy 2005). Alternative programs provide for participation of target populations in constructive and healthy activities like drug-free dances, youth or adult leadership activities, visits to community drop-in centers, and community service activities. A community-based process enhances the ability of the community to more effectively provide prevention and treatment services for alcohol, tobacco, and drug-use disorders. Activities in this process include community and volunteer training, coalition building, and networking. Early intervention programs are designed to assist someone just beginning to abuse drugs in order to modify his or her behavior. Activities range from user education to formal intervention and referral for treatment.

Educational activities are designed to enhance decision-making skills, the ability to cope with stress, and success with problem solving. Examples of these types of activities include classroom or small-group sessions, parenting and family management classes, and peer leader programs. Environmental activities focus on changing the written and unwritten community standards, codes, and attitudes that tend to tolerate, accept, or even support the abuse of drugs. This includes, at the very least, reviewing school and community drug-use policies. Informational programs are intended to increase awareness regarding the nature and extent of drug use, abuse, and addiction and their effects on individuals, families, and communities. Information can be provided via clearinghouse resource centers, media campaigns, public service announcements, speaking engagements, and health fairs. Problem identification and referral programs focus on those who have engaged in illegal use of alcohol or tobacco or who have begun to use illicit drugs. Strategies to combat such use include assistance programs for employees and students as well as DUI education programs.

Summary

The use of illegal drugs in the United States continues to rise, and this has a direct affect on schools and other organizations that provide sport and recreational opportunities. Where drug use is an issue, drug testing becomes an important consideration for those in charge. This issue of drug testing is tied to both state and federal law. As state actors, public institutions such as park and recreation departments and public schools must follow the dictates of the Fourth Amendment to the U.S. Constitution as well as any particular provisions from the state constitutions that apply to them. Therefore, it is critical that these public providers of sport and recreational opportunities understand the legal requirements as they relate to drug testing. Additionally, understanding the relevant issues in creating and implementing a drug testing plan is of critical importance. These issues are based upon both legal and practical considerations. The suggested components of a drug testing plan outlined in this chapter are designed to assist those sport and recreation providers who, either by choice or mandate, are faced with the task of implementing a plan.

Real-World Application

Scenario

Coach Taylor is the head football coach of the local high school team. Before the season started several parents came to him expressing concern that they suspected some of the players were using performance-enhancing drugs, and they wanted the school to implement a drug testing plan. The parents had been told by their sons that some of the star athletes were using steroids that are undetectable and were obtaining them from one of the players on the team. Coach Taylor denied that there was steroid use by any of his players and refused to implement a drug testing plan. Later that season, one of the players is arrested for attempting to sell steroids to an undercover police officer posing as a high school student. The player admits to selling drugs to six current football players. The school superintendent calls Coach Taylor into his office and tells him that he must implement a drug testing plan to determine if any of his players are using illegal drugs.

Practitioner Action

Coach Taylor's superintendent is correct: the coach does need a drug testing plan in place. After visiting several Web sites and talking to local community leaders, parents, law enforcement officials, the school's attorney, and school districts with established drug testing plans, Coach Taylor creates a plan for his team. He also visits several drug testing labs to observe their procedures and obtain an estimate of the cost of implementing a plan. He realizes that athletes need to be educated about the harm that using drugs can cause not only to them but to their family and community.

Questions

1. What do you think should be the basic elements of Coach Taylor's drug testing plan?

2. How would you tailor a plan to accommodate other types of extracurricular programs and activities like basketball, track and field, and wrestling? What elements would be similar? What would be different?

3. Would your program be any different if you were a college or professional coach? What elements would be similar? What elements would be different?

Equipment, Premises, Instruction, and Supervision

chapter objectives

After reading this chapter, you will have a thorough understanding of the following:

Threshold Issue 1: Understanding Issues Relevant to Maintaining and Providing Proper Equipment and Premises

Threshold Issue 2: Recognizing Key Issues in Providing Adequate Instruction and Supervision

Common sources of injuries in sport and recreation include dangerous or improper equipment, hazardous premises, improper instruction, and improper supervision. Each of these issues is obviously quite comprehensive in scope. The purpose of this chapter is not to provide an in-depth discussion of each issue. Much has been written on these issues and is available in books and articles. (The Sport and Recreation Law Association [SRLA] maintains a list of books and articles on its Web site [http://srlaweb.org] that have some very good information on these issues.) It is the purpose of this chapter to address key aspects of the broad issues and then, importantly, to provide direction in terms of finding information on recommendations, standards, and guidelines relevant to these issues.

Threshold Issue 1: Understanding Issues Relevant to Maintaining and Providing Proper Equipment and Premises

Equipment and premises must be in good working order to ensure the safety and well-being of your organization's participants. Understanding how to care for equipment and how to maintain playing surfaces is vital.

Equipment

Equipment issues are clearly at the forefront of importance for sport and recreation supervisors. It is important that supervisors not only provide protective or safety equipment, but also instruct participants as to how to properly use and care for the equipment, as well as perform basic safety inspections. These inspections would act as a supplement to inspections provided by the coach or sport supervisor. Manufacturer recommendations regarding inspection and maintenance of equipment should be followed. Also, all instructions and relevant documentation should be retained. All equipment should be properly fitted and participants shown how to properly wear it. It likewise must be appropriate for the activity and the physical size and skill level of participants.

A case example that illustrates the importance of providing proper equipment involves an injury to a high school football player. Richard Locilento was a senior at John A. Coleman Catholic High School and was participating in an annual, informal intramural tackle football game. The game was officiated by two instructors from the school, and no protective equipment was provided. Locilento sustained a dislocated shoulder while attempting to tackle another player. He filed suit, alleging that the school failed to properly supervise the game and provide necessary equipment and training. At trial, the jury held for Locilento, and the school appealed. The higher court reasoned that the likelihood of injury was greater because of the school's failure to provide the necessary protective equipment (*Locilento v. John A. Coleman Catholic High School* 1987).

Playing tackle football without protective equipment might seem like an extreme example. However, consider whether a similar result might occur if a young girl is hit in the face by a softball where a catcher's mask was neither required nor made available, or where shin guards were not made available for young soccer players.

With the importance of providing, maintaining, and often requiring proper and safe equipment of obvious importance, it is necessary to understand how and where to find information regarding important equipment issues. For collegiate and high school sports, information on equipment is readily available and provided for your reference in this chapter. For recreational activities and sports, guidance can be found in a variety of sources (see table 9.1).

For collegiate sports, information on recommended safety equipment is provided in the *2005-2006 NCAA Sports Medicine Handbook*. The *Handbook* provides information on mandatory equipment and prohibited items for the following sports: baseball, basketball, fencing, field hockey, football, gymnastics, ice hockey, lacrosse, shooting, soccer, snow skiing, softball, swimming and diving, track and field, volleyball, water polo, and wrestling. The *2005-2006 NCAA Sports Medicine Handbook* is available online at www.ncaa.org/library/sports_sciences/sports_med_handbook/2005-06/2005-06_sports_medicine_handbook.pdf. Other safety equipment issues addressed separately in the *Handbook* include guidelines for fitting and removing helmets, eye safety, and mouth protection.

For high school sports, information on protective equipment is available from the National Federation of State High School Associations through their Web site: www.nfhs.org. Equipment issues are covered in their Sports and Rules Information. This is a valuable source of information for high school coaches and administrators.

For sport activities, equipment that protects the face and head is of critical importance. Table 9.1 provides selected resources for obtaining safety recommendations for sport equipment that protects the player's head, face, eyes, and mouth.

Table 9.1 Standards and Recommendations on Selected Protective Sport Equipment

Safety issue	Organization	Home page	Document	Web site
Eye protection	American Society for Testing and Materials (ASTM)	www.astm.org	"Standard Specification for Eye Protectors for Selected Sports" "Standard Safety Specification for Eye and Face Protective Equipment for Hockey Players" (These documents are available for purchase from the ASTM. For more information regarding an ASTM standard or product please contact customer support at 610-832-9585 or via e-mail at service@astm.org.)	www.astm.org/cgi-bin/SoftCart.exe/NEWSITE_JAVASCRIPT/index.shtml?L+mystore+gfqh3818+1119041184
	National Collegiate Athletic Association (NCAA)	www2.ncaa.org	"2005-2006 NCAA Sports Medicine Handbook: "Eye Safety in Sports"	www.ncaa.org/library/sports_sciences/sports_med_handbook/2005-06/2005-06_sports_medicine_handbook.pdf
	American Academy of Pediatrics (AAP)	www.aap.org	"Protective Eyewear for Young Athletes"	http://aappolicy.aappublications.org/cgi/reprint/pediatrics;113/3/619.pdf

(continued)

Table 9.1 *(continued)*

Safety issue	Organization	Home page	Document	Web site
Head, face, and mouth protection	American Camping Association (ACA)	www.acacamps.org	"Protective Headgear (ACA Camp Accreditation Standard PD-21)"	www.acacamps.org/ accreditation/ stdsglance.php
	American Academy of Orthopaedic Surgeons	www.aaos.org	"Helmet Use in Skiing"	www.aaos.org/ wordhtml/position.htm
	American Academy of Pediatric Dentistry	www.aapd.org	"Prevention of Sports-Related Injuries"	www.aapd.org/pdf/ sports.pdf
	ASTM	www.astm.org	"Standard Specification for Head and Face Protective Equipment for Ice Hockey Goaltenders" "Standard Specification for Face Guards for Youth Baseball" "Standard Specification for Helmets Used in Recreational Bicycling or Roller Skating" "Standard Specification for Helmets Used for Down Hill Mountain Bicycle Racing" "Standard Specification for Helmets Used for BMX Cycling" "Standard Test Method for Shock-Attenuation Characteristics of Protective Headgear for Football" "Standard Specification for Protective Headgear Used in Horse Sports and Horseback Riding" "Standard Specification for Head and Face Protective Equipment for Ice Hockey Goaltenders" "Standard Performance Specification for Ice Hockey Helmets" "Standard Specification for Helmets Used in Short Track Speed Ice Skating (Not to Include Hockey)" "Standard Specifications for Helmets Used in Skateboarding and Trick Roller Skating" "Standard Specification for Helmets Used in Recreational Bicycling or Roller Skating" "Standard Specification for Helmets Used for Recreational Snow Sports" (These documents are available for purchase from the ASTM. For more information regarding an ASTM standard or product please contact customer support at 610-832-9585 or via e-mail at service@astm.org.)	www.astm.org/cgi-bin/SoftCart.exe/ NEWSITE_ JAVASCRIPT/index.sh tml?L+mystore+gfqh3 818+1119041184
	NCAA	www.ncaa.org	"2005-2006 NCAA Sports Medicine Handbook": "Guidelines for Helmet Fitting and Removal in Athletics"	www.ncaa.org/library/ sports_sciences/ sports_med_ handbook/2005-06/ 2005-06_sports_ medicine_ handbook.pdf

Safety issue	Organization	Home page	Document	Web site
Head, face, and mouth protection *(continued)*	National Operating Committee on Standards for Athletic Equipment	www.nocsae.org	"Standard Performance Specification for Newly Manufactured Football Helmets." "Standard Performance Specification for Recertified Football Helmets." "Standard Performance Specification for Newly Manufactured Baseball/Softball Batter's Helmets" "Standard Performance Specification for Newly Manufactured Baseball/Softball Catcher's Helmets With Faceguards" "Standard Performance Specification for Newly Manufactured Youth Baseballs" "Standard Performance Specification for Newly Manufactured Hockey Helmets" "Standard Performance Specification for Newly Manufactured Lacrosse Helmets With Faceguards" "Standard Performance Specification for Newly Manufactured Lacrosse Face Protectors" "Standard Performance Specification for Recertified Lacrosse Helmets"	www.nocsae.org/ standards/ documents.html

Each sport has its own necessary safety equipment. Make sure your athletes have the proper equipment and that it is inspected and maintained according to manufacturer recommendations.

Premises

When planning to develop, renovate, or perform extensive maintenance on facilities, an expert in facilities should be consulted in the early stages. Various agencies, associations, and organizations publish standards and guidelines that may affect your facility. There are also laws and regulations that may apply.

These may include, but are not limited to, the Occupational Safety and Health Administration, Americans with Disabilities Act, American Society for Testing and Materials, American National Standards Institute, AAHPERD's Council on Facilities and Equipment, ACSM's Health/Fitness Facility Standards and Guidelines, as well as various local and state health and fire codes.

To reduce the risk of injury, administrators, teachers, and coaches of sport and recreational activities should take reasonable precautions to provide a safe environment. Part of doing so includes inspecting facilities for risks. Administrators, teachers, and coaches can be held liable for an injury caused by hazards they should have discovered. Additionally, if they are aware of a hazard they may be held liable if they failed to take reasonable steps to remedy the hazard or to adequately warn participants of it.

Facility and equipment inspections may be classified according to type and frequency. An inspection may be generalized for an entire facility, or tailored to focus on a designated location. Inspections should be conducted regularly, and may occur daily, weekly, monthly, seasonally, or annually (Maloy 2001; Peterson & Hronek 1997). The frequency of the inspections depends on several factors including but not limited to manufacturer recommendations, facility and equipment standards, condition of the facility and equipment, and the amount of usage. Generally, the higher the risk, the more frequent the inspections should be. Daily inspections can be developed to address such risks as checking for water or debris on activity courts, holes in fields, or for doors that should be locked. Less frequent inspections can provide a more specialized inspection for equipment, facilities, and premises including things such as frayed cables on an exercise machine, loose boards on bleachers, or loose anchors for soccer goals (Maloy, 2001). Also, periodic inspections should be conducted to determine if facilities are compliant with all code requirements for equipment such as emergency lighting and fire extinguishers.

If a hazard is detected, it should be corrected immediately. If it cannot be immediately repaired or replaced, cordon off the area, warn participants, take the damaged equipment away, cancel or modify the activity, or do whatever else is necessary to provide a reasonably safe environment. Participants also can be taught how to perform basic safety inspections of the facility and equipment that they will be using. These inspections should supplement the inspection being performed by the coach, teacher, or supervisor. Participants should be instructed to report immediately any obvious or questionable defects to the supervisor.

Using an inspection report or checklist, administrators, teachers, and coaches can document their inspections. If faced with litigation, the sponsoring organization's proof that they sufficiently inspected for risks may prevent or limit liability. Inspection checklists should be created and then approved by an organization's administration and legal counsel. This type of documentation should be retained for the length of the state's statute of limitations.

For a turf management checklist developed by the Sports Turf Association, see page 124 in appendix A.

Regularly scheduled maintenance of facilities and equipment is another component of providing a reasonably safe environment. Regular maintenance helps to reduce risks that might be overlooked during inspection. Maintenance should be performed according to manufacturer's recommendations. Formal documentation of preventive maintenance measures should also be carefully retained.

In *Byrd v. State* (1994), the court ruled that the state fulfilled its duty to maintain a park in a safe condition by conducting daily inspections and correcting defects as soon as possible. Although all potential risks can never be fully eliminated, the court ruling in *Byrd* shows that an effective, formalized facility and equipment inspection program, coupled with a preventive maintenance plan, may help protect administrators, teachers, coaches, and the sponsoring organization from liability.

Facilities and equipment should meet or exceed the relevant recommended space and safety specifications (e.g., unobstructed space around playing area, size and thickness of matting, number and size of signage). Finally, facilities should be secure when they are not open and intended for use.

Threshold Issue 2: Recognizing Key Issues in Providing Adequate Instruction and Supervision

Instruction and *supervision* have different meanings, and it's important to understand the differences. This threshold issue outlines the differences.

Instruction

Coaches, physical educators, and other physical activity providers are expected to select activities that are appropriate for the ability levels and ages of their participants. It is further expected that instruction is proper, accurate, and delivered in a manner that maximizes the potential for participant success. Instruction should be supplemented with warnings regarding the inherent dangers of the activity; the provision of proper safety equipment and protective measures; and appropriate feedback, which allows the participant to evaluate and modify his or her performance (Dougherty 2002). Dougherty (2002) recommends the following instructional guidelines:

- Activities should be selected that are within the reasonable abilities of participants.

- Participants should be warned of the inherent risks in an activity. Safety rules should be explained and regularly enforced.

- All instruction should be consistent with the latest, professionally accepted standards, guidelines, and information. Prior to instructing, one should be familiar with curriculum materials, specific activity and sport standards and guidelines, and relevant safety information. Physical activity providers should thoroughly understand the activities they teach or coach.

- Participant readiness should be individualized. Evaluation and screening, documentation, and individualized progressions are keys to safety and success.

- The use of comprehensive lesson plans that document sound instructional strategies and reasonable progressions are important to instructional success.

- Participants should not be required or coerced to perform when they are, by their own admission, afraid or unprepared for the task.

- Regular feedback and corrective instruction should be provided.
- Injured or ill participants should not be allowed to participate without appropriate medical clearance.
- In activities where there is a probability of physical contact, steps should be taken to minimize the risk associated with mismatches. A mismatch may be defined as an inequity in the size, strength, or ability of the competitors that, if not properly controlled, can unreasonably increase the risk to the undermatched athlete (Dougherty et al., 2002). Size, physical maturity, skill, experience, and fatigue are important factors that should be considered when matching participants. Be especially alert to mismatches with participants that have substantially different levels of conditioning, those recovering from injury, those with physical or mental challenges, and those overly fatigued. Always determine if it is necessary or beneficial to allow any adult to participate in an activity or if it would create a potentially dangerous mismatch. If it is reasonably foreseeable that the situation may lead to a mismatch and a possible injury, teachers and coaches should proceed very cautiously. If adults are allowed to participate, consider creating guidelines for their behaviors. It may be appropriate to discuss potential dangers and to establish rules for their participation (e.g., regarding their intensity levels).

See the Safety Guidelines Finder in appendix B for links to documents that provide safety information on various activities.

Supervision

Supervisors of sport and recreational programs have a great deal of responsibility. They hold a unique relationship with those under their care. Examples of this type of relationship include teacher–student, coach–athlete, recreation supervisor–participant, and supervisor–facility user. The responsibility of the supervisor is to exercise reasonable care for the protection of participants under his or her supervision. To meet this responsibility, it is important to have a supervisory plan. A plan is outlined here to address key issues in supervision. It is intended as a tool to provide guidance in planning.

- **Consider the circumstances.** When developing a supervisory plan, it is important to consider the circumstances (e.g., type of activity, skill and maturity of participants, level of risk). The type of supervision is dependent on the circumstances and can be simply categorized as one of two types: general or specific. General supervision involves staying within sight and hearing of participants. The supervisor can hear and see what is happening on the court or field but is not necessarily in close contact with the participants. An example would be a person who is supervising a basketball game or tennis match. Participants are usually older and more mature, or more skilled, and the activity is lower risk. By contrast, specific supervision involves staying within close contact and proximity of participants. The supervisor is providing hands-on assistance or is immediately ready to do so. Examples would include supervision of young, beginning swimmers, gymnasts, or cheerleaders. Participants are usually younger and less mature, or less skilled, and the activity is higher risk. It is important to plan the type of supervision based upon the considerations relevant to both the activity and participants.

• **Have the proper qualifications.** Supervisors should have the requisite qualifications (e.g., education, experience, or certification). Examples of certifying agencies are provided in table 9.2. In addition to having the appropriate qualifications, there should be enough supervisors to properly oversee the activity, and they should be located in the proper positions to supervise the activity.

Table 9.2   Certifying Agencies in Sport and Recreation

Organization	Home page	Certifications
Adventure Experiences	www.advexp.com	Challenge course and ropes courses certification
Aerobics and Fitness Association of America	www.afaa.com	Many types of fitness certifications
American College of Sports Medicine	www.acsm.org	Health/Fitness and exercise certification
American Council on Exercise	www.acefitness.org	Fitness certifications
American Red Cross	www.redcross.org	A variety of first aid, CPR, and water safety certifications
National Athletic Trainers' Association Board of Certification	www.bocatc.org	Athletic training certification
National Exercise Trainers Association	www.ndeita.com	Fitness certifications
National Recreation and Park Association	www.nrpa.org	Recreation certification
National Strength and Conditioning Association	www.nsca-lift.org	Strength and conditioning certifications

• **Provide safety information first.** Every supervisory plan should begin with safety. It should be documented that instructions involved safety first. While true of all activities, it is particularly important where children are involved. Warnings should also be given regarding inherent dangers in the activity.

• **Have a plan for replacements.** Circumstances often arise that might pull a supervisor away from his or her assigned area of responsibility. When this happens, the participants still might need supervision. This would be especially true where specific supervision is preferred. A supervisory plan should include the identification of a person who has the requisite knowledge, training, and qualifications to properly supervise the activity until the primary supervisor returns.

• **Plan for progression.** Participants often learn in stages and are able to advance to higher-risk activities or levels only after progressing in skill to that point. It is important to have a plan that will ensure that participants are not placed in situations above their skill level that would pose an unreasonable risk of harm to them. A plan should teach safety first and move participants to higher-risk situations only when their skill and ability levels will allow.

• **Consider an emergency action plan.** For medical emergency action plans, please refer to chapter 2. Communication, training, certification, and emergency equipment are all important aspects of preparing for emergencies.

For examples of action plans and safety guidelines for various organized sports, see page 126 in appendix A.

Summary

A key question in many injury-related lawsuits is whether the injured participant was physically capable of successful participation and whether they were properly prepared and instructed. While certain risks may be necessary, they should be well-thought out and justified, and the potential for participant injury must be minimized (Dougherty 2002). In an effort to reduce injuries and maximize participant success, proper and accurate instruction must be appropriately provided. Coaches and other physical activity providers should continue to update and refine their instructional skills. Attending conferences, workshops, and in-service trainings can assist with this.

It is important that supervisors not only provide protective or safety equipment but also instruct participants as to how to properly use, care, and inspect the equipment. Additionally, some safety equipment is mandatory, and therefore supervisors and coaches must require that it be worn or used. Fortunately, there is guidance from professional organizations regarding the use of sport and recreational equipment. This chapter has provided links to some of these valuable resources.

Supervisors of sport and recreational programs have a great deal of responsibility. Therefore, to help meet this responsibility, a supervisory plan is a valuable tool. This chapter provided some key elements of a supervisory plan. The plan that you develop, with these or additional elements, will be of value to you in helping to provide a reasonably safe sport or recreation program.

Real-World Application

Scenario

Sally saw a need in her community to start a softball league for young girls. After speaking with some of her friends and coaches at the local high school who offered their encouragement, Sally contacts parents, registers children, reserves a field, and arranges for old equipment to be donated from the high school. She starts the league with children ages 8 through 13. On the first day of practice, she hands out bats and gloves and organizes the teams. She forms two groups organized by age. She then sends them to one of two fields: one for the younger girls and one for the older ones. Arriving late is an eight-year-old girl. Sally welcomes the girl and tells her that she can either play with the older girls or wait until next time since the group with younger girls is full. The older girls need a catcher. The girl wants badly to play, so Sally gives her a glove and puts her with the older girls. She does not have a catcher's mask. Shortly after the girl enters the practice game, she is hit by a foul ball. Fortunately, she turns her head just in time to only receive a glancing blow to the cheek that causes a small bruise. When the girl's mother learns what happened, she is furious. Sally quickly learns that she needs guidance on safety issues.

Practitioner Action

Sally is right. She does need guidance on safety measures for her softball league. After visiting several Web sites, talking with safety experts and representatives from professional associations, and studying the safety procedures of other coaches and leagues, she develops her own plan. Sally realizes that providing proper, well-fitted equipment is essential from a safety standpoint. She also learns that matching and progression are critical parts of a safety plan. Information about equipment is readily available via the Internet and of great value. Information regarding matching and progression is also easy to access and implement. Improving the safety of the program is beneficial for Sally, the participants, and their parents.

Questions

1. Based on a sport of your choosing, determine the recommended or required safety equipment for use in that activity. Provide the justification for the use of that safety equipment.

2. Using the information available in this chapter, provide a justification for convincing others of the importance of catcher's masks and other safety equipment for softball.

3. What instructional information and guidance can be provided to the coaches?

Playground Safety

chapter objectives

After reading this chapter, you will have a thorough understanding of the following:

Threshold Issue 1: Deciding Whether to Comply With CPSC and ASTM Guidelines and Standards

Threshold Issue 2: Knowing the Key Issues of the CPSC and ASTM Guidelines and Standards

Playground safety has become a leading risk management concern in the field of sport and recreation. Managers of park and recreation departments, resorts, activity centers, schools, and other places where playgrounds are present should be aware of safety considerations for playgrounds and resources on information. Industry guidelines and standards, statutes, case law, and common practice all have a place in determining the standard of care for playgrounds. Additionally, the potential for injury on playgrounds, as illustrated in the following section, is well documented. Given the availability and specificity of playground safety guidelines, and the known potential for injury on playgrounds, managers have both an ethical and legal responsibility to provide for a reasonably safe play environment.

Playground Injuries

Each year, more than 200,000 children ages 14 and younger are treated for playground-related injuries in the United States (Tinsworth and McDonald 2001). Children ages 5 to 9 are at greatest risk. They have higher rates of emergency room visits for playground injuries than any other age group (Phelan et al. 2001). Additionally, for all age groups who use playgrounds, about 45 percent of the injuries are severe—fractures, internal injuries, concussions, dislocations, and amputations (Tinsworth and McDonald 2001).

The majority of all nonfatal playground injuries (approximately 75 percent) occur on public playground equipment at schools and daycare centers (Phelan et al. 2001). The major cause of playground injuries to children is falling onto the surfacing under the equipment. According to the U.S. Public Interest Research Group's fifth nationwide survey of public playgrounds conducted in 2000, 80 percent of the 1,024 playgrounds surveyed lacked adequate protective surfacing. Also, 31 percent of slides and climbing equipment did not have an adequate fall zone (U.S. Public Interest Research Group 2002). On public playgrounds, more injuries occur on climbers than on any other equipment (Tinsworth and McDonald 2001).

Guidelines and Recommendations

Several organizations provide guidelines and recommendations for playground safety. Further information and links to their recommendations are provided in table 10.1. Sport and recreation managers should be aware of these organizations and their recommendations for playground safety. If your organization plans to build or renovate playgrounds on your premises, these recommendations will prove especially valuable. The following section contains further suggestions from the Consumer Product Safety Commission (CPSC).

Threshold Issue 1: Deciding Whether to Comply With CPSC and ASTM Guidelines and Standards

The first decision to make is whether to build a new playground or renovate an existing one in accordance with the CPSC guidelines. This is a threshold issue that should be decided based on consultation with an attorney or another competent

Table 10.1 Guidelines and Standards for Playgrounds

Organization	Home page	Document type	Document	Web site
American Society for Testing and Materials	www.astm.org	Standards for playground equipment and surfacing	"Standard Guide for ASTM Standards on Playground Surfacing" "Standard Specification for Engineered Wood Fiber for Use as a Playground Safety Surface Under and Around Playground Equipment" "Standard Specification for Determination of Accessibility of Surface Systems Under and Around Playground Equipment" "Standard Consumer Safety Performance Specification for Playground Equipment for Public Use" "Standard Consumer Safety Performance Specification for Home Playground Equipment" (These documents are available for purchase from the ASTM. For more information regarding an ASTM standard or product please contact customer support at 610-832-9585 or via e-mail at service@astm.org.)	www.astm.org/cgi-bin/SoftCart.exe/ NEWSITE_ JAVASCRIPT/index.shtml?L+mystore+gfqh3818+1119041184
Consumer Product Safety Commission	www.cpsc.gov	Playground safety guidelines	"Handbook for Public Playground Safety"	www.cpsc.gov/cpscpub/pubs/325.pdf

authority in your community or organization. To better prepare you for making this important decision, you should consider the following.

Familiarity With Resources

When planning and building a new playground, you should be familiar with the Consumer Product Safety Commission's "Handbook for Public Playground Safety." The handbook contains safety guidelines designed to help planners create a reasonably safe play environment. The guidelines serve to lessen the probability and severity of injury to children, and fewer injuries mean fewer potential lawsuits. They are based on design specifications developed by engineers and playground safety experts. It is also wise to consult organizations that have specialized knowledge of playground safety. Several organizations are devoted either fully or substantially to playground safety. They provide such things as published standards and guidelines, playground safety certification programs, publications, and references to Web sites. These organizations are listed in table 10.2.

Legal Mandates

Some states have laws that require public playgrounds to comply with CPSC guidelines, while others condition funding for the creation of a playground on meeting the guidelines. Check your state laws and seek consultation as to whether your state mandates compliance.

Community Standards

You should know whether other playgrounds in your area have complied with CPSC guidelines if you are planning to build or renovate play facilities. If it

Table 10.2   Organizations Providing Playground Safety Resources

Organization	Home page	Address and phone	Information provided
American Alliance for Health, Physical Education, Recreation and Dance	www.aahperd.org	1900 Association Dr. Reston, VA 20191-1598 Phone: 800-213-7193	Publications and resources
American Society for Testing and Materials	www.astm.org	100 Barr Harbor Dr. West Conshohocken, PA 19428-2959 Phone: 610-832-9585 Fax: 610-832-9555	Published playground safety standards (available for purchase)
Association for Childhood Education International	www.acei.org	17904 Georgia Ave. Suite 215 Olney, MD 20832 Phone: 800-423-3563	Publications and resources for parents
Consumer Product Safety Commission	www.cpsc.gov	United States Consumer Product Safety Commission Washington, DC 20207 Phone: 800-638-2772	Published safety guidelines and additional information
International Play Equipment Manufacturers Association	www.ipema.org	1924 N. Second Street Harrisburg, PA 17102 Phone: 888-944-7362 Fax: 717-238-9985	Publications and resources for the playground equipment industry
National Program for Playground Safety	www.uni.edu/playground	School of HPELS, WRC 205 University of Northern Iowa Cedar Falls, IA 50614 Phone: 800-554-PLAY Fax: 319-273-7308	Excellent resource for a wide variety of playground issues
National Recreation and Park Association	www.nrpa.org	22377 Belmont Ridge Road Ashburn, VA 20148-4150 Phone: 703-858-0784 Fax: 703-858-0794	Safety certification course, publications, and resources

appears that the majority of others have complied with the CPSC guidelines and you have not, you should be concerned about whether these guidelines might be viewed as a community standard that could possibly increase your liability if a child is injured on your playground.

Lawsuits

The potential for liability is an important consideration when you are planning the design and construction of any new or existing facility. This is especially true when applied to playgrounds. The outcome of personal injury lawsuits is highly dependent on the circumstances of each case. Many cases are brought forth as a result of a child falling from a piece of equipment to the hard ground below. Supervision is sometimes an issue. Another source of litigation involves the modification of existing equipment, resulting in injury. In many cases, compliance with the CPSC and American Society for Testing and Materials (ASTM) guidelines and standards is at issue in the lawsuit. So although it is uncertain whether a case will hinge on compliance, it will often be introduced into the record by the injured party where playground equipment is at issue. This is why knowledge of

Resources, standards, and the law all influence playground safety guidelines.

playground safety and consultation with an expert in your area before building, renovating, or modifying your playground is important.

Threshold Issue 2: Knowing the Key Issues of the CPSC and ASTM Guidelines and Standards

The National Recreation and Park Association (NRPA) is quite active in playground safety. The organization houses the National Playground Safety Institute (NPSI) that offers Playground Safety Inspector courses and certification. Information on these certification programs can be found at www.nrpa.org. The NPSI provides valuable resources on playgrounds through published sources. One of these publications is a brochure available from the NRPA titled *The Dirty Dozen: Are They Hiding in Your Child's Playground?* It outlines 12 of the leading causes of injury on playgrounds, all of which correspond to the CPSC guidelines for playground safety. The issues addressed in the following section mirror those listed in *The Dirty Dozen* and are important to consider when evaluating existing playgrounds or building new ones. These issues provide a starting point in learning about playground issues and hazards. As mentioned, it is important to investigate all available resources (including those listed in table 10.2) when developing your plan for playground safety.

Playground Surfacing

Nearly 75 percent of all injuries on playgrounds result from a child being injured in a fall from equipment (U.S. Public Interest Research Group 2002). The CPSC has specific information regarding guidelines for surfacing material. The guidelines are based on technical specifications that relate to both the height of a potential fall and the cushioning properties of surface materials. Loose fill materials and soft rubber mats are suggested types of surfacing. Astroturf, blacktop, and packed earth are obviously not recommended. What might not be so obvious is that even recommended types of surfacing materials must be maintained properly to ensure that they retain their ability to cushion a fall. For example, loose sand or wood mulch might become a poor surfacing material if it becomes hard-packed or unevenly distributed due to weather, repeated use, or lack of maintenance. Also, shredded tires might have sufficient cushioning properties but pose a burn hazard if exposed to direct sunlight in a hot environment. The CPSC and ASTM provide guidance on playground surfacing. Budget considerations and common sense also play an important role in the selection of playground surfacing materials.

For a public playground safety checklist from the CPSC, see page 134 in appendix A.

Fall Zones and Equipment Spacing

Even when the surfacing is properly cushioned, the area under and around each piece of playground equipment (the "fall zone") must be clear of potential hazards. You do not want a child to fall off a piece of playground equipment and strike an object below or near it. Therefore, the CPSC recommends that the fall zone be covered with protective surfacing material and clear of hazards at least 6 feet (1.8 meters) in all directions from the edge of stationary play equipment. The CPSC also has adapted fall-zone guidelines for slides and swings. In addition to having an area free of hazards in the fall zone, it is important to space equipment properly. You want to avoid problems associated with overcrowding. Children might wish to jump from one piece of equipment to another, or a child might fall from a climber and strike another piece of equipment as he or she falls. Special considerations exist for swings and moving equipment.

Protrusion and Entanglement Hazards

The potential for injury on playgrounds exists in circumstances where a child is impaled or cut by a piece of equipment or equipment hardware. Bolts, rungs, and handholds that protrude from a piece of equipment pose the threat of injuring an eye, causing a cut, or creating a puncture wound. Training and equipment are available to identify and measure protrusion hazards. Additionally, entanglement hazards that pose the threat of strangulation are important to look for on playgrounds. Entanglement can occur when strings or other items worn around a child's neck get caught on components of playground equipment, such as on open S-hooks, protrusions, or equipment conditions that are favorable for entanglement at the top of slides. The NPSI Playground Safety Inspector course provides training in the identification of both protrusion and entanglement hazards.

This playground is reasonably safe for children in several regards: It has a soft woodchip surface, it's free of ragged or sharp edges, and it is a proper distance from other play equipment, such as swings.

Entrapment

Another potential hazard on playgrounds is entrapment. Entrapment occurs when a body part—the head, arm, or a leg—becomes trapped between two rungs or other opening on a piece of playground equipment. The primary concern is strangulation, in which case a child's torso passes through an opening but their head becomes lodged. Openings at the top of slides, between platforms, and on climbers are key areas of concern for entrapment. The CPSC recommends there be no openings on playground equipment that measure between 3.5 and 9 inches (9 and 23 centimeters). The rationale is that an opening less than 3.5 inches (9 centimeters) should be small enough to prevent a child's torso from passing through, while an opening greater than 9 inches (23 centimeters) should be large enough to allow the whole body and head to pass through.

Fall Prevention

Small children need protection from falling when playing on elevated surfaces like platforms and walkways. As such, guardrails should be of sufficient height and provide adequate protection from falls. The CPSC has guidelines specific to fall prevention for preschool-age children, since this group is often at the greatest risk of injury.

See the Safety Guidelines Finder in appendix B for links to documents that provide safety information on various activities.

Trip Hazards

The potential for injury due to tripping is important to address. Human-created hazards, such as exposed concrete footings (where the ground has washed away from the concrete used to anchor a piece of equipment), border materials like railroad ties, and surfacing material that is not maintained and has become uneven are all potential tripping hazards. Additionally, natural hazards like tree stumps, roots, and rocks pose a tripping hazard. Proper maintenance should serve to eliminate or greatly reduce the risk of injury due to these types of hazards.

Supervision

Regular, proper maintenance is essential to keeping a playground safe.

Supervision is a key component of playground safety. It is estimated that more than 40 percent of all playground injuries are directly related to a lack of proper supervision. Therefore, parents or caregivers must be in a position to observe children at play. The caregiver should place himself or herself in the best position to observe, and the playground should be designed and constructed to allow for reasonable observation.

Age-Appropriate Equipment

Play equipment and environments should be appropriate for the age of the children using them. Playgrounds for preschool-age children should be separate from playgrounds intended for school-age children. Appropriate signage must be in place so that parents and caregivers know which play areas are safe for the children they are supervising.

Crush Points, Shearing, and Sharp Edges

Sharp edges on playground equipment have the potential to cut a child. For example, a sharp piece of metal on a slide might cut a child as he or she slides past the object. Another hazard is a crush point. A child might have a hand or finger crushed by the fulcrum point on a merry-go-round, seesaw, or swing. Inspect these components regularly.

Maintenance, Inspections, and Audits

Regular, proper maintenance is essential for keeping a playground safe. Inspections are usually conducted on a frequent, regular schedule to look for common playground hazards. Audits are performed more infrequently but provide a more in-depth inspection and analysis of playground hazards. Both inspections and audits are important for ensuring a safe play environment.

Recommended Exclusions

For more information on identifying and controlling lead paint, see page 135 in appendix A.

Certain playground components are considered dangerous. The CPSC has therefore recommended they not be part of a public playground. Heavy swings (for example, animal-figure swings and multiple-occupancy glider-type swings), free swinging ropes that may fray or form a loop, and swinging exercise rings and trapeze bars are not recommended for public playgrounds. Additionally, a playground component painted with lead paint or wood treated with arsenic is unsafe and should be prohibited.

Summary

Playground safety has become a tremendously important issue for recreation providers. Litigation resulting from playground injuries occurs frequently these days. Furthermore, the number of reported injuries on playgrounds remains high. Recreation providers have a wealth of information pertaining to playground safety at their fingertips. With organizations such as the NRPA providing leadership in the area and the CPSC and ASTM providing guidelines and standards, the bar has been raised for safety on playgrounds. Thus, from both an ethical and legal standpoint, it is critical that sport and recreation providers make informed and reasoned decisions regarding the safety of both existing and planned playgrounds.

Real-World Application

Scenario

Caroline recently took a position as the director of her town's recreation and parks department. With this job, she is responsible for eight parks, five of which have playgrounds. As she is nearing the end of her first month on the job, and the end of a particularly busy day, an angry mother bursts into her office with a complaint. Caroline assures the parent that she is willing to listen and be of help. This calms the woman and she tells Caroline the story of what happened to her six-year-old son earlier that day. They had gone to a playground in one the town's parks around 2:00 that day. As she was sitting and watching her son play she looked away only for a moment, and when she looked back she was horrified to see her son falling to the ground. After making sure that her son wasn't injured, she talked to him and learned that he had climbed to the top of a tall metal slide and was in the process of sliding down when he noticed that the slide was burning him. The slide is metal and was in direct sunlight. In a great deal of pain, he rolled off the slide about half way down. As he fell, he just missed a low fence that was placed only a few feet from the slide. The ground was hard-packed but fortunately he suffered only some minor bruises. The woman felt both relieved that a tragedy had been avoided and upset that such danger would exist in the playground. After listening to the woman, Caroline realizes that she has a responsibility to provide reasonably safe playgrounds and that she must do something about the problem.

Practitioner Action

Caroline is right to be concerned about the safety of children in her town's playgrounds. After visiting several Web sites; talking with legal counsel, industry experts, and representatives from professional associations like NRPA; and learning what other parks are doing with regard to playground safety, she takes action. Caroline learns about playground safety courses offered through the NRPA and many resources readily available on the Web. She also becomes aware of the guidelines set forth by the CPSC and the playground safety standards of the ASTM. She learns that the fence is too close to the slide and that there are types of playground surfacing material that would better cushion a fall. She also learns of the burn hazard potential of metal slides. With this knowledge, Caroline is able to improve the safety of playgrounds in her town and avoid further situations like this one.

Questions

1. After reviewing the CPSC "Handbook for Public Playground Safety," select several playgrounds and identify hazards that exist on those playgrounds.

2. What is the probability of risk associated with the identified hazards? How severe could injuries associated with these hazards potentially be?

3. What would you do to decrease or eliminate the risk of injury?

Aquatic Safety

chapter objectives

After reading this chapter, you will have a thorough understanding of the following:

Threshold Issue 1: Understanding Compliance Issues Relevant to Local, State, and Federal Laws and Codes

Threshold Issue 2: Recognizing Key Issues in Aquatic Program Safety

The purpose of this chapter is to introduce general safety and liability issues involved with the operation of public and semipublic aquatic programs. The chapter is not intended as a substitute for appropriate training and certification.

Every year millions of Americans visit swimming pools, rivers, lakes, and beaches to participate in various forms of aquatic activities. Swimming and its related activities are among the most popular leisure-time activities in the United States today. It is estimated that more than 125 million Americans swim annually. Almost one million public and semipublic pools exist in the United States (Griffiths 2003). The United States Lifesaving Association, which is concerned with statistics on open water (beaches) as opposed to those associated with pools, reported that attendance at beaches in the United States was over 238,000,000 in 2003 (United States Lifesaving Association 2004). Annually, more than 70 million Americans participate in recreational boating. Annual boat registrations have increased from just over 10 million in 1988 to more than 12.8 million in 2002.

Unfortunately, and partly as a result of this increasing participation, there have been numerous injuries and deaths and a subsequent increase in legal action (Connaughton and Spengler 2000). All too often aquatic activities result in permanent mental or physical impairment, or even death. Three incidents against which aquatic operators must guard against are drownings, near-drownings, and spinal cord injuries resulting in paralysis.

Types of Aquatic Incidents

Drowning is defined as submersion asphyxia with death occurring within 24 hours of the incident. Near-drowning, on the other hand, is submersion that results in the victim being transported to a hospital for treatment but is not severe enough to result in death within 24 hours after the incident (Kearns 1990; Thanel 1998). Paralysis is the complete or partial loss of the ability to move and results when the spinal cord is severed or damaged (American Red Cross 1995).

In 2000, 3,281 people drowned in the United States (Centers for Disease Control and Prevention 2004a). However, according to Kearns (1990), the number of drownings is vastly underreported. For example, a person who dies 10 days after a water-submersion incident will not have drowning listed as a cause of death on their death certificate.

Near-drownings are common and also generally underreported. For each drowning that occurs, approximately three to four near-drownings occur (American Red Cross 1995; Centers for Disease Control and Prevention 2003). Osinski (1990) estimates that during the summer months 50 near-drownings occur each day. Fifteen percent of children who are admitted for near-drowning die in the hospital (National Safe Kids Campaign 2004). Other near-drowning victims are resuscitated but are left with temporary or permanent physical or mental damage. Up to 20 percent of near-drowning victims suffer severe, permanent neurological disability (National Safe Kids Campaign 2004). The quality of life for these victims varies greatly. Many require costly long-term medical and nursing care. Typical medical

See the Safety Guidelines Finder in appendix B for links to documents that provide safety information on various activities.

costs for a near-drowning victim can range from $75,000 for initial treatment to $180,000 per year for long-term health and medical care (National Safe Kids Campaign 2004).

In 2002, the U.S. Coast Guard received reports for 5,705 boating incidents. During the same year, 4,062 boating participants were reported injured and 750 died in boating incidents. Among those who died, an estimated 8 out of 10 were not wearing life jackets (Centers for Disease Control and Prevention 2004).

Another area of concern for aquatic professionals is the number of injuries and deaths that result from headfirst entries into shallow water. Paralyzing injuries from diving and sliding are much more common than is generally believed. They account for approximately 10 percent of all spinal cord injuries. An estimated 1,000 diving-related spinal cord injuries occur annually in the United States (American Red Cross 1995). However, it should be noted that in 80 years of *competitive* diving in the U.S., there is no record of a death or a catastrophic injury involving a supervised practice or diving competition (Clement 2003).

Headfirst entries into shallow water cause the overwhelming majority of diving injuries. According to Gabriel (1992), 86 percent of diving accidents occur in shallow water 5 feet (1.5 meters) deep or less. Thirteen percent occur in water that is 5 to 9 feet (1.5 to 2.7 meters) deep. While the true number of spinal cord injuries that occur in pools (as compared to other bodies of water) is not known, authorities estimate that 30 to 40 percent of them may be pool-related (DeVivo and Sekar 1997; Gabrielsen 1987).

Drownings, near-drownings, and spinal cord injuries are a substantial source of liability for aquatic organizations. These tragedies can be very expensive, especially for the defense, as awards and settlements in excess of $1 million are not uncommon (Sobo 1998). Besides the financial costs, they have destroyed careers, closed programs, increased insurance costs, and caused tremendous amounts of emotional stress for those involved. At the very least, they are hardly good for public relations. Negative publicity about drownings and serious injuries may tarnish an organization's image and possibly decrease business income (Connaughton and Spengler 2000).

Aquatic sites can be analyzed from several viewpoints with regard to safety and liability. Site design, construction of the facility, maintenance, operation, and supervision of the site can all be part of this analysis. Many injury and wrongful death cases have involved allegations relating to maintenance, management, and supervision. In addition to drownings, near-drownings, and spinal cord injuries, other risks present in aquatic programs can result in illness, injuries, deaths, and liability. These include incidents involving slips and falls, entrapments, marine and aquatic life, recreational water illnesses, and pool chemicals.

To see the 12 steps set out by the Centers for Disease Control and Prevention for preventing recreation water illness, see page 138 in appendix A.

In aquatic programs it is impossible to completely eliminate the risk of injury and death. However, it is possible to minimize that risk, and in today's litigious society it has become imperative for aquatic administrators to do so. The management of aquatic programs is becoming increasingly complicated, especially in the area of protecting the welfare of the public. The American Red Cross has been quick to point out that the responsibility for facility safety lies with the administration at each site.

Guidelines and Recommendations

There are several methods to reduce aquatic injuries, drownings, and liability. Many injuries and drownings occur as a result of a lack of attention to well-known safety practices and guidelines. Careful investigation of aquatic injuries and drownings has shown that many of them could have been prevented.

Several national associations and governing bodies associated with aquatics have published guidelines and recommendations regarding the safe operation of aquatic programs. Further information and links to their recommendations are provided in table 11.1.

Table 11.1   Aquatic Guidelines and Recommendations

Activity	Organization	Home page	Document	Web site
Camping	American Camping Association	www.acacamps.org	ACA accreditation standards, including aquatics	www.acacamps.org/accreditation/hyes.php
Lifeguarding, lifeguard management, aquatic safety	American Red Cross	www.redcross.org	Lifeguarding and aquatic safety training, lifeguard management course information	www.redcross.org/services/hss/aquatics
Scouting	Boy Scouts of America	www.scouting.org	"Guide to Safe Scouting: Aquatics Safety" "Age-Appropriate Guidelines for Activities" (see "Aquatics")	www.scouting.org/pubs/gss/gss02.html www.scouting.org/nav/enter.jsp?s=xx&c=ds&terms=Age+appropriate+guidelines&x=15&y=11
Aquatic safety	National Recreation and Park Association	www.nrpa.org	Aquatic Facility Operator Course information	www.nrpa.org/content/default.aspx?documentId=751
	Ellis & Associates: International Aquatic Safety and Risk Management Consultants	www.jellis.com	"National Pool and Waterpark Lifeguard Training Program" information	www.jellis.com/programs/lifeguarding/default.html
Swimming pools	National Swimming Pool Foundation	www.nspf.org/index.html	U.S. state codes for beaches and swimming pools	www.nspf.org/state.html www.nspf.org/cpo.html
	Association of Pool and Spa Professionals	www.theapsp.org/	Certified Pool Operator information) "Technical Standards ANSI/NSPI"	www.theapsp.org/ProfessionalResources/Technical+Standards/
Beach safety and open-water lifeguarding	United States Lifesaving Association	www.usla.org	"USLA Guidelines for Open Water Lifeguard Agency Certification" *Open Water Lifesaving—The United States Lifesaving Association Manual*	www.usla.org/Train+Cert/agenciescert.asp www.usla.org/Train+Cert/text.asp
Waterparks	World Waterpark Association	www.waterparks.org	"Considerations for Operating Safety"	www.waterparks.org/other_pub.asp?itemId=18
Canoeing	American Canoe Association	www.acanet.org	Safety resources	www.acanet.org/safety/safety.lasso

Activity	Organization	Home page	Document	Web site
Boating	U.S. Coast Guard Office of Boating Safety	www.uscgboating.org	State boating laws	www.uscgboating.org/ regulations/boating_laws.htm
	Personal Water-craft Industry Association	www.pwia.org/ index.html	Boating safety and education	www.pwia.org/issues/ boatsafeeducation.html
	National Safe Boating Council	www.safeboatingcoun cil.org/	"National Boating Education Standards"	www.nasbla.org/pdf/Education/ Standards_JAN_04.pdf
Pool safety	U.S. Consumer Product Safety Commission	www.cpsc.gov	Pool and spa safety publica-tions	www.cpsc.gov/cpscpub/pubs/ chdrown.html
Pool standards	American Society for Testing and Materials	www.astm.org	Standards on swimming pool fencing, vacuum releases, safety covers, and more	Home page: search "swimming pool"
Aquatic therapy and rehabilitation	Aquatic Therapy and Rehab Insti-tute	www.atri.org	"Safety Standards for Aquatic Therapy and Rehabilitation Practitioners"	www.atri.org/articles/ Standards.pdf
Lifeguard effective-ness	Centers for Dis-ease Control and Prevention	www.cdc.gov	"Lifeguard Effectiveness: A Report of the Working Group"	www.cdc.gov/ncipc/lifeguard/ lifeguard.htm
Recreational water illnesses	Centers for Dis-ease Control and Prevention	www.cdc.gov	Recreational water illnesses How to prevent recreational water illnesses	www.cdc.gov/healthyswimming www.cdc.gov/healthyswimming/ prevent.htm

Threshold Issue 1: Understanding Compliance Issues Relevant to Local, State, and Federal Laws and Codes

While recommendations and guidelines can be (and in many cases should be) followed, laws and codes *must* be followed. Some may affect aquatic programs in general (like the Americans With Disabilities Act and Occupational Safety and Health Act), while others specifically affect program operation (like specific codes for swimming pools, beaches, water slides, and so on). Many state and local public health departments have jurisdiction over public and semipublic swimming pools as well as other aquatic facilities (e.g., beaches, lakes, water parks) in their area. Requirements often vary greatly from one jurisdiction to another and may effect bathing loads, or the number of swimmers in a pool at any given time; water quality and sanitation; signage; the required presence of certified lifeguard(s); the presence of emergency equipment, including a ring buoy, a shepard's crook, a backboard, a first-aid kit, and so on; telephone access; depth markings; protective fencing; and record keeping. Failure to follow a code may result in civil punishment and liability.

Lawsuits have been brought in response to a wide array of injuries or deaths allegedly resulting from failure to comply with regulations regarding specific safety equipment, the depth of the water, the use of depth markers; the presence of safety ropes or a supervisor or lifeguard, the level of training maintained by lifeguards, hours of operation, sanitation, the number of patrons, warning signs, telephone access, and lighting. Compliance with statutory and regulatory requirements is imperative. Carefully maintain documentation of compliance.

These laws and codes are usually easy to obtain. Most state and local jurisdictions print manuals presenting their requirements, often through their health departments. Many are also available online. Questions regarding compliance should be directed to the regulatory body.

The following case provides a tragic example of failing to comply with state regulations regarding pool operation and safety. In *First Overseas Investment Corporation v. Cotton* (1986), a wrongful death suit was brought against a hotel by the estate of the plaintiff who drowned in the hotel swimming pool. On the day in question, Mr. Cotton went swimming in the shallow end of the pool. The water was very cloudy because the pool attendant dumped a bucketful of soda ash into it that morning. Two hotel guests observed the plaintiff swimming, but when they looked back about one minute later he was gone. They went to the side of the pool but did not see him. They told the pool attendant that they thought Mr. Cotton was in the pool. The two guests began swimming and searching the bottom of the pool. They testified that they did not find him until they were practically on top of him. One ran down to the beach to get a lifeguard. The lifeguard attempted to revive Mr. Cotton, but his efforts were unsuccessful, as were the efforts of a rescue squad that arrived at the scene shortly after.

Testimony indicated that 12 to 20 minutes elapsed between the time the guests first started looking for Mr. Cotton and when resuscitation efforts were first made. According to expert testimony, there was a high probability of survival if he had been rescued four to five minutes after disappearing. It was the plaintiff's contention that Mr. Cotton would have been rescued within four to five minutes and would not have drowned if the hotel had complied with the Florida Department of Health and Rehabilitative Services (HRS) rules regarding pools of that size. The rules dealt specifically with the proper functioning of filtration systems, the clearness of the water, the first-aid training of the person responsible for supervision and safety, and the supply and maintenance of lifesaving and first-aid equipment, including an elevated lifeguard chair.

Expert testimony indicated that soda ash should not have been dumped directly into the pool and that a bucketful was 10 to 12 times more than needed. Soda ash increases turbidity and makes the water cloudy until completely filtered. The pool attendant testified that the pool's filtration system was inoperable. He further testified that he had no training in first aid or in the use of lifesaving equipment. The pool did not have lifesaving equipment—such as a shepherd's crook, an elevated lifeguard chair, or first-aid equipment—on hand.

The trial court stated that violations of the regulations of the HRS entailed negligence. All of the regulations at issue were designed to ensure a clear view of swimmers in distress and the capability of saving them from drowning. On appeal, the trial court's verdict for the plaintiff was affirmed.

Threshold Issue 2: Recognizing Key Issues in Aquatic Program Safety

Judicial expectations regarding the various aspects of aquatic operation are often reflected in case law and can be translated into guidelines for handling unavoidable injuries, just as they are instructive in preventing avoidable injuries. This section will discuss several relevant cases.

Aquatic Operators Must Warn Patrons of Injury Risks and Dangers

Failure to warn is an increasingly frequent allegation in negligence litigation. Do not assume that patrons appreciate the possibility and consequences of an injury. Risks must be identified, as well as the types and severity of injuries that can reasonably be expected to occur because of participation. Swimmers and divers must be told how to avoid injuries. Warnings should be written, accompanied by verbal interpretation, and followed by frequent reminders.

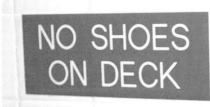

The proper signage will help keep program participants safe.

In the field of aquatics, warnings often appear on signs. Inexperience, age, reading ability, or difficulty with the language in which the signs are printed might prevent some people from understanding the signs. Therefore, signs should contain both printing and graphics that convey messages that cannot be misunderstood. Use multilingual signs where needed. Post signs in highly visible areas where they are unlikely to be missed. Courts have ruled that certain wording on signs has been ineffective in providing an adequate warning. Laws therefore may require specific wording for certain signs. These signs should be posted without alterations of any of the wording. It is also recommended that signs meet the expectations of the legal counsel for your program or organization.

A case that highlights the importance of warnings is *Miller v. United States* (1979), in which a 20-year-old plaintiff was awarded $1 million for injuries he sustained in a diving accident at a national wildlife refuge. The plaintiff walked onto the pier to about 10 feet (3 meters) from its end and noticed a man off the end of the pier in water up to his shoulders who appeared to be treading water. Other people were also in the water about one-third of the way out to the end of the pier. The plaintiff asked a person who was in the water at the end of the pier about the water. This person responded that it was "fine." One of the plaintiff's friends even assured him that the spot was "perfect" for swimming. Most significant, there were no warnings of any kind. The plaintiff dove into the water, which was only about 3 feet (.9 meter) deep, striking his head on the bottom and causing severe injuries that resulted in quadriplegia. The risk was a hidden one of which the plaintiff had no comprehension or awareness. The court found that he exercised ordinary care for his own safety. The court affirmed a $1 million verdict, holding that the defendant—in this case the federal government—was negligent because it failed to post warning signs prohibiting diving. The area was unsafe for diving because the water was murky and shallow. Even though the government knew that people had previously used this area for swimming and diving and its own safety plan recommended warning signs, it took no steps to warn of the danger.

Aquatic Operators Are Expected to Provide Adequate Supervision

The need for reasonable supervision is well illustrated by the decisions of several courts that have held operators liable for injuries resulting from poor supervision. Although lifeguards are not required at all swimming facilities, most experts would agree that the presence of a sufficient number of conscientious and qualified lifeguards contributes greatly to the safety of any aquatic program. Case law has established that a lifeguard must exercise a high degree of care in the performance of his or her job.

The type of supervision must be adequate for the size of the site, the number and type of users, the activities being conducted, and the environmental conditions present. The number of lifeguards required and the degree of supervision are proportional to the danger that is known or can reasonably be expected. Patrons participating in high-risk activities, weak swimmers and those unable to swim, young children, and physically or mentally challenged patrons must be kept under particularly close supervision.

Lifeguards should not be given additional responsibilities above and beyond those normally assigned to them. No duty should interfere with a lifeguard's primary responsibility to ensure safety of patrons. The following case is an example of what can happen when a lifeguard is performing duties unrelated to patrons' safety.

In *Corda v. Brook Valley Enterprises, Inc.* (1983), the only lifeguard on duty was removing umbrellas and making other preparations for an approaching storm when a patron drowned. The lifeguard testified that he was away from his post for less than two and one-half minutes. The court held that the lifeguard owed the plaintiff a duty to exercise the care that a reasonably prudent person who was serving as a lifeguard at the club would have exercised. The court held that there was enough evidence presented for the jury to conclude that the lifeguard had not acted in a manner consistent with that duty. Additionally, the court held that it was up to the jury to decide whether the defendant acted reasonably in not providing two lifeguards when the responsibilities of the position included maintenance.

The *Corda* case is an excellent example of why provisions must be made for alternatives if lifeguards are involved in any other duty besides supervising patrons. This may be accomplished by having more than one lifeguard on duty, requiring all patrons to exit the water before the guard leaves his or her station, or employing a separate staff person to perform any ancillary duties.

Aquatic Operators Are Expected to Formulate and Enforce Safety Rules

Certain rules and regulations are necessary for promoting a safe environment. They must be consistently and regularly enforced. Aquatic operators have been held liable in several cases when they did not follow or enforce their own safety rules and, as a result, patrons were injured. An aquatic operator may also be held liable for not eliminating horseplay (such as running, pushing, wrestling, and other boisterous activities) if it could have been prevented by the aquatic staff but was not, and it resulted in injury of a patron.

Aquatic Operators Are Expected to Provide Proper Staff Instruction and Training

Administrators should not only try to prevent injuries but should also plan for them. Lifeguards should be provided with training specifically related to the facility at which they work. The knowledge and skill level of all lifeguards should be assessed periodically regardless of the certifications they hold. Update practices to reflect changes in currently accepted procedures. The appropriateness of rescue techniques has been an issue in several negligence lawsuits.

Written emergency action plans should be designed specifically for each facility. Make sure that all employees know what is expected of them in the event of an emergency. These plans should be regularly rehearsed and modified when needed. It is also recommended that these plans meet the expectations of the program's legal counsel and insurance provider. See chapter 2 for additional information.

Administrators should not rely on in-service training alone to keep lifeguards' skills sharp. Simulated emergencies (also referred to as mock drills) for water assists and rescues and first aid bring a sense of reality to lifeguard training. If the staff are accustomed to dealing with emergencies in practice, they may be better able to deal with them when they actually occur.

Aquatic Operators Are Expected to Provide Safe Facilities and Equipment

To reduce the chances of an injury, facilities and equipment must meet existing standards; be properly designed and maintained; and be inspected regularly for defects, wear, and tampering. Aquatic operators have been held liable in several cases for deaths or injuries that resulted from cloudy or dark water as seen earlier in the *Cotton* case, inadequate water depth, electrified water, objects in the water, and defects in the facility. Regularly check lifesaving and first-aid equipment to see that it is in good working condition.

Some states and local authorities set regulations requiring that certain equipment be present. Violators of these regulations could be held negligent in the event of an injury or drowning. Cases in this category center on whether the unavailability or inadequacy of rescue equipment was the proximate cause of the injury or drowning.

Develop regular inspection and maintenance schedules for all aspects of the facility and equipment. These inspections may be best accomplished with the aid of appropriate forms and checklists. This will make the review process less time consuming, more efficient, and more effective. Finally, carefully retain all checklists.

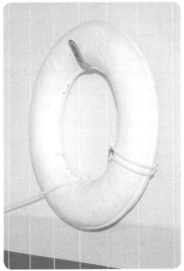 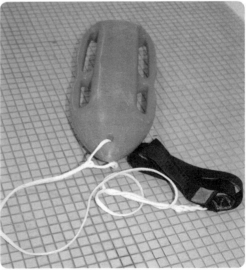

Proper safety and rescue equipment is a must for any aquatic program.

An example of failure to inspect and maintain is seen in *Brown v. Southern Ventures Corp.* (1976), where a lawsuit was brought by the surviving spouse and children of a man who drowned in a motel swimming pool while attending a football-game party at the motel. At some point during the evening the decedent went to the pool area. His body was later found floating in the shallow end. There were no witnesses to the incident. The cement coping (slanted tile border), which extended approximately 1 inch (2.5 centimeters) over the edge of the pool wall, was loose and in a somewhat shaky condition. A former swimming pool contractor and maintenance man testified that he had inspected the pool and had found that approximately 25 percent of the coping around the pool had to be replaced and that some pieces were completely loose. An employee of the motel testified that he had noticed some loose coping and had reported that condition to the motel manager some time before Mr. Brown's death, although the manager denied that such information was given to her. The court found that loose coping would have been more hazardous to a person standing on it than coping that was firmly cemented. The court held that the motel breached its duty when it failed to maintain the pool in a safe condition, that the dangerous condition was the most plausible explanation of the decedent's entry into the pool, and that the decedent had not been intoxicated to such a degree as to cause or contribute to his death. A regular inspection most likely would have uncovered the condition of the coping.

To see recommendations for public spas by the Centers for Disease Control and Prevention, see page 142 in appendix A.

Administrators should identify potentially hazardous areas, equipment, and activities through a regular inspection process. Hazardous areas or defective equipment should be repaired or removed, or access to them should be prevented. Additionally, all local and state codes regarding aquatic facilities and equipment should be strictly obeyed.

Aquatic Operators Are Expected to Secure Their Facilities When Not Open for Use

Several operators have been held liable for injuries or deaths that resulted from failing to adequately close and lock their facilities. An aquatic facility that is accessible during off-hours is often an invitation to disaster. Every reasonable precaution should be taken to prevent unauthorized use. Failure to do so could result in the aquatic operator being liable.

For an example of an aquatic emergency action plan, see page 143 in appendix A.

Summary

Swimming and related activities are among the most popular leisure-time pursuits in the United States today. Moreover, swimming and other aquatic ventures have become very popular for fitness and rehabilitation purposes. Unfortunately, there have also been numerous aquatic-related injuries and deaths. Proper supervision and sound risk management will reduce the number of injuries, deaths, and subsequent lawsuits. This will make aquatic areas safer and more enjoyable places in which to recreate, exercise, and work.

Real-World Application

Scenario

Since they recently installed a new in-ground swimming pool, Mr. and Mrs. Smith, owners of Happy Days Summer Camp, are particularly excited about this year's upcoming camp. They have been planning for the many different aquatic programs and activities that will be offered. Mrs. Smith contacts one of the returning camp counselors, a certified lifeguard, about meeting to prepare the pool for opening day. In preparation for the meeting, the lifeguard e-mails Mrs. Smith to inquire about many safety issues, including lifeguard training, coverage and supervision, pool rules, signage, depth markers, emergency equipment, local codes and regulations, pool chemistry, and emergency planning. The Smiths have not considered most of the issues about which the lifeguard is concerned and realize they have much to do before opening the pool.

Practitioner Action

The lifeguard is correct. There are many safety and risk management factors to consider when operating an aquatic facility. After viewing several Web sites, consulting the local board of health and American Red Cross chapter, and visiting several other similar pools in the community, the owners developed a sound risk management plan for operating their new pool.

Questions

1. What rules, warnings, and signage should be used for the Happy Days Summer Camp pool?
2. What safety equipment may be required? Even if it is not required, what safety equipment should the pool have?
3. What factors should be considered when determining how many lifeguards to use?

Appendix A

Additional Information for Sport and Recreation Managers

The following pages offer you real-life action plans, state laws, and checklists that will further your understanding of the importance of action plans. Use this information as you begin to create your own specific action plans for your organization.

1   *Medical Emergency Action Plan—Injury Report Form* *115*

2   *Background Check Application Information* *116*

3   *Sample Child Pick-Up Authorization Form* *117*

4   *Emergency Action Plan for Lightning* *118*

5   *Interpreting OSHA's Bloodborne Pathogens Standards* *119*

6   *Sample State Law* *122*

7   *Turf Management Checklist* *124*

8   *Examples of Organized Sport Safety Guidelines* *126*

9   *Public Playground Safety Checklist* *134*

10   *Identifying and Controlling Lead Paint* *135*

11   *Steps to Prevent Recreation Water Illness* *138*

12   *Public Spas* *142*

13   *Sample Aquatic Emergency Action Plan* *143*

Medical Emergency Action Plan—Injury Report Form

The following injury report form is part of the emergency action plan from the University of Florida's Living Well Fitness Program.

Recreational Sports Injury Report Form

Department of Recreational Sports
P.O. Box 118212 Room 200 SRFC
Gainesville, Florida 32601-8212

Date _____ / _____ / _____

Participant Information

Last   First   MI

Name: _____

UF ID#: __ / __ Check all that apply: Student ☐ Faculty ☐ Staff ☐ Male ☐ Female ☐ Visitor ☐

Phone: _____ Date of Birth _____ / _____ / _____

Street/Apt   City   Zip

Address: _____

Insurance: School ☐ Personal Health ☐ Other ☐ _____

Injury Information

Injury Location (Facility): _____

Activity During Injury: _____ Time of Injury _____ AM PM

How Injury Occurred & Other Information: _____

_____

First Aid Applied: ☐ _____

Body Part: _____ Side _____

Check all that apply: Previous Injury ☐ Tape/Brace on Injured Area ☐ Pain ☐ Swelling ☐ Discoloration ☐

Personnel on Duty: 1 _____

(Print Clearly)   2 _____

For use by Athletic Trainer   Athletic Training/Sports Medicine Center

Additional Evaluation: _____

_____

Athletic Trainer on Dury: 1. _____ Ph: _____ / _____

Suspected Injury: Please check box

Abrasion ☐   Concussion ☐   Contusion (Bruise) ☐   Dis/Subluxation ☐

Fracture ☐   Sprain ☐   Strain ☐   Other ☐ _____

Treatment: _____

Ambulance Called ☐   If checked, where was the individual sent: Shands ☐ North Florida ☐ AGH ☐

Referred to: Infirmary ☐ ATMSC ☐ Other ☐ _____

Medical Release Form Given: Continued Activity? Yes, with Approval ☐ No ☐ Yes, Against Advice ☐

The University of Florida and the Department of Recreational Sports do not carry any type of accident or insurance policy on the participants involved in the activities and programs.

Reprinted with permission of the University of Florida Department of Recreational Sports

Last Name

First

MI

The following is a list of sample items to consider in an employment or volunteer application for a youth sport or recreation position. Consultation with a competent attorney and others must be made before creating an application. This list is intended only as a starting point in the development of an application.

Information for Applications

General Information

Name

Application date

Position sought

Address

Home phone number

Business phone number

E-mail address

Date of birth

Social Security Number

Level of education

Occupation

Job title

Employer

Relevant Job Related Information

Relevant skills and training

Interest in this position

Previous volunteer and work experience (type of job, place, and dates)

Relevant past experiences

Community work or affiliations

Organization memberships

Certifications

Whether have children in the program

References

Background

Motor vehicle information (e.g., drivers license information, history of accidents or traffic violations)

Criminal convictions with description of each offense (e.g., nature, date, disposition, etc.)

Whether applicant has been refused participation in any other youth sport programs (if yes, explain)

Permission and Hold Harmless (Waiver of Liability) Language

- Language might be included that is designed to show that the applicant gives their permission to have a background check conducted (e.g., criminal and child abuse records)

- Language might be included that is designed to show that the applicant gives their permission to have credentials/records provided on the application verified (e.g. driver's license, DMV record, etc.)

- Language might be included that is designed to make clear that employment or volunteer work is conditional on the organization not receiving any inappropriate background information

- Language might be included that is designed to protect both the organization and the provider(s) of the background information from liability (e.g., defamation, invasion of privacy)

- Language might be included that is designed to allow the organization to refuse hiring or appointing for volunteer work a person (with inappropriate background information) who has worked for the organization before or who is already working for the organization

- Language might be included that is designed to certify that the answers provided on the application are true and correct, and that pertinent facts have not been knowingly withheld

Signature and date

The form might also contain a nondiscrimination statement

The following form is an example of a child pick-up authorization form.

Child Pick-Up Authorization Form

Name of child _____ Parent/Guardian _____

I hereby give permission for the following people to pick up my child. Photo identification will be required to verify the identity of the person picking up my child.

1. Name _____ Relationship _____

2. Name _____ Relationship _____

3. Name _____ Relationship _____

In the event that I as the parent/guardian am not able to pick up my child, I understand that I must give verbal permission for one of the above people to pick up my child.

_____   _____
Parent/Guardian signature   Date

_____   _____
Parent/Guardian signature   Date

The following is an example of an emergency action plan for lightning storms. This was created by the National Lightning Safety Institute in Louisville, Colorado (National Lightning Safety Institute 2005).

Emergency Action Plan for Lightning Storms

4.5.1 City of Louisville Playing Fields

General Information

Lightning's behavior is random and unpredictable. Being prepared and ready to quickly respond are the best defenses against the hazards posed by lightning.

Lightning Safety Program for Playing Fields

At the first signs of lightning or thunder, leave the playing field. Go to your vehicle and take shelter there with the windows rolled up. ("If you can hear it [thunder], clear it [suspend activities].")

Avoid rain and sun shelters and dugouts. These are not safe from lightning.

Avoid going underneath trees. Trees attract lightning.

Avoid metal fences, gates, and tall light and power poles.

Wait 30 minutes after the last observation of lightning or thunder before you leave the shelter. Game officials will signal a resumption of activities.

4.5.2 City of Louisville Outdoor Parks

General Information

Lightning's behavior is random and unpredictable. Being prepared and ready to quickly respond are the best defenses against the hazards posed by lightning.

Lightning Safety Program for City Parks

At the first signs of lightning or thunder, leave the playing field. Go to your vehicle and take shelter there with the windows rolled up. ("If you can hear it [thunder], clear it [suspend activities].")

Avoid the rain and sun shelters in the park.

These are not safe from lightning.

Avoid going underneath trees. Trees attract lightning.

Avoid metal fences, gates, and tall light and power poles.

Wait 30 minutes after the last observation of lightning or thunder before you resume outdoor activities.

4.5.3 City of Louisville Swimming Pools

General Information

Lightning's behavior is random and unpredictable. Being prepared and ready to quickly respond are the best defenses against the hazards posed by lightning.

Our pools are connected to a much larger surface area via underground water pipes, gas lines, electric and telephone wiring, and so on. A lightning strike to this metallic network in one place may induce shocks elsewhere. This is so both for indoor and outdoor pools.

Lightning Safety Program for Pools

At the first signs of lightning or thunder, the pools will be evacuated. ("If you can hear it [thunder], clear it [suspend activities].") They will remain cleared for 30 minutes after the last observed lightning or thunder.

Patrons should leave the pool and the surrounding area. Seek shelter inside the main building or in a fully enclosed vehicle with the windows up.

Avoid waiting under tall trees, umbrellas, or near electric power lines.

Avoid use of showers or other contact with water.

Avoid use of the telephone.

Avoid contact with metal objects.

Teach this safety slogan: "If you can see it, flee it; if you can hear it, clear it."

Reprinted with permission of the National Lightning Safety Institute. www.lightningsafety.com/nlsi_pls/lsvl_plans.html.

The following three letters show how bloodborne pathogens standards established by the Occupational Safety and Health Administration (OSHA) have been interpreted based on inquiries to OSHA from practitioners in various fields.

Letter One: Lifeguard Training

Dear Mr. Smith:

Thank you for your October 23, 2003, letter to the OSHA's Directorate of Enforcement Programs. This letter constitutes OSHA's interpretation only of the requirements discussed and may not be applicable to any question(s) not delineated within your original correspondence. You had specific questions regarding an employer's responsibility to provide training to lifeguards as required by 1910.1030, OSHA's bloodborne pathogens standard. Your question has been restated in the following section, and it is followed by OSHA's response.

Question: Can an employer require potential lifeguards to obtain training that meets the requirements of 29 CFR 1910.1030(g)(2)(i) through (g)(2)(ix)(c) prior to being employed, and can the employer then only be responsible to follow up with an on-site orientation?

Reply: No. An employer whose employees have occupational exposure to blood or other potentially infectious materials (OPIM) must provide training at the time of initial assignment [1910.1030(g)(2)(ii)(A)] and at least annually thereafter [1910.1030(g)(2)(ii)(C)]. 29 CFR 1910.1030(g)(2)(i) requires that such training "be provided at no cost to the employee and during working hours." OSHA interprets this to mean that the employer is responsible for providing this training regardless of whether the employee previously worked in a similar job for another employer or was given training by another employer prior to taking the current position. The requirements of the bloodborne pathogens standard are performance-based, and compliance is determined on a facility-by-facility basis. The standard is very detailed on the minimum elements of a training program that an employer must provide [1910.1030(g)(2)(vii)]. Many of the elements are very specific to the facility or circumstances that employees will encounter at a particular facility. For instance, the employer must include "information on the appropriate actions to take and persons to contact in an emergency involving blood or OPIM" [1910.1030(g)(2)(viii)(J)] and must also include "an explanation of the procedure to follow if an exposure incident occurs, including

the method of reporting the incident and the medical follow-up that will be made available." It would be difficult for an employer to ensure that these and several other of the workplace-specific elements of a training program are met by relying on training performed by another employer or facility.

Please keep in mind that the annual refresher training need only cover the topics listed in 1910.1030(g)(2)(vii) to the extent needed [OSHA CPL 02-02-069 (formerly CPL 2-2.69) XIII.G.4]. This means that employees who return to the same facility from year to year for lifeguard duties need not be given an exact reproduction of the previous year's training.

Employers are also required to maintain records of the training. 29 CFR 1910.1030(h)(2) states that training records shall include information specifying, among other things, "the contents or a summary of the training sessions and the names and qualifications of persons conducting the training." It would be difficult for an employer to have a reliable summary of the training provided by an outside party. Employees with bloodborne pathogen exposure are required to be given the opportunity to ask and have questions answered during the training. This would also be difficult for an employer to verify if the training was conducted prior to the employee becoming employed.

Thank you for your interest in occupational safety and health. We hope you find this information helpful. OSHA requirements are set by statute, standards, and regulations. Our interpretation letters explain these requirements and how they apply to particular circumstances, but they cannot create additional employer obligations. This letter constitutes OSHA's interpretation of the requirements discussed. Note that our enforcement guidance may be affected by changes to OSHA rules. Also, from time to time we update our guidance in response to new information. To keep apprised of such developments, you can consult OSHA's Web site at www.osha.gov. If you have any further questions, please feel free to contact the Office of Health Enforcement at 202-693-2190.

Sincerely,

Richard E. Fairfax, Director
Directorate of Enforcement Programs

From the Occupational Health & Safety Administration (OSHA), a division of the U.S. Department of Labor.

(continued)

Letter Two: Trainers and Team Physicians

Dear Dr. Jones:

This is in response to your letter of December 30, 1992, in which you made proposals regarding the OSHA regulation 29 CFR 1910.1030, "Occupational Exposure to Bloodborne Pathogens." Specifically, your proposals pertained to the sporting arena, both at the amateur and professional level. We regret the delay in providing this response.

The bloodborne pathogens standard provides protections to employees with occupational exposure. The term "occupational exposure" is defined under the standard as reasonably anticipated skin, eye, mucous membrane, or parenteral contact with blood or other potentially infectious materials that may result from the performance of an employee's duties. It is the employer's responsibility to determine which, if any, employees have occupational exposure.

We agree with you that "trainers and team physicians will always be considered to have reasonably anticipated contact with body fluids." However, we note that you have made proposals for modifying the manner in which wounds are currently handled in the sporting arena in order to avoid occupational exposure to other employees, including players. These proposals include requiring that every player who is noted to have a wound of any sort be immediately removed from the game by appropriately protected trainers and team physicians and that the player not be allowed to return to the game until an occlusive dressing has been applied to the abrasion or wound. This athlete would also continue to wear this dressing in the training room and in the shower following the event. You also recommended that mouth protectors be used to decrease the opportunity for lacerations to players' mouths and to avoid biting injuries and that players be responsible for keeping their mouth protectors in a safe location away from other players.

Your suggestions appear to be well reasoned and effective. We would encourage you to implement any and all of the previously mentioned procedures that you feel are appropriate.

Because there is no employer–employee relationship at the amateur level of sports, OSHA has no jurisdiction over the manner in which player safety and health are achieved. However, your suggestions could certainly be implemented as part of sound public health policy.

We hope this information has addressed your concerns. Thank you for your interest in employee safety and health.

Sincerely,

Roger A. Clark, Director
Directorate of Compliance Programs

From the Occupational Health & Safety Administration (OSHA), a division of the U.S. Department of Labor.

Letter Three: Summer Camps and Conference Centers

Dear Dr. White:

This is in response to your inquiry of May 7, concerning the applicability of the OSHA regulation, 29 CFR 1910.1030, "Occupational Exposure to Bloodborne Pathogens." Specifically, you asked about coverage of employees of summer camps and conference or retreat centers. We apologize for the delay in this response.

Employees who have occupational exposure to blood or other potentially infectious materials (OPIM) are covered by this standard. Occupational exposure is defined as reasonably anticipated skin, eye, mucous membrane, or parenteral contact with blood or OPIM that may result from the performance of an employee's duties. One of the central provisions of the standard is that employers are responsible for identifying job classifications that have occupational exposure. Due to the nature of activities in which camp members participate, both minor and major injuries can be expected. Employees who are expected to stabilize or treat these injuries, for example, a camp nurse, may reasonably be expected to have occupational exposure. If counselors, sports coaches, and other staff who work with campers are responsible for rendering first aid, they would also be covered by the standard.

With this in mind, we will answer your specific questions in the order presented in your letter.

1. "To whom in the camp community does the vaccination requirement apply?"

The vaccination requirement, as well as all other provisions of the standard, applies to all employees who have occupational exposure. However, OSHA has recently issued a policy statement specifying that failure to offer the hepatitis B vaccine preexposure to employees who render first aid only as a collateral duty will be considered a *de minimis* violation carrying no penalties, provided that a number of conditions are met.

This new policy does not apply to your employees who render medical assistance or emergency response activities on a regular basis, such as camp nurses and doctors; they must be offered the vaccine preexposure, in accordance with paragraphs (f)(1) and (2) of the standard.

2. "Is it adequate to provide the immunization for [only] the camp's health care staff or primary first-aid provider?"

The hepatitis B vaccine must be given to all employees who have occupational exposure, with the exception noted previously for first-aid providers.

3. "Is [the bloodborne] rule intended to apply to camp lifeguards at pools, rivers, and lakes?"

It is the employer's responsibility to determine which, if any, of the employees have occupational exposure. Lifeguards are generally considered to be emergency responders and are therefore considered to have occupational exposure.

4. "Do persons with first-aid training or incidental responsibilities require vaccination?"

The key to this issue is not whether employees have been trained in first aid but whether they are also designated as responsible for rendering medical assistance. While employees may be trained in first aid and cardiopulmonary resuscitation (CPR), not all of them will necessarily be designated to render first aid. Employees who primarily provide first aid or emergency response duties must be vaccinated. Employees who are designated to provide first aid as a collateral duty are covered by the first-aid policy as described previously. The standard excludes employees who perform unanticipated "Good Samaritan acts" from coverage by the standard since such an action does not constitute "occupational exposure."

5. "Is it reasonable for the vaccine to be required of seasonal employees?"

Yes. An employer is obligated to offer the hepatitis B vaccine to those employees covered by the standard who are currently employed. Those workers with occupational exposure should be offered the required inoculations scheduled in the series while they are in your employ. If the third injection, for instance, would be due after the employee has ended their term of employment, the employer would not be obligated to offer it. If the employee (for example, the camp nurse or doctor) is one who returns to your employ the following season and is required to be offered the hepatitis B vaccine series, it would obviously be to your advantage to see that the series is completed and to arrange for payment for the last dose.

Your health care professional in charge of administering this program should consult the U.S. Public Health Service's recommendations for administering injections when the series is interrupted. Although optimal protection is not conferred until after the third dose, increasing immunity is conferred with each successive dose of the vaccine.

We hope this information is responsive to your concerns. Thank you for your interest in worker safety and health.

Sincerely,

Roger A. Clark, Director
Directorate of Compliance Programs

From the Occupational Health & Safety Administration (OSHA), a division of the U.S. Department of Labor.

The following is a California state law regarding the use of automated external defibrillators (AEDs). It is provided as an example of what one state has mandated with regard to the responsibilities placed on those who choose to use AEDs. Consult your own state law and an attorney to determine your own rights and responsibilities regarding AEDs.

California State Law and AEDs

California Civil Code (2005). This statute outlines liability protections for AED use.

§1714.21

(a) For purposes of this section, the following definitions shall apply:

    (1) "AED" or "defibrillator" means an automated or automatic external defibrillator.

    (2) "CPR" means cardiopulmonary resuscitation.

(b) Any person who, in good faith and not for compensation, renders emergency care or treatment by the use of an AED at the scene of an emergency is not liable for any civil damages resulting from any acts or omissions in rendering the emergency care.

(c) A person or entity who provides CPR and AED training to a person who renders emergency care pursuant to subdivision (b) is not liable for any civil damages resulting from any acts or omissions of the person rendering the emergency care.

(d) A person or entity that acquires an AED for emergency use pursuant to this section is not liable for any civil damages resulting from any acts or omissions in the rendering of the emergency care by use of an AED, if that person or entity has complied with subdivision (b) of Section 1797.196 of the Health and Safety Code.

(e) A physician who is involved with the placement of an AED and any person or entity responsible for the site where an AED is located is not liable for any civil damages resulting from any acts or omissions of a person who renders emergency care pursuant to subdivision (b), if that physician, person, or entity has complied with all of the requirements of Section 1797.196 of the Health and Safety Code that apply to that physician, person, or entity.

(f) The protections specified in this section do not apply in the case of personal injury or wrongful death that results from the gross negligence or willful or wanton misconduct of the person who renders emergency care or treatment by the use of an AED.

(g) Nothing in this section shall relieve a manufacturer, designer, developer, distributor, installer, or supplier of an AED or defibrillator of any liability under any applicable statute or rule of law.

California Health and Safety Code §1797.196 (2005).

This statute provides information regarding requirements for AED use.

(a) For purposes of this section, "AED" or "defibrillator" means an automated or automatic external defibrillator.

(b) In order to ensure public safety, any person who acquires an AED shall do all of the following:

 (1) Comply with all regulations governing the training, use, and placement of an AED.

 (2) Notify an agent of the local EMS agency of the existence, location, and type of AED acquired.

 (3) Ensure all of the following:

  (A) That expected AED users complete a training course in cardiopulmonary resuscitation and AED use that complies with regulations adopted by the Emergency Medical Services (EMS) Authority and the standards of the American Heart Association or the American Red Cross.

  (B) That the defibrillator is maintained and regularly tested according to the operation and maintenance guidelines set forth by the manufacturer, the American Heart Association, and the American Red Cross, and according to any applicable rules and regulations set forth by the governmental authority under the federal Food and Drug Administration and any other applicable state and federal authority.

  (C) That the AED is checked for readiness after each use and at least once every 30 days if the AED has not been used in the preceding 30 days. Records of these periodic checks shall be maintained.

  (D) That any person who renders emergency care or treatment on a person in cardiac arrest by using an AED activates the emergency medical services system as soon as possible, and reports any use of the AED to the licensed physician and to the local EMS agency.

  (E) That there is involvement of a licensed physician in developing a program to ensure compliance with regulations and requirements for training, notification, and maintenance.

From Cal.Civ.Code §1714.21 and Cal. Health & Safety Code §1797.196 (2005).

The following checklist was developed by the Sports Turf Association. Use this as an example of the type of checklist you can develop to make sure your premises are reasonably safe.

Soccer Checklist

The Sports Turf Association feels it is important to make the public aware of some of the safety measures that are necessary for sport turf today. The following suggestions will assist you in attaining better, safer sport turf. These suggestions are based on "Guidelines for Sport-Field Maintenance, Work Plan for Soccer," by Ron Dubyk, *Sports Turf Newsletter,* Vol 1, Issue 3, January 1988. Updated by the Sports Turf Association 1999.

Item	Comments	April	May	June	July	Aug	Sept	Oct	Nov
Spring cleanup	Clean-up winter debris and lay out lines of play (use a transit).	*	*						
Goal posts	Install prior to May; remove after October. Repaint or repair during the winter.	*	*					*	*
Goal nets	Check daily and repair or replace as needed, in accordance with Guidelines for Movable Soccer Goal Safety.		*	*	*	*	*	*	
Field use	By permit only, ideally May through October. Play should be suspended due to inclement weather; this is determined by staff.		*	*	*	*	*	*	
Litter	Inspect daily for rocks, glass, and other debris.	*	*	*	*	*	*	*	
Benches and bleachers	Inspect daily and repair as necessary. Repaint in the off-season.		*	*	*	*	*	*	
Weed spraying or I.P.M.	Use a broad spectrum herbicide (mecoprop, dicamba, 2,4D), following the recommended rates. Subject to local bans. Post signs.	*	*					*	
Insects and disease	Resolve as diagnosed.			*	*	*	*		
Irrigation	Energize irrigation system and make necessary repairs by May; winterize system in October. Maintain an equivalent of 1 inch (2.5 centimeters) of rainfall.		*	*	*	*	*	*	
Mowing	Mow to a height of 1.75 inches (4.4 centimeters). Mow an average of three times every two weeks.		*	*	*	*	*	*	
Line striping	Lines should be applied every week using a mixture of white latex paint and water (1:1 ratio). The use of non-selective herbicide may cause rutting or a tripping hazard.		*	*	*	*	*	*	
Aerating and slicing	Use a core-type aerator; break up and redistribute the cores in two directions.		*	*	*	*	*		

Item	Comments	April	May	June	July	Aug	Sept	Oct	Nov
Soil testing	Test at the end of the season.							*	
Sod repairs	Repair at the end of the season; usually needed around goal mouth and center field areas. Use a snow fence for protection.							*	
Signage	Prepare signs in the off-season. Secure signs in a visible and vandal-proof area. Inspect daily when in use.		*	*	*	*	*	*	
Fencing	Maintain and repair as necessary.		*	*	*	*	*	*	
Lighting	Inspect regularly; replace and repair as required.		*	*	*	*	*	*	
Topdressing	Drag mat in two directions. Mixture depends on the existing field soil, drainage, use, etc. Recommend higher sand proportions.		*	*	*	*	*	*	
Overseeding	Watch fertilizer ratio and use 1:2:1 at 12 kgN/ha (0.25 pounds per 1,000 square feet) in each direction when overseeding. Use a turf-type perennial ryegrass; spring seeding is recommended.		*				*	*	
Fertilizing	Based on annual soil samples; apply 4:1:2 or 5:1:2 at 12 kgN/ha (0.25 pounds.N per 1,000 square feet) in each direction. At least one-half of the nitrogen should be in slow-release form. See 'Overseeding' above for fertilizer rates during the overseeding operation.	*	*	*	*	*	*	*	Dormant
Documentation	Maintain ongoing, daily records of all of the above items, including date, name of site, and name of inspector.	*	*	*	*	*	*	*	

Have you established an inspection routine, using written forms to pinpoint hazards and dangers? Ensure an individual is designated for repairs and to follow-up and correct any defects. Are your personnel trained in preventive and corrective turf and field maintenance programs?

This memo was produced as a public service. For further information, please contact

Sports Turf Association
328 Victoria Road South
Guelph, ON, N1H 6H8

Phone: 519-763-9431
Fax: 519-766-1704
info@sportsturfassociation.com

Here, you'll find three examples of action plans and safety guidelines from the U.S. Consumer Product Safety Commission (CPSC): one for movable soccer goals, one for baseball safety, and one for the importance of helmets in preventing injury. Use these three examples as you create specific safety plans for your organization.

Guidelines for Movable Soccer Goal Safety

Introduction

This handbook presents guidelines for the installation, use, and storage of full-size or nearly full-size movable soccer goals. The CPSC believes these guidelines can help prevent deaths and serious injuries resulting from soccer goals tipping over. Publication of the handbook is intended to promote greater safety awareness among those who purchase, install, use, and maintain movable soccer goals.

These guidelines are intended for use by parks and recreation personnel, school officials, sports equipment purchasers, parents, coaches, and any other members of the general public concerned with soccer goal safety.

These guidelines are intended to address the risk of movable soccer goal tipping over. They are not CPSC standards, nor are they mandatory requirements. Therefore, the Commission does not endorse them as the sole method to minimize injuries associated with soccer goals.

Soccer Goal Injuries and Deaths

According to the 1994 National Soccer Participation Survey (Soccer Industry Council of America), over 16 million persons in the United States play soccer at least once a year. Seventy-four percent (over 12 million) of these persons are under the age of 18. Soccer ranks fourth in participation for those under 18, following basketball, volleyball, and softball and well ahead of baseball, which has an annual participation of 9.7 million.

There are approximately 225,000 to 500,000 soccer goals in the United States. Many of them are unsafe because they are unstable and are either unanchored or not properly anchored or counterbalanced. These movable soccer goals pose an unnecessary risk of tipping over when children climb on them or hang from the crossbar.

The CPSC knows of four deaths in 1990 alone and at least 21 deaths during the past 16 years (1979-1994) associated with movable soccer goals. In addition, an estimated 120 injuries involving falling goals were treated each year in U.S. hospital emergency rooms during the period 1989 through 1993. Many of the serious incidents occurred when the soccer goals tipped over onto the victim. Almost all of the goals involved in these occurrences appeared to be "home-made" by high school shop classes, custodial members, or local welders, not professionally manufactured. These "home-made" goals are often very heavy and unstable.

The majority of movable soccer goals are constructed of metal, typically weighing 150 to 500 pounds (68 to 227 kilograms). The serious injuries and deaths are a result of blunt force trauma to the head, neck, chest, and limbs of the victims. In most cases this occurred when the goal was accidentally tipped onto the victim. In one case an 8-year-old child was fatally injured when the movable soccer goal he was climbing tipped over and struck him on the head. In another case, a 20-year-old male died from a massive head trauma when he pulled a goal down on himself while attempting to do chin-ups. In a third case, while attempting to tighten a net to its goal post, the victim's father lifted the back base of the goal causing it to tip over and strike his 3-year-old child on the head, causing a fatal injury.

High winds can also cause movable soccer goals to fall over. For example, a 9-year-old was fatally injured when a goal was tipped over by a gust of wind. In another incident, a

19-year-old goalie suffered stress fractures to both legs when the soccer goal was blown on top of her.

Rules of Soccer

From the Federation of International De Football Association. 1993. Laws of the Game: Guide for Referees.

> "Goalposts and crossbars must be made of wood, metal, or other approved material as decided from time to time by the International Football Association Board. They may be square, rectangular, round, half-round, or elliptical in shape."
>
> "Goalposts and crossbars made of other materials and in other shapes are not permitted. The goalposts must be white in color."
>
> "The width and depth of the crossbar shall not exceed 5 inches (12 centimeters)."

From the National Federation of State High School Association's 1994-95 National Federation Edition-Soccer Rules Book.

Design and Construction Guidelines

While a movable soccer goal appears to be a simple structure, a correctly designed goal is carefully constructed with counterbalancing measures incorporated into the product. The common dimensions of a full-size goal are approximately 24 feet (7.3 meters) in width by 8 feet (2.4 meters) in height and 5 feet (1.5 meters) in depth (see figure A.1). The stability of a soccer goal depends on several factors. One effective design alternative uses a counterbalancing strategy by lengthening the overall depth of the goal to effectively place more weight further from the goal's front posts (that is, placing more weight at the back of the goal). A second design selects lightweight materials for the goal's front posts and crossbar and provides much heavier materials for the rear ground bar and frame members. This tends to counterbalance the forces working to tip the goal forward. Another design uses a heavy rear framework and folds flat when not in use, making the goal much less likely to tip over. Finally, after these various designs are considered, it is imperative that all movable soccer goals be anchored firmly in place at all times.

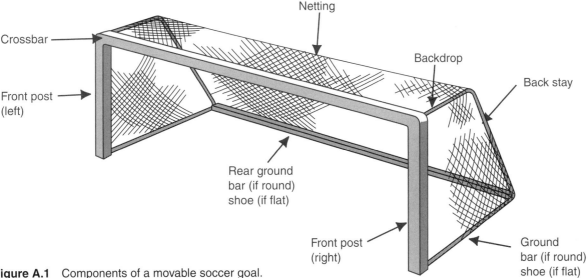

Figure A.1   Components of a movable soccer goal.

Anchoring, Securing, and Counterweighting Guidelines

A properly anchored and counterweighted movable soccer goal is much less likely to tip over. Remember to secure the goal to the ground (preferably at the rear of the goal), making sure the anchors are flush with the ground and clearly visible. It is imperative that all movable soccer goals be anchored properly (see figure A.2). There are several different ways to secure your soccer goal. The number and type of anchors to be used will depend on a number of factors, such as soil type, soil moisture content, and total goal weight.

(continued)

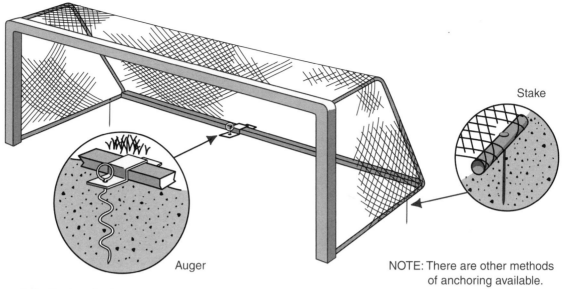

Stake

Auger

NOTE: There are other methods of anchoring available.

Figure A.2 Goal anchoring.

Auger-Style Anchor

This style anchor is "helical"-shaped and is screwed into the ground (see figure A.3). A flange is positioned over the ground shoes (bars) and rear ground shoe (bar) to secure them to the ground. A minimum of two auger-style anchors (one on each side of the goal) are recommended. More may be required, depending on the manufacturer's specifications, the weight of the goal, and soil conditions.

Semipermanent Anchor

This anchor type is usually composed of two or more functional components. The main support requires a permanently secured base that is buried underground. One type of semipermanent anchor connects the underground base to the soccer goal by means of two tethers (see figure A.4a). Another design utilizes a buried anchor tube with a threaded

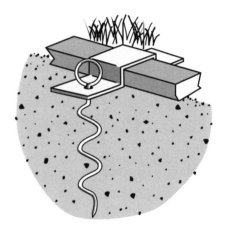

Figure A.3 Auger-style anchor.

opening at ground level (see figure A.4b). The goal is positioned over the buried tube and the bolt is passed through the goal ground shoes (bar) and rear ground shoe (bars) and screwed into the threaded hole of the buried tube.

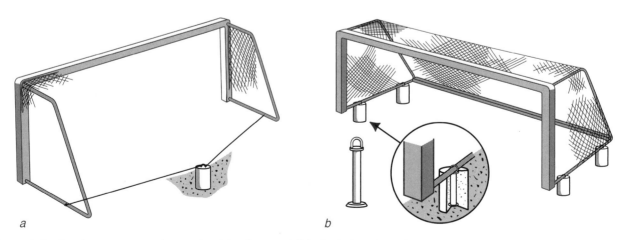

a

b

Figure A.4 Semipermanent anchors using *(a)* tethers and *(b)* a buried anchor tube.

Peg- or Stake-Style Anchors (Varying Lengths)

Typically, two to four pegs or stakes are used per goal (more for heavier goals) (see figure A.5). The normal length of a peg or stake is approximately 10 inches (25 centimeters). Care should be taken when installing pegs or stakes. Pegs or stakes should be driven into the ground with a sledgehammer as far as possible and at an angle, if possible, through available holes in the ground shoes (bars) and rear ground shoe (bar) to secure them to the ground. If the peg or stake is not flush with the ground, it should be clearly visible to persons playing near the soccer goal. Stakes with larger diameters or textured surfaces have greater holding capacity.

J-Hook Stake-Style Anchor

This style is used when holes are not predrilled into the ground shoes (bars) or rear ground shoe (bar) of the goal. Similar to the peg- or stake-style anchor, this anchor is hammered, at an angle if possible, directly into the earth. The curved (top) position of this anchor fits over the goal member to secure it to the ground (see figure A.6). Typically, two to four stakes of this type are recommended (per goal), depending on stake structure, manufacturer's specifications, the weight of the goal, and soil conditions. Stakes with larger diameters or textured surfaces have greater holding capacity.

Sandbags and Counterweights

Sandbags or other counterweights could be an effective alternative on hard surfaces, such as artificial turf at an indoor facility, where the surface cannot be penetrated by a conventional anchor (see figure A.7). The number of bags or weights needed will vary and must be adequate for the size and total weight of the goal being supported.

Net Pegs

These tapered, metal stakes should be used to secure only the net to the ground (see figure A.8). Net pegs should not be used to anchor the movable soccer goal.

Figure A.5 Peg- or stake-style anchor.

Figure A.6 J-hook anchor.

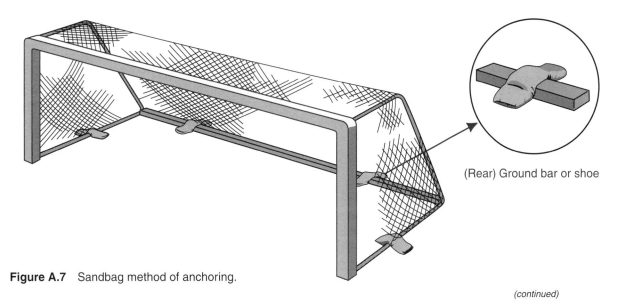

Figure A.7 Sandbag method of anchoring.

(Rear) Ground bar or shoe

(continued)

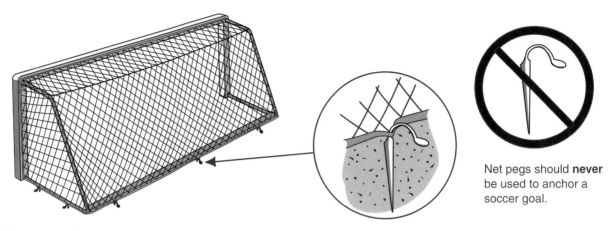

Net pegs should **never** be used to anchor a soccer goal.

Figure A.8 Net pegs.

Guidelines for Goal Storage or Securing When Goal is Not in Use

The majority of the incidents investigated by the CPSC did not occur during a soccer match. Most of the incidents occurred when the goals were unattended. Therefore, it is imperative that all goals be stored properly when not being used. When goals are not being used, always remove the net and take appropriate steps to secure goals: Place the goal frames face to face and secure them at each goalpost with a lock and chain (see figure A.9).

Alternatively, you can lock and chain the goalposts to a suitable fixed structure, such as a permanent fence (see figure A.10).

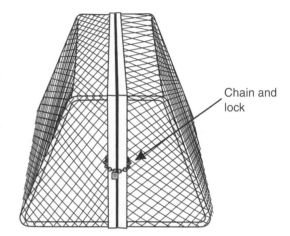

Chain and lock

Figure A.9 Join goal faces and lock them together using a chain and lock.

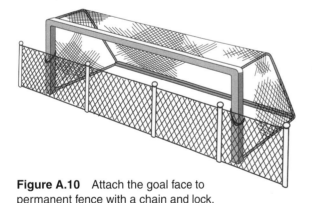

Figure A.10 Attach the goal face to permanent fence with a chain and lock.

Lock unused goals in a secure storage room after each use. If applicable, fully disassemble the goals for seasonal storage or fold the face of the goal down and lock it to its base.

Conclusions and Safety Tips

- Securely anchor or counterweight movable soccer goals at all times.
- Anchor or chain one goal to another; to itself in a folded-down position; or to nearby fence posts, dugouts, or any other similar sturdy fixture when not in use. If this is not practical, store movable soccer goals in a place where children cannot access them.
- Remove nets when goals are not in use.
- Check for structural integrity and proper connecting hardware before every use. Replace damaged or missing parts or fasteners immediately.
- Never allow anyone to climb on the net or goal framework.

- Ensure that safety and warning labels are clearly visible—placed under the crossbar and on the sides of the downposts at eye level (see figure A.11).
- Fully disassemble goals for seasonal storage.
- Always exercise extreme caution when moving goals, and allow adequate manpower to move goals of varied sizes and weights. Movable soccer goals should only be moved by authorized and trained personnel.
- Always instruct players on the safe handling of and potential dangers associated with movable soccer goals.
- Movable soccer goals should only be used on level (flat) fields

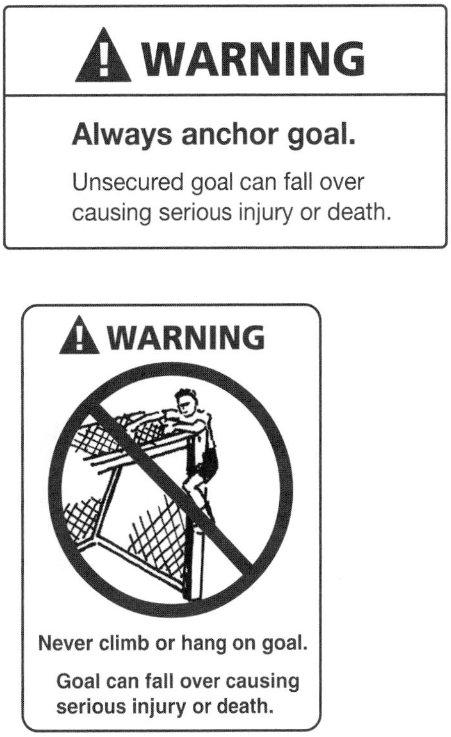
WARNING
Always anchor goal.
Unsecured goal can fall over causing serious injury or death.
WARNING
Never climb or hang on goal.
Goal can fall over causing serious injury or death.
a
b

Figure A.11 Various warning labels.

List of Soccer Organizations

Federation of International De Football Association
Hitzigweg 11,8030
Zurich, Switzerland
Telephone: 41-1-384-9595

National Federation of State High School Associations
P.O. Box 690
Indianapolis, IN 46206
Telephone: (317) 972-6900

National Collegiate Athletic Association
700 W. Washington St., P.O. Box 6222
Indianapolis, IN 46206-6222
Telephone: (317) 917-6222

For Further Information

For further information on soccer goal anchors or to obtain free soccer goal warning labels (see figure A.11), safety alerts and bulletins, and additional copies of this document, please contact

The Coalition to Promote Soccer Goal Safety
c/o Soccer Industry Council of America
200 Castlewood Dr.
North Plain Beach, FL 33408

Call any of these Coalition telephone numbers:

800-527-7510

800-334-4625

800-243-0533

800-531-4252

You can also write the Consumer Product Safety Commission
Washington, DC 20207

To report a dangerous product or a product-related injury, call CPSC's toll-free hotline at 800-638-2772 or CPSC's teletypewriter at 800-638-8270. Consumers can get recall information via Internet gopher services at www.cpsc.gov or report product hazards to info@cpsc.gov.

From the U.S. Consumer Product Safety Commission (CPSC). www.cpsc.gov/cpscpub/pubs/326.html

(continued)

Baseball Safety

The CPSC wants you and your family to be safe when playing baseball. The CPSC announced that softer-than-standard baseballs, safety-release bases, and batting helmets with face guards could significantly reduce the number and severity baseball-related injuries to children each year.

Baseball, softball, and teeball are among the most popular sports in the United States, with an estimated 6 million children ages 5 to 14 participating in organized leagues and 13 million children participating in nonleague play. In 1995, hospital emergency rooms treated an estimated 162,100 children for baseball-related injuries.

The CPSC collected and analyzed data on baseball-, softball-, and teeball-related injuries to children to determine specifically how these children were injured and what safety equipment could prevent such injuries. The CPSC found that baseball protective equipment currently on the market may prevent, reduce, or lessen the severity of more than 58,000 injuries occurring to children each year. Softer-than-standard balls (see figure A.12) may prevent, reduce, or lessen the severity of the 47,900 ball-impact injuries to the head and neck.

Batting helmets with face guards (see figure A.13) may prevent, reduce, or lessen the severity of about 3,900 facial injuries occurring to batters in organized play.

Figure A.12   A soft-core ball.

Safety-release bases (see figure A.14) that leave no holes in the ground or parts of the base sticking up from the ground when the base is released may prevent, reduce, or lessen the severity of the 6,600 base-contact sliding injuries occurring in organized play.

Figure A.13   A batting helmet with face guard.

Figure A.14   A safety-release base.

The CPSC protects the public from unreasonable risks of injury or death from 15,000 types of consumer products under the agency's jurisdiction. To report a dangerous product or a product-related injury and for information on CPSC's fax-on-demand service, call CPSC's hotline at 800-638-2772 or CPSC's teletypewriter at 800-638-9270. To order a press release through fax-on-demand, call 301-504-0051 from the handset of your fax machine and enter the release number. Consumers can obtain this release and recall information at CPSC's Web site at www.cpsc.gov. Consumers can report product hazards to info@cpsc.gov.

From the U.S. Consumer Product Safety Commission (CPSC). www.cpsc.gov/cpscpub/pubs/329.pdf

Wearing Helmets to Prevent Sport-Related Head Injuries

The CPSC estimates that about 3 million head injuries related to consumer products were treated in hospital emergency rooms in 1988. About 440,000 of these were injuries, such as concussions and skull fractures. Many of these accidents occurred when helmets could have been worn.

The Commission's study of head injuries showed that these four products or activities led to a large number of head injuries that were treated in hospital emergency rooms (see figure A.15).

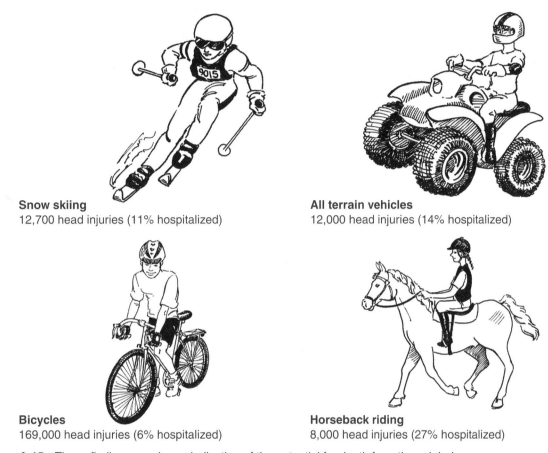

Snow skiing
12,700 head injuries (11% hospitalized)

All terrain vehicles
12,000 head injuries (14% hospitalized)

Bicycles
169,000 head injuries (6% hospitalized)

Horseback riding
8,000 head injuries (27% hospitalized)

Figure A.15 These findings may be an indication of the potential for death from these injuries.

Many people do not wear helmets. Fewer than 1 out of 10 bicyclists wear helmets. Three-quarters of all-terrain vehicle (ATV) drivers with head injuries were not wearing helmets.

There are several nationally recognized voluntary safety standards for helmets. These standards require helmets to absorb the energy of an impact to lessen or prevent head injuries. Crushable, expanded plastic foam can serve this purpose. Many helmets also have a hard outer shell to protect against collision with a sharp object.

To reduce head injuries, bicyclists, ATV drivers, horseback riders, and skiers should wear the helmet appropriate for their respective activity.

Here is a quick checklist for public playground safety. Use this checklist to help make sure your organization's, local community's, or school's playground is a reasonably safe place to play.

Playground Safety Checklist

1. Make sure surfaces around playground equipment have at least 12 inches (30.5 centimeters) of wood chips, mulch, sand, or pea gravel. The surface can also consist of mats made of safety-tested rubber or rubber-like materials.

2. Check that protective surfacing extends at least 6 feet (1.8 meters) in all directions from play equipment. For swings, be sure surfacing extends to twice the height of the suspending bar both in front and behind it.

3. Make sure play structures more than 30 inches (76 centimeters) high are spaced at least 9 feet (2.7 meters) apart.

4. Check for dangerous hardware, like open S-hooks or protruding bolt ends.

5. Make sure spaces that could trap children, such as openings in guardrails or between ladder rungs, measure less than 3.5 inches (9 centimeters) or more than 9 inches (23 centimeters).

6. Check for sharp points or edges in equipment.

7. Look out for tripping hazards, like exposed concrete footings, roots, tree stumps, and rocks.

8. Elevated surfaces, like platforms and ramps, should have guardrails to prevent falls.

9. Check playgrounds regularly to see that equipment and surfacing are in good condition.

10. Carefully supervise children on playgrounds.

From the U.S. Consumer Product Safety Commission (CPSC). www.cpsc.gov/cpscpub/pubs/327.html

Appendix A

The following information is from the CPSC. Use this information as you create an action plan for identifying and controlling lead paint.

CPSC Staff Recommendations for Identifying and Controlling Lead Paint on Public Playground Equipment

To reduce the risk of childhood lead poisoning, the CPSC staff recommends the following strategy for identifying and controlling the lead paint hazard associated with older public playground equipment. The strategy complements the framework described in the 1995 "Guidelines for the Evaluation and Control of Lead-Based Paint Hazards in Housing" that was developed by the U.S. Department of Housing and Urban Development (HUD) and other federal agencies to support the requirements of Title X (The "Residential Lead-Based Paint Hazard Reduction Act of 1992"). The guidelines are available for a fee by calling HUD at 800-245-2691.

Some states and localities require the services of licensed or certified professionals to identify, address, and correct lead paint hazards. Individual state and local health departments, lead poison prevention programs, housing authorities, the Environmental Protection Agency (EPA) National Network of Lead Training Centers (413-545-5201), or the National Lead Information Center (800-424-LEAD) can provide help in locating qualified professionals in each area.

When and How to Check and Test Playground Equipment for Lead Hazards: Lead Hazard Assessment

A lead hazard assessment for playground equipment may include a visual inspection, examination of records, paint testing, characterization of the hazard, identification of potential control measures, and a plan for establishing the priority for the implementation of control measures.

Conduct a visual inspection of the playground and equipment. The visual inspection should include the following:

- Examine the condition of the entire painted surface. Any painted surface that has not been repainted after 1977 should be assumed to contain lead, since the ban on lead paint did not come into effect until 1978. Even if the surface has been repainted after 1977, the paint should be considered suspect unless records

have been maintained showing that nonleaded paint was used. Also, the original paint may contain lead, and it may become available for ingestion when the repainted surface deteriorates.

- Identify areas of visible paint chips and dust accumulation. Lead chips and dust are generated as lead paint deteriorates over time due to weathering, aging, and moisture or is disturbed in the course of renovation or repair. Check for the presence of paint chips underneath the playground equipment.

- Evaluate the need for significant structural repairs or changes to the equipment that are likely to affect the integrity and condition of the painted surface.

Evaluate the results of the visual inspection

If the paint is intact and in overall good condition, there is no visible paint dust or paint chips, and significant repairs or equipment changes are not needed, one of two alternatives can be taken: monitoring (periodic visual inspection) or laboratory testing to determine if the paint contains lead. Lead paint is not considered to be a hazard until it deteriorates. Accordingly, the CPSC recommends that such equipment be monitored (that is, visually inspected) on a regular basis to ensure that the paint has not deteriorated. This inspection can be coordinated with regular safety inspections. For information on playground safety, consult the CPSC "Handbook for Public Playground Safety." The handbook is available from the CPSC (800-638-2772 or info@cpsc.gov). If at any time the painted surface begins to deteriorate, paint samples should be collected and analyzed for lead.

Instead of regular monitoring, owners or managers may wish to immediately collect and test paint samples for lead. However, as long as the paint is intact the CPSC does not believe that testing is necessary. If laboratory testing is conducted on intact paint and the presence of lead is confirmed, continued monitoring can be implemented as a control measure to ensure that the paint does not

(continued)

deteriorate. If the visual inspection indicates the need for significant structural repairs or changes to the equipment that are likely to affect the integrity and condition of the painted surface (that is, will result in peeling, cracking, chipping, chalking, and so on), the paint should be tested to determine if it contains lead before any repair work begins.

If the paint is in a deteriorating condition (as noted by its peeling, cracking, chipping, or chalking), paint samples should be collected from several locations on the playground equipment (sampling each type and color of paint) for laboratory testing. Red, orange, yellow, green, and brown are the colors most likely to contain lead. Check with the laboratory that will be analyzing the paint samples to determine whether trained professionals are needed to collect samples.

Paint samples should be analyzed by an accredited laboratory according to standard methods for total lead analysis (for example, ASTM, EPA, or Association of Official Analytical Chemists standards). Studies conducted by the CPSC, EPA, and HUD indicate that lead test kits do not accurately and reliably discriminate between paint with lead and paint without lead. And lead test kits are not designed to tell you the amount of lead present. If portable X-ray fluorescence (XRF) analyzers are used to screen for lead, follow-up analysis by a laboratory is also needed. XRF measurements have a large margin of error compared to laboratory analysis. They are not reliable when used to test curved surfaces, such as might be found on playground equipment.

Evaluate the results of the laboratory tests.

- If the laboratory analysis indicates that the paint contains lead levels that are equal to or exceed 0.5 percent by weight and the paint is deteriorated, the extent of the hazard should be characterized and control measures undertaken. Owners or managers may consider control measures for lead paint between 0.06 and 0.5 percent. However, priority should be given to implementing control measures for deteriorating paint at or above 0.5 percent.

- The EPA is currently developing an addendum to their July 14, 1994 (60 Federal Register: 47248), guidance on lead-based paint, lead-contaminated dust, and lead-contaminated soil. The addendum will address the issue of soil and playgrounds.

- Playground equipment should be inspected and regularly maintained to ensure that it meets safety guidelines and provides a safe environment for children, regardless of whether it contains lead paint.

Characterize the Hazard.

The surface area of paint containing 15 micrograms (ug) of lead that a child would need to ingest over about 15 to 30 days to exceed a blood lead level of 10 micrograms of lead per decilitre of blood (ug/dl) was estimated by the CPSC. The surface area was estimated using a range of lead concentrations that have been found, or might be found, in playground paint samples and the easily extracted lead percentages (that is, the bioavailability surrogate representing the amount of lead absorbed by the body) found in samples tested by the CPSC's Health Sciences Laboratory.

How to Control the Lead Hazard from Public Playground Equipment: Lead Hazard Controls

Just knowing that a playground has paint containing lead may not indicate if there is a hazard. The CPSC staff does not consider playground equipment with lead paint that is intact and in good condition to be a hazard. Therefore, continued monitoring is essential, and may be an appropriate control measure for intact paint containing lead.

Over time, paint will deteriorate due to exposure to changing weather conditions and normal wear and tear. If that paint contains lead, it does present a hazard once it deteriorates and requires attention. Priority should be given to controlling deteriorating leaded paint on public playground equipment containing lead in amounts equal to or exceeding 0.5 percent by weight. Because playground equipment is intended for use by children, consideration of measures that permanently eliminate the potential hazard posed by lead paint are recommended. In general, interim control measures for playground equipment may be considered appropriate if the playground is slated for repair or the equipment is expected to be replaced within a few years.

While interim control measures often have a lower initial cost than permanent control measures, they require regular monitoring and reevaluation to ensure that the lead paint is still intact. In some cases, permanent control measures may be more cost-effective over the long-term than interim control measures when the cost of monitoring is considered.

The CPSC contacted city officials in a few cities that have already implemented control measures for playgrounds with leaded paint.

Interim Control Measures

Stabilize and cover the lead paint surface with non-leaded paint or an encapsulant. Because outdoor metal and wood playground equipment is continually subject to deterioration due to exposure to sunlight, heat, moisture, and wear and tear through normal play activities, covering the lead paint surface with nonleaded paint or encapsulants will only temporarily reduce human exposure to lead. Covering the lead paint surface requires ongoing and regular monitoring because lead paint is still present and may become hazardous in the future. Sanding, scraping, and using power tools to prepare the surface to be repainted or encapsulated can increase the hazard by spreading lead paint chips and dust. Precautionary measures outlined in the 1995 HUD Guidelines and the 1996 EPA Section 402 Rule, "Lead Requirements for Lead-Based Paint Activities," should be followed to ensure that lead control measures are conducted safely.

Encapsulants are coatings that provide a barrier between the lead paint and the environment. They vary in their effectiveness and how long they are expected to last. The degree of adherence depends on the encapsulant used and the substrate to which it will be applied. While some encapsulants may last for many years, they were developed for use in interior spaces. Their effectiveness and longevity in outdoor environments where they are subject to deterioration from changing weather conditions is uncertain. Therefore, encapsulants for playground equipment should be considered only as an interim measure.

In addition, according to the 1995 HUD guidelines, encapsulants are generally not effective on metal surfaces that are prone to rust or corrosion unless a proper corrosion-control primer is used before the application of the encapsulant.

Playground equipment that has been covered with an encapsulant or nonleaded paint requires regular monitoring throughout the life of the equipment. Such monitoring would allow detection if the surface does not remain in good condition throughout changing weather conditions and wear due to normal play activities.

Permanent Control Measures

Replacing playground equipment or component parts that contain lead paint is the most definitive way to eliminate the risk of lead poisoning from exposure to lead paint on playground equipment. Contracting with a professional will reduce the likelihood of environmental contamination during replacement, especially if the paint is in poor condition and likely to be disturbed. Because of varying regulations regarding hazardous waste storage, transport, and disposal, state and local health departments or environmental agencies should be contacted to find out what laws are applicable.

To remove lead paint permanently, a lead paint removal professional who is trained, certified, or licensed to remove lead hazards should be used. Removing lead paint improperly can increase the hazard by spreading lead chips and dust around the play area. Individual state and local health departments or environmental agencies can help you locate qualified contractors. Surfaces should be repainted with paint containing no more than 0.06 percent lead, according to CPSC regulations.

From the U.S. Consumer Product Safety Commission (CPSC). http://www.cpsc.gov/cpscpub/pubs/lead/6006.html

The Centers for Disease Control and Prevention (CDC) has created these 12 steps to prevent recreation water illness (RWI). Use these steps as you create your own specific action plan.

Twelve Steps for the Prevention of RWIs

Step 1: Lead Your Staff

Making a choice to integrate an RWI protection plan into an existing facility risk management plan is the single greatest decision you can make to protect swimmers from RWIs. Take the lead, outline your vision, show your commitment to your staff, and put yourself at the forefront of the aquatics field. Decide that RWI protection is a priority; back it up with resource investment and commitment, and that will set the tone for the rest of the staff.

Step 2: Develop Partnerships

Building a communication bridge to your health department and other aquatic facilities is a great way to get information about other outbreaks occurring in your community. If you start to hear about outbreaks associated with other pools, daycare centers, schools, and other such facilities where your swimmers attend, take proactive measures and increase vigilance to protect your pool. Increase education of staff, swimmers, and visiting daycare groups. If a pool closes because of a suspected outbreak, that does not mean that all of the swimmers should descend on your pool without giving them some education about RWI prevention. Work with your health department to get the word out when a potential RWI outbreak is occurring. Remind them that one of the messages to send out whenever a diarrheal outbreak is occurring is "don't swim when ill with diarrhea." Use your communication networks and the media to circulate this message. Protect your facility, make the contacts early, and build a communication network so that you are aware of the health status of your community at all times.

Step 3: Educate Pool Staff

1. Ensure that the pool operator, at a minimum, has taken part in a standardized training course given by aquatics professionals.

2. Integrate the "P-L-E-As" for Healthy Swimming (see step 4) into staff training.

3. Promote good hygiene and safety around the pool by knowing the "P-L-E-As" for Healthy Swimming.

4. Inform parents that unhealthy behaviors at poolside and elsewhere are no longer acceptable. Parents told the CDC that they wanted to be able to rely on the lifeguards for help and enforcement.

5. Ensure that all staff know the critical role of water testing, proper testing methods, the importance of dual chlorine and pH control (a fact sheet is available at www.cdc.gov/healthyswimming/ph_chlorine.htm), and how to respond if disinfectant levels are not adequate.

6. Make sure that staff can explain, in a way that is inoffensive and acceptable to parents, why behaviors such as using public tables and chairs for diaper changing is a health risk. This may require that an older, more experienced staff member be assigned to the kiddie pool.

7. Distribute educational materials, such as Healthy Swimming aquatics staff newsletters, fact sheets, and question and answer sheets.

Maintaining pool water quality according to existing public health requirements will prevent the spread of most recreational water illnesses (RWIs).

Step 4: Educate Swimmers and Parents

1. Educate your season pass holders. You may choose to begin by educating them first since they may feel more ownership of the facility and want to make the facility as safe as possible.

2. Educate your daily patrons. You might hand out prevention messages ("P-L-E-As" for Healthy Swimming or a CDC brochure) as patrons enter the pool or park area.

3. Remember that people care about their health, so a good lead-in might be something like the following: "To ensure the health and safety of all our visitors, we ask that you remember to follow these easy "'P-L-E-As for Healthy Swimming.'"

    PLEASE don't swim when you have diarrhea. This is especially important for kids in diapers.

    PLEASE don't swallow the pool water.

PLEASE practice good hygiene. Take a shower before swimming and wash your hands after using the toilet or changing diapers.

PLEASE take your kids on bathroom breaks or check diapers often.

PLEASE change diapers in a bathroom and not at poolside.

PLEASE wash your child thoroughly (especially the rear end) with soap and water before swimming.

4. Consider implementing a short safety and RWI orientation for larger groups before they enter the pool complex. This is especially important for groups with young children (see step 10).

Step 5: Maintain Water Quality and Equipment

Keep the chemical feed equipment and chemicals at optimal levels within state and local government regulations. This includes maintaining the disinfectant at regulated levels, usually 1 to 3 parts per million (ppm); optimal pH (7.2 to 7.8); alkalinity of 80 to 120 ppm; calcium hardness of 200-400 ppm; and total dissolved solids below 2,500 milligrams per liter. As you know, poor pH control can compromise chlorine's effectiveness as a disinfectant. Make sure all of your staff realize this. Remember that maintaining recommended chlorine and pH levels will prevent most bacterial outbreaks, such as those caused by E. coli.

When germs get into the scum (biofilm) layer, they can be protected from disinfection. Scrubbing the pool or spa to break up that scum layer is important. Don't let germs take up residence in your pool or spa.

Be sure to monitor chlorine regularly where the chlorine is needed—at poolside. You should be able to prevent waterparks, pools, or hot tubs from running out of chlorine through regular monitoring and pumphouse and systems checks. Ensure regular and thorough maintenance of the recirculation and filtration equipment to provide maximum filtration.

Step 6: Evaluate Aquatic Facility Design

If you are building a new waterpark, get feedback from your industry colleagues and public health experts about the safety and protection features you need to consider in the design stage. Pool designers will respond to you, their customer, if you are clear that your public health needs are a high priority and you consider it an investment in safe operations.

Evaluate Your Filtration System

If your kiddie pool filtration system is connected with other pools, fecal contamination can be dispersed from the kiddie pool to the other pools. The best situation is one in which there is a separate filtration system for the kiddie pool. Increasing the water turnover rates in kiddie pools may decrease the length of time that swimmers are exposed to contaminating germs. This decision needs to be made in collaboration with your state and local regulators and design consultants to avoid causing suction injuries. This may require installation of antivortex drain covers (with no top openings and automatic cut-off valves) or other technology.

Evaluate Your Form of Disinfection

There is a great deal of interest in new technologies that disinfect pool water, including ozone, ultraviolet (UV) irradiation, and mixed oxidants. They look promising. Seek out the experts for the latest information but keep in mind that you are still going to need some residual disinfectant in the pool when using ozone and UV. Dropping disinfectant in the pool may put swimmers at greater risk if the pool becomes contaminated.

Evaluate Your Hygiene Facilities

Are there adequate numbers of toilets, diaper-changing stations, and showers? Are they safe? Are they close to where they are needed? Address these issues in the design phase, if possible. Your pool will continue to be used as a restroom if you are not proactive in assuring that patrons have what they want. Down the drain versus in your pool is a major RWI prevention measure. See step 8 for more information on hygiene facilities.

Step 7: Institute Disinfecting Guidelines

Even if you are not required to do so, have a written fecal accident response policy and keep records of all fecal accidents, chlorine and pH level measurements, and any major equipment repairs or changes. This may help you respond more efficiently to any problems. You may have little control over a toddler's soiling your kiddie pool, but you do have control over how you document and respond to this occurrence. Also put policies in place for responding to vomiting and body fluid spills. Check your state and local codes for existing information or the CDC's Healthy Swimming Web site (www.cdc.gov/healthyswimming) for guidance. Develop training materials for staff so that they can respond appropriately, document the response, and communicate to patrons why (under some circumstances) it is critical to close the pool for some period of time.

Step 8: Evaluate Hygiene Facilities

In parent interviews, parents uniformly said they change diapers at poolside because changing rooms were unclean, poorly maintained, or had

(continued)

inadequate diaper-changing facilities. Here are some questions that you could ask to improve your facilities:

- Do you have an adequate number of facilities?
- Are they safe?
- Are the facilities close to the pool?
- Are the facilities well maintained (stocked and cleaned)?
- Would you walk barefoot in them as your patrons do?
- Are the diaper-changing facilities usable, safe, and close to hand-washing facilities?
- Do you have showers with warm water?

If possible, address these issues in the design phase. Ask your patrons for feedback. Your pool will continue to be used as a restroom if you are not proactive in assuring that patrons have what they want.

If your facility is large enough, determine the utility of hiring a person just to maintain the restrooms or consider remodeling your diaper-changing stations. Both improvements may be good investments if they increase the number of parents and children who use them. Install diaper-changing cabanas with soap and running water close to the kiddie pools. This is a great way to discourage parents from changing diapers on tables or lounge chairs. It can also help mothers who are keeping an eye on other kids.

Although difficult, keep pushing to get swimmers to shower (yes, a soap and water, back-end shower) before using the pool. Dirt, sweat, and fecal matter should go down the drain, not into your pool. Train staff to recognize risky behavior, such as changing a child on public tables or chairs. Have them educate patrons about why this is a health risk.

Step 9: Develop a Bathroom-Break Policy

Parents will continue to want to see regular chlorine testing and appropriate disinfection following fecal accidents. Therefore, why not reduce fecal accidents by helping parents get their children to the bathroom by scheduling an hourly break for disinfectant testing and bathroom use? Staff should let patrons know that this break provides optimal timing for bathroom use. Additionally, to prevent transmission of germs, you should ensure that the bathrooms are clean, that they are stocked with toilet paper, and that they have ample soap for hand washing. If parents ask, tell them this policy not only reduces fecal contamination but also should reduce the amount of urine in the pool that uses up disinfectant that could be

killing germs. All of the combined chlorine that stings patrons' eyes and brings in complaints could be reduced if patrons start urinating in the restroom rather than in the pool.

Step 10: Create a Special Policy for Large Groups of Young Children

If you allow large groups of toddler-aged children in the pool (for example, from daycare centers), consider the following:

- Require RWI orientation training for the care providers, and make sure they understand that your pool, like most daycare centers, also excludes children ill with diarrhea.
- Keeping toddler-aged children in the pools specifically designated for them.

Step 11: Post and Distribute Health Information

Consider providing signage in a conspicuous location before pool entry. Rotate this information and keep it updated.

Encourage swimmers to shower with soap and water before entering the pool. This could reduce the risk of pool contamination by removing invisible fecal matter from their bottoms. A quick rinsing over a swimsuit with cold water will not do much good. Facility staff, managers, and home pool owners should consider having hot water available in shower facilities used by swimmers.

Post your last pool inspection report and let your customers know you intend to do your part to protect their health. Restaurants do it and many people choose to patronize the "best performers."

The recreational water sector is not the only sector that needs to participate in the educational process. Parents have told the CDC that they would like to receive this message from various sources before they arrive at the pool. Public health officials have already begun to educate swimmers by making prevention messages available to the general public.

Step 12: Develop an Outbreak or Emergency Response Plan

The best advice is to be prepared. If an outbreak does occur, are you ready? Do you have a plan? Most pool staff already have a risk management plan for injuries and drowning, but many do not have plans for managing an RWI outbreak.

- Develop a policy to follow in the event that you begin getting calls from the public or the health department starts an investigation. Part of this plan should include a strategy to communicate with the local health department and media.

- Appoint a spokesperson to ensure that a consistent response is given to outside sources (callers, media, the health department, and others) and that these sources have a clear contact person.
- Talk to your colleagues who have experience. It can be difficult if an outbreak occurs and you are not ready to speak with reporters.

- Develop a communication network. If you hear about problems let your health department know. Alert other pool operators in the community of problems as well.
- Collaborate with your local health department. This is always important, plus the investigation may indicate a source unrelated to the pool.
- Support the investigation. If the pool is the source of the outbreak, the investigation can often reveal how or why illness was transmitted. This information leads to better illness prevention strategies that can help everyone.

From the Centers for Disease Control and Prevention (CDC). www.cdc.gov/healthyswimming/twelvesteps.htm.

The CDC has created the following recommendations for operating and using public spas. Use this information as you create your own specific action plan.

Recommendations for Operating and Using Public Spas

In addition to swimming pools, it's important to have steps in place for spas. The following tips will be helpful in creating an action plan for spas.

Spa operation

- Obtain operator training recommended by the state or local authority. Suggested national training courses are listed at www.cdc.gov/healthyswimming/courses.htm.
- Maintain free chlorine or bromine levels continuously between 2 to 5 ppm.
- Test disinfectant levels at least daily (hourly when in heavy use).
- Maintain the pH level of the water at 7.2 to 7.8.
- Scrub spa surfaces if they have a slime layer.
- Maintain the filtration and recirculation system according to manufacturer recommendations.
- Drain and replace all or portions of the water on a weekly to monthly basis, depending on usage and water quality.
- Treat the spa with a biocidal shock treatment on a daily to weekly basis, depending on water quality and frequency of water change.
- Cover spas, if possible, to minimize loss of disinfectant and reduce the levels of environmental contamination (for instance, from debris and dirt).
- Maintain accurate daily records of disinfectant and pH measurements.
- Educate spa users about appropriate use through signs, handouts, and so on.

Spa users

- Shower or bathe with soap before entering the spa.
- Observe limits, if posted, on the maximum allowable numbers of bathers.

Additional spa safety

- Prevent the temperature from exceeding 104 degrees Fahrenheit (40 degrees Celsius).
- If pregnant, consult a physician before spa use, particularly in the first trimester.
- Exclude children less than 5 years of age from using spas.*
- Maintain a locked safety cover for the spa, when possible.
- Prevent entrapment injuries with appropriate drain design and configuration.

* The authors recommend also seeing www.aap.org/family/homewatr.htm.

From the Centers for Disease Control and Prevention (CDC). www.cdc.gov/healthyswimming/pdf/cdc_qt_spa.pdf

The following excerpts are from the aquatic emergency action plan of the Willis R. Casey Aquatic Center at North Carolina State University. Use this plan as an example of how to construct your own specific aquatic emergency action plan. The Willis R. Casey Aquatic Center action plan can be viewed in its entirety at www.ncsu.edu/aquatics/pdf_files/eap_f04_revised.pdf.

Emergency Action Plan: Willis R. Casey Aquatic Center

Emergency Equipment and Its Location

Whistle

Each instructor, coach, and lifeguard should have a whistle readily available. Although a whistle will be attached to each lifeguard stand, each instructor, coach, and lifeguard should provide his or her own whistle and utilize the following signals while on duty:

- One long whistle blast: to clear the pool (for example, during an electrical storm or to close the pool at the end of the day)
- Multiple long whistle blasts: to alert other rescuers that an accident has happened and a rescue is necessary

Two-Way Radios

In addition to using the whistle to attract the attention of other aquatic staff and lifeguards, a two-way radio can be used to obtain assistance from the aquatics director and other facilities staff. During each lifeguard shift, there should be a two-way radio located at each lifeguard stand in the pool being used for recreational swimming and also one that is carried by the roving lifeguard. If the roving lifeguard is in the water participating in drills to improve his or her skills or fitness, the two-way radio should be on the secondary lifeguard stand during that time period. The two-way radios are to be used for necessary aquatic business, not for chatting. The two-way radios should be turned on and the channel selector turned to channel 12, subchannel 24. A radio check should be conducted at the beginning of each shift to ensure that communications are properly established among all lifeguards on the shift. Please do not pick up the radio by the antenna. The following call numbers will be used for communicating on the two-way radio:

CG2 or Carmichael 2 is Larry Brown, aquatics director

801   Lifeguard stand #1 on the northwest side of the 50-meter pool

802   Lifeguard stand #2 on the northeast side of the 50-meter pool

803   Lifeguard stand #3 on the southwest side of the 50-meter pool

804   Lifeguard stand #4 on the northwest side of the 25-yard (23-meter) pool

805   Lifeguard stand #5 on the east side of the 25-yard (23-meter) pool

806   Roving lifeguard

807   Shift supervisor for the lifeguards

To communicate with another person, first state the call number of the person you are calling followed by "This is (your own call number), over." The term "over" means that you expect communication from the person to whom you are talking. When you finish your communication with the person and you do not desire further communication, end your message with "out" instead of "over." For example, if the aquatics director (CG2) is calling the roving lifeguard (806), he could say, "806, this is CG2, over." "This is 806, over." "806, what is the temperature reading in the 25-yard pool, over." "CG2, this is 806. The temperature in the 25-yard pool is 86 degrees. Over." "806, this is CG2. Thanks for your help. Out."

The Carmichael Gymnasium Student Staff is found on channel 3 of the 10-channel radio located on the desk in the lifeguard office. Their call numbers are as follows:

101   Facility manager (student supervising entry into Carmichael Gymnasium). The facility manager should be informed when the pool has been closed at the end of the day.

102   Main entrance. This student checks IDs and can set and cut off the main alarm system to the pool.

103   Student checking IDs at the lobby entrance where the old building attaches to the new addition.

104   Student checking IDs at the third-floor entrance.

(continued)

Emergency Transmitter

Each instructor, coach, and lifeguard should know the location and condition of the rescue equipment. An emergency transmitter is located on the right side hand railing of each lifeguard stand. Pressing the button on the emergency transmitter for one or two seconds notifies campus police that there is an emergency in the Aquatics Center that needs EMS help. When the transmitter activates campus police, it will also cause the red lights mounted on the outside wall of the aquatics director's office to blink. The transmitters are tested monthly to ensure that they are functioning properly. As an aquatics instructor or coach, you should inform your students about these emergency transmitters so that they can assist you with the emergency action plan as needed. Every student should know the location of the emergency transmitters and how to activate the emergency transmitter. The emergency transmitter should be activated immediately upon determining that EMS is needed. This implies that the emergency transmitter should be activated before making a rescue for a passive patron, as the passive patron will definitely need the care provided by EMS.

AEDs

An AED should be used when a pulse is undetectable in a patient. A wet patient must be on a spine board with drain holes, and the chest must be dried off with towels. The AED will indicate a shock is needed if the heart is in V-Tach or V-Fib (a disorganized and/or fast heart beat that effectively stops the heart from pump-ing). Two-way radios, cell phones, and free-flowing oxygen should be at least 6 feet (1.8 meters) away or, preferably, turned off while utilizing the AED. If the heart completely stops (is in assystole) or has a normal rhythm, no shock will be indicated. If no shock is indicated and the patron's heart is in assystole, follow the audio and visual prompts from the AED. If CPR is indicated by the AED prompts, administer CPR with supplemental oxygen using the MTV-100 regulator to increase the oxygen in the blood flow to the vital organs during compressions. This will increase the probability of successfully resuscitating the patient. The MTV-100 regulator works well in conjunction with the AED as the oxygen is not free-flowing but is only delivered to the patient when the button on the regulator is pressed.

Documentation

All incidents and rescues, active or passive, must be recorded on an incident report form. This will provide a permanent record that can be used for liability issues, to debrief regarding an incident, and to improve the performance in case of future incidents. Both the lifeguard and the aquatics instructor should jointly complete the incident form for incidents that occur in physical education classes and by the lifeguard and coach for injuries that occur during practices or meets. This document should be given to the aquatics director after it is completed and signed. If the aquatics director is not in his office, it should be taped to his desk in front of the keyboard of his computer.

Emergency Action Plan Flow Chart

Emergency Incident

Aquatic Staff's Awareness

Primary rescuer's	Whistle	Alerts second rescuer	Whistle	Alerts third and fourth rescuer
Reaction **Nonprimary rescuer with 2-way radio alerts aquatics director and 101**				
Passive	Active	Passive	Active	
1. Activate EMS and rescue	1. Equipment	1. Confirm EMS activation via red strobe light	1. Deliver oxygen, AED, and first aid equipment to side of pool	1. Clear pool patrons to lobby area
2. Equipment rescue	2. Remove from water	2. Deliver oxygen, AED, and first aid equipment to side of pool; clear pool if no other rescuers are on duty	2. Clear pool patrons to lobby, if needed	2. Confirm EMS activation via red strobe light and red phone
3. Remove from water (spinal injury?)	3. Assess and administer oxygen	3. Assist with basic life support	3. Assist with basic life support	3. Assist with basic life support
4. Start life support using oxygen	4. Activate EMS, if necessary			4. Escort EMS upon arrival at east door of 25-yard pool
5. Use AED				5. Contact aquatics director
Basic life support continues; advanced life support begins		EMTs take over; contact aquatics director by radio, cell phone, or pager		

Incident Report for ALL Injuries and Rescues

Incident Report Form

Date of report: _____ Date of incident: _____ Time of incident: _____

Injured Party Personal Data

Name: _____ Age: _____ Gender: Male _____ Female _____

Address: _____ City: _____ State: _____ Zip: _____

University status: Student: _____   Faculty: _____   Staff: _____   Other: _____

Phone numbers: Home: _____ Work: _____ Cell: _____

Family contact (name, relationship, and phone number): _____

_____ (   )_____

Incident Data

Location of the incident: Deck: _____   25 yd pool: _____   50 m pool: _____   Sun deck: _____

Description of incident: _____

_____

_____

_____

Was injury sustained?   Yes _____   No _____

If yes, describe injury: _____

_____

_____

_____

Care Provided

Describe care given

Primary survey: airway, breathing, circulation, severe bleeding, spinal management (AED, oxygen, inline stabilization) _____

_____

_____

_____

Did victim refuse first-aid attention by staff?   Yes _____   No _____

Victim's signature for refusal of care: _____ Witness: _____

Primary guard who provided care: _____ Shift supervisor: _____

Name(s) of other lifeguards involved: _____

EMS activated?   Yes _____   No _____   Emergency transmitter? _____ Pool phone? _____

Time of activation: _____ Time of arrival of public safety: _____ Time of arrival of EMS: _____

Name of paramedic taking over care: _____ Time of taking over care: _____

Was the victim transported to an emergency facility?   Yes _____   No _____

Where? _____

Witnesses:

1. Name: _____

    Address: _____ City: _____ State: _____ Zip: _____

    University status: Student: _____   Faculty: _____   Staff: _____   Other: _____

    Phone numbers: Home: _____   Work: _____   Cell: _____

2. Name: _____

    Address: _____ City: _____ State: _____ Zip: _____

    University status: Student: _____   Faculty: _____   Staff: _____   Other: _____

    Phone numbers: Home: _____   Work: _____   Cell: _____

If victim was not transported to an emergency facility, did person return to activity?   Yes _____   No _____

Victim's signature: _____

Facility Data

Number of guards on duty at the time of the incident: _____   Number of patrons in pool: _____

Condition of water at time of incident: _____

Report prepared by: _____ Time: _____

Contact Larry Brown, Aquatics Director: Home (—) —-—; Page: —-— Time: _____

If not serious, by radio or voicemail—Time: _____

Appendix B

Safety Guidelines Finder

This finder has been divided into two types of activities—water-based activities and land-based activities. Use this finder to locate documents that provide safety information for the activity in question.

The Web sites listed in this finder will take you to a specific document. However, we all know that Web sites are constantly changing. Therefore, if you cannot find the Web site listed, you may wish to access the main Web page for the organization that provides the information. The main Web page (or home page) is the address listed in the Web site column *up to the first single slash* (/). For example, the main Web page for the site www.aca-camps.org/accreditation/stdsglance.htm is simply www.aca-camps.org.

Some of the information presented in this finder is available online while some is available for a fee. Look for the following symbols to determine the availability of the information.

   ⚲ = Available as a free download

   🔒 = Information available for a fee or must be ordered

The table also identifies what chapters in this book contain additional information on safety issues relevant to the activity. To more easily access the Web sites listed in this finder, go to the book's companion Web site at www.HumanKinetics.com/RiskManagementInSportAndRecreation. The password for this site is riskmanagementwebsites.

Water-Based Activities

Activity	Organization	Title and description	Web site	Availability	Chapter link
Aquatics	American Society for Testing and Materials (ASTM) Documents from ASTM are available for purchase. For more information regarding an ASTM standard or product please contact customer support at 610-832-9585 or via e-mail at service@astm.org.	"Standard Provisional Specification for Manufactured Safety Vacuum Release Systems (SVRS) for Swimming Pools, Spas, and Hot Tubs" "Standard Guide for Fences for Residential Outdoor Swimming Pools, Hot Tubs, and Spas" "Standard Performance Specification for Safety Covers and Labeling Requirements for All Covers for Swimming Pools, Spas, and Hot Tubs" "Standard Specification for Pool Alarms" Water Rescue: "Standard Guide for Performance of a Water Rescuer—Level 1" "Standard Guide for Performance of a Water Rescuer—Level II" "Standard Guide for Performance of an Ice Rescuer—Level II" "Standard Practice for Single Person Cold Water Survival/Rescue Technique: Help Position" "Standard Practice for Multiple-Person Cold Water Survival/Rescue Technique: Huddle Position"	www.astm.org/cgi-bin/ SoftCart.exe/NEWSITE_ JAVASCRIPT/index.shtml?L +mystore+gfqh3818+11190 41184	🔒	11
	American Academy of Pediatrics (AAP)	"Swimming Programs for Infants and Toddlers" "Prevention of Drowning in Infants, Children, and Adolescents"	www.aap.org/policy/ re9940.html	🔓	11
	American Camping Association (ACA) Standards for Accreditation of Camps	PA-1–PA-19 covers aquatics supervisor qualifications, supervision of activity leaders, lookouts, supervision ratios, safety regulations, emergency procedures, first-aid kits, wheelchair procedures, safety systems, participant classification, swimming pools, natural bodies of water, aquatic sites away from camp, camper supervision off-site, lifeguard qualifications, staff swimming, first aid and cardiopulmonary resuscitation (CPR), scuba diving, and swimming lessons	www.acacamps.org/ accreditation/ stdsglanceintro.php	🔒	11
Boating	ACA Standards for Accreditation of Camps	PA-20–PA-35 covers watercraft supervisor qualifications—youth, watercraft safety—adults, family, staff (the ACA states that all-adult groups, families, and staff groups must have an appropriately certified person or use Personal Flotation Devices [PFD], follow safety regulations, and use a checkout system), first aid and CPR, PFDs, personal watercraft, watercraft activity orientation, watercraft instruction, motorized watercraft training, watercraft maintenance, public providers of swimming, public providers of boating, aquatic sites away from camp, and camper supervision	www.acacamps.org/ accreditation/ stdsglanceintro.php	🔒	11
	National Outdoor Leadership School (NOLS)	"NOLS Backcountry Lightning Safety Guidelines"	www.nols.edu/resources/ research/pdfs/lightningsafety guideline.pdf	🔓	5
	National Lightning Safety Institute (NLSI)	"Boating Lightning Safety"	www.lightningsafety. com/nlsi_pls/boating.html	🔓	5
	AAP	"Personal Watercraft Use by Children and Adolescents"	http://aappolicy.aappubl ications.org/cgi/reprint/ pediatrics;105/2/452.pdf	🔓	5

Activity	Organization	Title and description	Web site	Availability	Chapter link
Fishing	NOLS	"NOLS Backcountry Lightning Safety Guidelines"	www.nols.edu/resources/research/pdfs/lightningsafety guideline.pdf	🔓	5
Parasailing	ASTM	Parachute aircraft standards	www.astm.org/cgi-bin/SoftCart.exe/NEWSITE_JAVASCRIPT/index.shtml?L+mystore+gfqh3818+1119041184	🔒	5
Rafting	NOLS	"NOLS Backcountry Lightning Safety Guidelines"	www.nols.edu/resources/research/pdfs/lightningsafety guideline.pdf	🔓	5

Go to www.HumanKinetics.com/RiskManagementInSportAndRecreation to find links to these resources, as well as links to new or updated safety guidelines, or to suggest links that could be added to the Web site. The password for the site is riskmanagementwebsites.

Land-Based Activities

Activity	Organization	Title and description	Web site	Availability	Chapter link
Adventure and challenge activities	ACA Standards for Accreditation of Camps	PC-1–PA-16 covers adventure and challenge supervisor qualifications, staff skill verification, supervision of activity leaders, operating procedures, adventure and challenge equipment, equipment maintenance, equipment access control, spotters and belayers, site control of access to adventure/ challenge activity areas, annual inspection, first aid, safety orientation, competency demonstration, protective headgear, and public providers of adventure and challenge activities	www.acacamps.org/accreditation/stdsglanceintro.php	🔒	
All-Terrain Vehicles (ATVs)	American Academy of Orthopaedic Surgeons (AAOS)	"All-Terrain Vehicles"	www.aaos.org/wordhtml/position.htm	🔓	
	ACA Standards for Accreditation of Camps	"ATV Safety"	www.acacamps.org/accreditation/stdsglanceintro.php		
	AAP	"All-Terrain Vehicle Injury Prevention: Two-, Three-, and Four-Wheeled Unlicensed Motor Vehicles"	www.aappolicy.aappublications.org/cgi/content/full/pediatrics;105/6/1352	🔓	
Archery	ASTM	"Standard Test Method for the Determination of Percent of Let-Off for Archery Bows" "Standard Specification for Classification and Marking of Single-Lens Scopes for Use with Archery Bows" "Standard Test Method for Determining the Force-Draw and Let-Down Curves for Archery Bows" "Standard Test Methods for Archery Bowstring Component-Serving String Material" "Standard Specification for Determining the Rating Velocities of an Archery Bow"	www.astm.org/cgi-bin/SoftCart.exe/NEWSITE_JAVASCRIPT/index.shtml?L+mystore+gfqh3818+1119041184	🔒	
	ACA Standards for Accreditation of Camps	"Target Sport Safety"	www.acacamps.org/accreditation/stdsglanceintro.php	🔒	
Badminton	ASTM	"Standard Specification for Eye Protectors for Selected Sports"	www.astm.org/cgi-bin/SoftCart.exe/NEWSITE_JAVASCRIPT/index.shtml?L+mystore+gfqh3818+1119041184	🔒	9

(continued)

Activity	Organization	Title and description	Web site	Availability	Chapter link
Baseball	ASTM	"Standard Test Methods for Measuring High-Speed Baseball Bat Performance Factor" "Standard Specification for Face Guards for Youth Baseball" "Test Method for Compression-Displacement of Baseballs and Softballs" "Standard Test Method for Measuring Baseball Bat Performance Factor" "Standard Test Method for Measuring the Coefficient of Restitution (COR) of Baseballs and Softballs" "Standard Specification for Eye Protectors for Selected Sports" "Standard Guide for Construction and Maintenance of Skinned Areas on Sports Fields"	www.astm.org/cgi-bin/ SoftCart.exe/NEWSITE_ JAVASCRIPT/index.shtml?L +mystore+gfqh3818+11190 41184	🔒	9
	National Collegiate Athletic Association (NCAA)	"2005-2006 NCAA Sports Medicine Handbook": "Guidelines for Helmet Fitting and Removal in Athletics" "Protective Equipment" "Eye Safety" "Mouth Guards"	www.ncaa.org/library/ sports_sciences/sports_ med_handbook/2005-06/ 2005-06_sports_medicine_ handbook.pdf	🔓	9
	AAOS	"The Risks of Shoulder and Elbow Injury from Participation in Youth Baseball" "Use of Breakaway Bases in Preventing Recreational Baseball and Softball Injuries"	www.aaos.org/wordhtml/ position.htm	🔓	9
	AAP	"Protective Eyewear for Young Athletes" "Risk of Injury From Baseball and Softball in Children"	http://aappolicy.aappubl ications.org/cgi/reprint/ pediatrics;113/3/619.pdf http://aappolicy.aappubl ications.org/cgi/reprint/ pediatrics;107/4/782.pdf	🔓	9
Basketball	ASTM	"Standard Specification for Residential Basketball Systems" "Standard Test Method for Shock Attenuating Properties of Materials Systems for Athletic Footwear" "Standard Specification for Eye Protectors for Selected Sports" "Standard Practice for Fitting Athletic Footwear"	www.astm.org/cgi-bin/ SoftCart.exe/NEWSITE_ JAVASCRIPT/index.shtml?L +mystore+gfqh3818+11190 41184	🔒	9
	NCAA	"2005-2006 NCAA Sports Medicine Handbook" "Protective Equipment" "Eye Safety" "Mouth Guards"	www.ncaa.org/library/ sports_sciences/sports_ med_handbook/2005-06/ 2005-06_sports_medicine_ handbook.pdf	🔓	9
	AAP	"Protective Eyewear for Young Athletes"	http://aappolicy.aappubl ications.org/cgi/reprint/ pediatrics;113/3/619.pdf	🔓	9

Activity	Organization	Title and description	Web site	Availability	Chapter link
Bicycling	ASTM	"Standard Specification for Helmets Used in Recreational Bicycling or Roller Skating" "Standard Specification and Test Method for Rear-Mounted Bicycle Child Carriers" "Standard Specification for Condition 3 Bicycle Forks" "Standard Specification for Bicycle Serial Numbers" "Standard Specification for Helmets Used for Down Hill Mountain Bicycle Racing" "Standard Specification for Helmets Used for BMX Cycling"	www.astm.org/cgi-bin/ SoftCart.exe/NEWSITE_ JAVASCRIPT/index.shtml?L +mystore+gfqh3818+11190 41184	🔒	9
	ACA Standards for Accreditation of Camps	"Protective Headgear"	www.acacamps.org/ accreditation/ stdsglanceintro.php	🔒	9
	AAOS	"Helmet Use by Motorcycle Drivers and Passengers and Bicyclists"	www.aaos.org/wordhtml/ position.htm	🔓	
	AAP	"Bicycle Helmets"	http://aappolicy.aappubl ications.org/cgi/reprint/ pediatrics;108/4/1030.pdf	🔓	
Boxing	ASTM	"Standard Test Method for Shock-Absorbing Properties of Playing Surface Systems and Materials"	www.astm.org/cgi-bin/ SoftCart.exe/NEWSITE_ JAVASCRIPT/index.shtml?L +mystore+gfqh3818+11190 41184	🔒	
	NCAA	"2005-2006 NCAA Sports Medicine Handbook": "Use of the Head as a Weapon in Football and Other Contact Sports" "Protective Equipment" "Eye Safety" "Mouth Guards"	www.ncaa.org/library/ sports_sciences/sports_ med_handbook/2005-06/ 2005-06_sports_medicine_ handbook.pdf	🔓	9
	AAP	"Participation in Boxing by Children, Adolescents, and Young Adults"	http://aappolicy.aappubl ications.org/cgi/reprint/ pediatrics;99/1/134.pdf	🔓	6
Camping	NOLS	"NOLS Backcountry Lightning Safety Guidelines"	www.nols.edu/resources/ research/pdfs/lightningsafety guideline.pdf	🔓	5
Cheerleading	ASTM	"Standard Test Method for Shock-Absorbing Properties of Playing Surface Systems and Materials" "Standard Test Method for Characterization of Gymnastic Landing Mats and Floor Exercise Surfaces" "Standard Specification for Basic Tumbling Mats" "Standards Safety Specification for Components, Assembly, Use, and Labeling of Consumer Trampolines"	www.astm.org/cgi-bin/ SoftCart.exe/NEWSITE_ JAVASCRIPT/index.shtml?L +mystore+gfqh3818+11190 41184	🔒	9

(continued)

Land-Based Activities (continued)

Activity	Organization	Title and description	Web site	Availability	Chapter link
Climbing	ASTM	"Standard Specification for Climbing and Mountaineering Carabiners" "Standard Specification for Climbing Harnesses" "Standard Specification for Labeling of Climbing and Mountaineering Equipment"	www.astm.org/cgi-bin/ SoftCart.exe/NEWSITE_ JAVASCRIPT/index.shtml?L +mystore+gfqh3818+11190 41184	🔒	
	ACA Standards for Accreditation of Camps	"Spotters and Belayers"	www.acacamps.org/ accreditation/ stdsglanceintro.php	🔒	
	NOLS	"NOLS Backcountry Lightning Safety Guidelines"	www.nols.edu/resources/ research/pdfs/lightningsafety guideline.pdf	🔓	5
Dirt biking	AAOS	"Helmet Use by Motorcycle Drivers and Passengers and Bicyclists"	www.aaos.org/wordhtml/ position.htm	🔓	
	AAP	"Bicycle Helmets"	http://aappolicy.aappubl ications.org/cgi/reprint/ pediatrics;108/4/1030.pdf	🔓	
	ACA Standards for Accreditation of Camps	"Protective Headgear"	www.acacamps.org/ accreditation/ stdsglanceintro.php	🔒	
	NOLS	"NOLS Backcountry Lightning Safety Guidelines"	www.nols.edu/resources/ research/pdfs/lightningsafety guideline.pdf	🔓	5
Field hockey	ASTM	"Standard Specification for Eye Protectors for Selected Sports" "Standard Test Method for Shock-Absorbing Properties of Playing Surface Systems and Materials"	www.astm.org/cgi-bin/ SoftCart.exe/NEWSITE_ JAVASCRIPT/index.shtml?L +mystore+gfqh3818+11190 41184	🔒	9
	NCAA	"2005-2006 NCAA Sports Medicine Handbook": "Use of the Head as a Weapon in Football and Other Contact Sports" "Guidelines for Helmet Fitting and Removal in Athletics" "Protective Equipment" "Eye Safety" "Mouth Guards"	www.ncaa.org/library/ sports_sciences/sports_ med_handbook/2005-06/ 2005-06_sports_medicine_ handbook.pdf	🔓	9

Activity	Organization	Title and description	Web site	Availability	Chapter link
Fitness	ASTM	"Consumer Safety Specification for Stationary Exercise Bicycles" "Standard Specification for Fitness Equipment" "Standard Specification for Fitness Equipment and Fitness Facility Safety Signage and Labels" "Standard Test Methods for Evaluating Design and Performance Characteristics of Selectorized Strength Equipment" "Standard Specification for Selectorized Strength Equipment" "Standard Test Methods for Evaluating Design and Performance Characteristics of Motorized Treadmills"	www.astm.org/cgi-bin/SoftCart.exe/NEWSITE_JAVASCRIPT/index.shtml?L+mystore+gfqh3818+1119041184	🔒	2
	American College of Sports Medicine (ACSM)	"Automated External Defibrillators in Health/Fitness Facilities"(joint statement with American Heart Association [AHA]) Position stand on progression models in resistance training for healthy adults Position stand on exercise and physical activity for older adults "Recommendations for Cardiovascular Screening, Staffing, and Emergency Policies at Health/Fitness Facilities"– (joint position statement with AHA) Position stand on heat and cold illnesses during distance running Position stand on exercise and fluid replacement	www.acsm.org/publications/positionStands.htm	🔒	4, 7, 2
	AAP	"Strength Training by Children and Adolescents" "Intensive Training and Sports Specialization in Young Athletes" "Promotion of Healthy Weight-Control Practices in Young Athletes"	http://aappolicy.aappublications.org/cgi/reprint/pediatrics;107/6/1470.pdf http://aappolicy.aappublications.org/cgi/reprint/pediatrics;106/1/154.pdf http://aappolicy.aappublications.org/cgi/reprint/pediatrics;97/5/752.pdf	🔓	2
Football	ASTM	"Standard Specification for Football Helmets" "Standard Test Method for Shock-Attenuation Characteristics of Protective Headgear for Football" "Standard Specification for Shock-Absorbing Properties of North American Football Field Playing Systems as Measured in the Field" "Standard Test Methods for Comprehensive Characterization of Synthetic Turf Playing Surfaces and Materials" "Standard Test Method for Shock-Absorbing Properties of Playing Surface Systems and Materials"	www.astm.org/cgi-bin/SoftCart.exe/NEWSITE_JAVASCRIPT/index.shtml?L+mystore+gfqh3818+1119041184	🔒	9
	NCAA	"2005-2006 NCAA Sports Medicine Handbook": "Protective Equipment" "Eye Safety" "Transparent Eye Shield" "Exception Procedure for Football" "Mouth Guards" "Use of the Head as a Weapon in Football and Other Contact Sports" "Guidelines for Helmet Fitting and Removal in Athletics"	www.ncaa.org/library/sports_sciences/sports_med_handbook/2005-06/2005-06_sports_medicine_handbook.pdf	🔓	9
	Gatorade Sports Science Institute	"2002 GSSI Guidelines on Heat Safety in Football"	www.gssiweb.com/reflib/refs/566/attackheatill.cfm?pf=1&CFID=965482&CFTOKEN=30127001	🔓	4

(continued)

Land-Based Activities *(continued)*

Activity	Organization	Title and description	Web site	Availability	Chapter link
Go-carts	ASTM	"Standard Specification for Bearing, Roller, Needle: Thick Outer Ring With Rollers and Cage" "Standard Specification for Safety and Performance of Fun-Karts" "Standard Practice for the Classification, Design, Manufacture, and Operation of Concession Go-Karts and Facilities" "Standard Safety Guide for Consumer Recreational Use of Fun-Karts"	www.astm.org/cgi-bin/ SoftCart.exe/NEWSITE_ JAVASCRIPT/index.shtml?L +mystore+gfqh3818+11190 41184	🔒	
	ACA Standards for Accreditation of Camps	"Go-Kart Safety"	www.acacamps.org/ accreditation/ stdsglanceintro.php	🔒	
Golf	NLSI	"A Lightning Safety Mandate for the Game of Golf"	http://www.lightningsafety.com/ nlsi_pls/golfsafetyrecomme nd.html	🔓	5, 7
Gymnastics	ASTM	"Standard Test Method for Characterization of Gymnastic Landing Mats and Floor Exercise Surfaces" "Standard Specification for Basic Tumbling Mats" "Standard Safety Specification for Components, Assembly, Use, and Labeling of Consumer Trampolines"	www.astm.org/cgi-bin/ SoftCart.exe/NEWSITE_ JAVASCRIPT/index.shtml?L +mystore+gfqh3818+11190 41184	🔒	
	NCAA	"2005-2006 NCAA Sports Medicine Handbook": "Use of Trampoline and Minitramp" "Protective Equipment" "Mouth Guards"	www.ncaa.org/library/ sports_sciences/sports_ med_handbook/2005-06/ 2005-06_sports_medicine_ handbook.pdf	🔓	9
	AAP	"Trampolines at Home, School, and Recreational Centers"	http://aappolicy.aappubl ications.org/cgi/reprint/ pediatrics;103/5/1053.pdf	🔓	
Handball	ASTM	"Standard Specification for Eye Protectors For Selected Sports"	www.astm.org/cgi-bin/ SoftCart.exe/NEWSITE_ JAVASCRIPT/index.shtml?L +mystore+gfqh3818+11190 41184	🔒	9
	NCAA	"2005-2006 NCAA Sports Medicine Handbook" "Protective Equipment" "Eye Safety"	www.ncaa.org/library/ sports_sciences/sports_ med_handbook/2005-06/ 2005-06_sports_medicine_ handbook.pdf	🔓	9
Hiking	NOLS	"NOLS Backcountry Lightning Safety Guidelines"	www.nols.edu/resources/ research/pdfs/lightningsafety guideline.pdf	🔓	5

Activity	Organization	Title and description	Web site	Availability	Chapter link
Hockey	ASTM	"Standard Guide for Ice Hockey Playing Facilities" "Standard Specification for Head and Face Protective Equipment for Ice Hockey Goal-tenders" "Standard Performance Specification for Ice Hockey Helmets" "Standard Safety Specification for Eye and Face Protective Equipment for Hockey Players"	www.astm.org/cgi-bin/ SoftCart.exe/NEWSITE_ JAVASCRIPT/index.shtml?L +mystore+gfqh3818+11190 41184	🔒	9
	NCAA	"2005-2006 NCAA Sports Medicine Handbook": "Use of the Head as a Weapon in Football and Other Contact Sports" "Guidelines for Helmet Fitting and Removal in Athletics" "Protective Equipment" "Eye Safety" "Mouth Guards"	www.ncaa.org/library/ sports_sciences/sports_ med_handbook/2005-06/ 2005-06_sports_medicine_ handbook.pdf	🔓	9
	AAP	"Safety in Youth Ice Hockey: The Effects of Body Checking"	http://aappolicy.aappubl ications.org/cgi/reprint/ pediatrics;105/3/657.pdf	🔓	9
Horse racing	ASTM	"Standard Specification for Body Protectors Used in Horse Sports and Horseback Riding" "Standard Specification for Protective Head-gear Used in Horse Sports and Horseback Riding"	www.astm.org/cgi-bin/ SoftCart.exe/NEWSITE_ JAVASCRIPT/index.shtml?L +mystore+gfqh3818+11190 41184	🔒	
Horseback riding	ASTM	"Standard Specification for Body Protectors Used in Horse Sports and Horseback Riding" "Standard Specification for Protective Head-gear Used in Horse Sports and Horseback Riding"	www.astm.org/cgi-bin/ SoftCart.exe/NEWSITE_ JAVASCRIPT/index.shtml?L +mystore+gfqh3818+11190 41184	🔒	
	ACA Standards for Accreditation of Camps	PH-1–PA-13 covers Supervisor qualifica-tions, supervision of riding staff, supervision ratios, riding equipment, classifying horses, horse suitability, riding facilities, safety regulations and emergency procedures, safety orientation, first aid, rider classifica-tion, rider apparel, and public providers of horseback riding.	http://acacamps.org/ accreditation/ stdsglanceintro.php	🔒	2
Hunting and sport shooting	NOLS	"NOLS Backcountry Lightning Safety Guide-lines"	www.nols.edu/resources/ research/pdfs/lightningsafety guideline.pdf	🔓	5
	ACA Standards for Accreditation of Camps	"Target Sport Safety"	www.acacamps.org/ accreditation/ stdsglanceintro.php	🔒	
Ice skating	ASTM	"Standard Specification for Helmets Used in Short Track Speed Ice Skating (Not to Include Hockey)"	www.astm.org/cgi-bin/ SoftCart.exe/NEWSITE_ JAVASCRIPT/index.shtml?L+m ystore+gfqh3818+1119041184	🔒	9
Inline skating	ASTM	"Standard Specifications for Helmets Used in Skateboarding and Trick Roller Skating" "Standard Specification for Helmets Used in Recreational Bicycling or Roller Skating"	www.astm.org/cgi-bin/ SoftCart.exe/NEWSITE_ JAVASCRIPT/index.shtml?L+m ystore+gfqh3818+1119041184	🔒	9
	AAOS	"Injuries From In-line Skating"	www.aaos.org/wordhtml/ position.htm	🔓	
	AAP	"In-line Skating Injuries in Children and Ado-lescents	http://aappolicy.aappublica tions.org/cgi/content/full/ pediatrics;101/4/720	🔓	

(continued)

Activity	Organization	Title and description	Web site	Availability	Chapter link
Lacrosse	ASTM	"Standard Specification for Eye Protectors for Selected Sports" "Standard Test Method for Shock-Absorbing Properties of Playing Surface Systems and Materials"	www.astm.org/cgi-bin/ SoftCart.exe/NEWSITE_ JAVASCRIPT/index.shtml?L +mystore+gfqh3818+11190 41184	🔒	9
	NCAA	"2005-2006 NCAA Sports Medicine Handbook": "Use of the Head as a Weapon in Football and Other Contact Sports" "Guidelines for Helmet Fitting and Removal in Athletics" "Protective Equipment" "Eye Safety" "Mouth Guards"	www.ncaa.org/library/ sports_sciences/sports_ med_handbook/2005-06/ 2005-06_sports_medicine_ handbook.pdf	🔓	9
Martial arts	ASTM	"Standard Test Method for Shock-Absorbing Properties of Playing Surface Systems and Materials"	www.astm.org/cgi-bin/ SoftCart.exe/NEWSITE_ JAVASCRIPT/index.shtml?L +mystore+gfqh3818+11190 41184	🔒	9
	NCAA	"2005-2006 NCAA Sports Medicine Handbook" "Protective Equipment" "Eye Safety" "Mouth Guards"	www.ncaa.org/library/ sports_sciences/sports_ med_handbook/2005-06/ 2005-06_sports_medicine_ handbook.pdf	🔓	9
Motorcycle racing	AAOS	"Helmet Use by Motorcycle Drivers and Passengers and Bicyclists"	www.aaos.org/wordhtml/ position.htm	🔓	
Motorcy-cling	AAOS	"Helmet Use by Motorcycle Drivers and Passengers and Bicyclists"	www.aaos.org/wordhtml/ position.htm	🔓	
	ACA Standards for Accreditation of Camps	"Protective Headgear"	www.acacamps.org/ accreditation/ stdsglanceintro.php	🔒	
Mountain-eering	ASTM	"Standard Specification for Climbing and Mountaineering Carabiners" "Standard Specification for Climbing Harnesses" "Standard Specification for Labeling of Climbing and Mountaineering Equipment"	www.astm.org/cgi-bin/ SoftCart.exe/NEWSITE_ JAVASCRIPT/index.shtml?L +mystore+gfqh3818+11190 41184	🔒	
	NOLS	"NOLS Backcountry Lightning Safety Guidelines"	www.nols.edu/resources/ research/pdfs/lightningsafety guideline.pdf	🔓	5
Paintball	ASTM	"Standard Specification for Paintball Markers (Limited Modes)" "Standard Test Method for Evaluating Paintball Barrier Netting" "Standard Specification for Paintball Marker Barrel Blocking Devices" "Standard Guide for Installation of Paintball Barrier Netting" "Standard Specification for Paintballs Used in the Sport of Paintball"	www.astm.org/cgi-bin/ SoftCart.exe/NEWSITE_ JAVASCRIPT/index.shtml?L +mystore+gfqh3818+11190 41184	🔒	

Activity	Organization	Title and description	Web site	Availability	Chapter link
Playground	ASTM	"Standard Guide for ASTM Standards on Playground Surfacing" "Standard Specification for Engineered Wood Fiber for Use as a Playground Safety Surface Under and Around Playground Equipment" "Standard Specification for Determination of Accessibility of Surface Systems Under and Around Playground Equipment" "Standard Consumer Safety Performance Specification for Playground Equipment for Public Use" "Standard Consumer Safety Performance Specification for Home Playground Equipment"	www.astm.org/cgi-bin/ SoftCart.exe/NEWSITE_ JAVASCRIPT/index.shtml?L +mystore+gfqh3818+11190 41184	🔒	10
	Consumer Product Safety Commission (CPSC)	Handbook for Public Playground Safety"	www.cpsc.gov/cpscpub/pubs/ 325.pdf	🔓	10
Racquetball	ASTM	"Standard Specification for Eye Protectors for Selected Sports"	www.astm.org/cgi-bin/ SoftCart.exe/NEWSITE_ JAVASCRIPT/index.shtml?L +mystore+gfqh3818+11190 41184	🔒	9
	NCAA	"2005-2006 NCAA Sports Medicine Handbook": "Eye Safety"	www.ncaa.org/library/ sports_sciences/sports_ med_handbook/2005-06/ 2005-06_sports_medicine_ handbook.pdf	🔓	9
Rodeo	ASTM	"Standard Specification for Body Protectors Used in Horse Sports and Horseback Riding" "Standard Specification for Protective Headgear Used in Horse Sports and Horseback Riding"	www.astm.org/cgi-bin/ SoftCart.exe/NEWSITE_ JAVASCRIPT/index.shtml?L +mystore+gfqh3818+11190 41184	🔒	
Roller skating	ASTM	"Standard Specifications for Helmets Used in Skateboarding and Trick Roller Skating" "Standard Specification for Helmets Used in Recreational Bicycling or Roller Skating"	www.astm.org/cgi-bin/ SoftCart.exe/NEWSITE_ JAVASCRIPT/index.shtml?L +mystore+gfqh3818+11190 41184	🔒	9
Rugby	ASTM	"Standard Test Method for Shock-Absorbing Properties of Playing Surface Systems and Materials"	www.astm.org/cgi-bin/ SoftCart.exe/NEWSITE_ JAVASCRIPT/index.shtml?L +mystore+gfqh3818+11190 41184	🔒	9
	NCAA	"2005-2006 NCAA Sports Medicine Handbook": "Use of the Head as a Weapon in Football and Other Contact Sports" "Protective Equipment" "Mouth Guards"	www.ncaa.org/library/ sports_sciences/sports_ med_handbook/2005-06/ 2005-06_sports_medicine_ handbook.pdf	🔓	9
Skateboarding	ASTM	"Standard Specifications for Helmets Used in Skateboarding and Trick Roller Skating"	www.astm.org/cgi-bin/ SoftCart.exe/NEWSITE_ JAVASCRIPT/index.shtml?L +mystore+gfqh3818+11190 41184	🔒	9
	AAP	"Skateboard and Scooter Injuries"	http://aappolicy.aappubl ications.org/cgi/reprint/ pediatrics;109/3/542.pdf	🔓	9

(continued)

Activity	Organization	Title and description	Web site	Availability	Chapter link
Sledding	ASTM	"Standard Specification for Helmets Used for Recreational Snow Sports"	www.astm.org/cgi-bin/ SoftCart.exe/NEWSITE_ JAVASCRIPT/index.shtml?L +mystore+gfqh3818+11190 41184	🔒	
	AAOS	"Sledding Safety"	www.aaos.org/wordhtml/ position.htm	🔓	
Snow-boarding	ASTM	"Standard Terminology Relating to Snow-boarding" "Standard Specification for Helmets Used for Recreational Snow Sports"	www.astm.org/cgi-bin/ SoftCart.exe/NEWSITE_ JAVASCRIPT/index.shtml?L +mystore+gfqh3818+11190 41184	🔒	9
	AAOS	"Helmet Use in Skiing and Snowboarding"	www.aaos.org/wordhtml/ position.htm	🔓	9
Snow skiing	ASTM	"Standard Practice for Selection of Release Torque Values for Alpine Ski Bindings" "Standard Practice for Functional Inspections and Adjustments of Alpine Ski/Binding/Boot Systems" "Specification for Ski Binding Test Devices" "Standard Test Method for Verification of Ski Binding Test Devices" "Standard Specification for Helmets Used for Recreational Snow Sports"	www.astm.org/cgi-bin/ SoftCart.exe/NEWSITE_ JAVASCRIPT/index.shtml?L +mystore+gfqh3818+11190 41184	🔒	9
	AAOS	"Helmet Use in Skiing"	www.aaos.org/wordhtml/ position.htm	🔓	9
Snow-mobiling	AAP	"Snowmobiling Hazards"	http://aappolicy.aappubl ications.org/cgi/reprint/ pediatrics;106/5/1142.pdf	🔓	
Soccer	ASTM	"Guide for Safer Use of Movable Soccer Goals" "Standard Safety and Performance Specification for Soccer Goals" "Standard Test Method for Shock-Absorbing Properties of Playing Surface Systems and Materials"	www.astm.org/cgi-bin/ SoftCart.exe/NEWSITE_ JAVASCRIPT/index.shtml?L +mystore+gfqh3818+11190 41184	🔒	9
	CPSC	Guidelines for movable soccer goal safety	www.cpsc.gov/cpscpub/prerel/ prhtml99/99106.html	🔓	9
	NCAA	"2005-2006 NCAA Sports Medicine Handbook": "Protective Equipment" "Mouth Guards"	www.ncaa.org/library/ sports_sciences/sports_ med_handbook/2005-06/ 2005-06_sports_medicine_ handbook.pdf	🔓	9

Activity	Organization	Title and description	Web site	Availability	Chapter link
Softball	ASTM	"Standard Specification for Eye Protectors for Selected Sports" "Test Method for Compression-Displacement of Baseballs and Softballs" "Standard Test Method for Measuring the Coefficient of Restitution (COR) of Baseballs and Softballs" "Standard Test Method for Measuring Softball Bat Performance Factor" "Standard Guide for Construction and Maintenance of Skinned Areas on Sports Fields"	www.astm.org/cgi-bin/ SoftCart.exe/NEWSITE_ JAVASCRIPT/index.shtml?L +mystore+gfqh3818+11190 41184	🔒	9
	NCAA	"2005-2006 NCAA Sports Medicine Handbook" "Protective Equipment" "Eye Safety" "Mouth Guards"	www.ncaa.org/library/ sports_sciences/sports_ med_handbook/2005-06/ 2005-06_sports_medicine_ handbook.pdf	🔓	9
	AAOS	"Use of Breakaway Bases in Preventing Recreational Baseball and Softball Injuries"	www.aaos.org/wordhtml/ position.htm	🔓	9
	AAP	"Risk of Injury From Baseball and Softball in Children"	http://aappolicy.aappubl ications.org/cgi/reprint/ pediatrics;107/4/782.pdf	🔓	9
Squash	ASTM	"Standard Specification for Eye Protectors for Selected Sports"	www.astm.org/cgi-bin/ SoftCart.exe/NEWSITE_ JAVASCRIPT/index.shtml?L +mystore+gfqh3818+11190 41184	🔒	
	NCAA	"2005-2006 NCAA Sports Medicine Handbook": "Eye Safety"	www.ncaa.org/library/ sports_sciences/sports_ med_handbook/2005-06/ 2005-06_sports_medicine_ handbook.pdf	🔓	9
Tennis	ASTM	"Standard Guide for Construction and Maintenance of Grass Tennis Courts" "Standard Practice for Construction of Chain Link Tennis Court Fence" "Standard Guide for Specifying Industrial and Commercial Chain Link Fence" "Standard Practice for Fitting Athletic Footwear"	www.astm.org/cgi-bin/ SoftCart.exe/NEWSITE_ JAVASCRIPT/index.shtml?L +mystore+gfqh3818+11190 41184	🔒	9
Track and field	ASTM	"Standard Specification for Pole Vault Landing Systems" "Standard Specification for Synthetic Surfaced Running Tracks"	www.astm.org/cgi-bin/ SoftCart.exe/NEWSITE_ JAVASCRIPT/index.shtml?L +mystore+gfqh3818+11190 41184	🔒	9
	ACSM	Position stand on heat and cold illnesses during distance running	http://www.acsm-msse.org/ pt/pt-core/template-journal/ msse/media/1296.pdf	🔓	9

(continued)

Land-Based Activities *(continued)*

Activity	Organization	Title and description	Web site	Availability	Chapter link
Trampolines	ASTM	"Standard Safety Specification for Components, Assembly, Use, and Labeling of Consumer Trampolines"	www.astm.org/cgi-bin/ SoftCart.exe/NEWSITE_ JAVASCRIPT/index.shtml?L +mystore+gfqh3818+11190 41184	🔒	
	NCAA	"2005-2006 NCAA Sports Medicine Handbook": "Use of Trampoline and Minitramp"	www.ncaa.org/library/ sports_sciences/sports_ med_handbook/2005-06/ 2005-06_sports_medicine_ handbook.pdf	🔓	
	AAOS	"Trampolines and Trampoline Safety"	www.aaos.org/wordhtml/ position.htm	🔓	
	AAP	"Trampolines at Home, School, and Recreational Centers"	http://aappolicy.aappubl ications.org/cgi/reprint/ pediatrics;103/5/1053.pdf	🔓	
Wrestling	ASTM	"Standard Specification for Competition Wrestling Mats" "Standard Test Method for Shock-Absorbing Properties of Playing Surface Systems and Materials"	www.astm.org/cgi-bin/ SoftCart.exe/NEWSITE_ JAVASCRIPT/index.shtml?L +mystore+gfqh3818+11190 41184	🔒	9
	ACSM	Position stand on weight loss in wrestlers.	http://www.acsm-msse.org/ pt/pt-core/template-journal/ msse/media/0696b.pdf	🔒	
	NCAA	"2005-2006 NCAA Sports Medicine Handbook": "Skin Infections in Wrestling" "Weight Loss—Dehydration" "Mouth Guards" "Protective Equipment"	www.ncaa.org/library/ sports_sciences/sports_ med_handbook/2005-06/ 2005-06_sports_medicine_ handbook.pdf	🔓	4, 9

These guidelines, recommendations, and standards do not purport to address all of the safety concerns associated with each activity. It is the responsibility of the user of these guidelines, recommendation, and standards to establish appropriate safety and health practices and determine the applicability of regulatory limitations prior to use.

Go to www.HumanKinetics.com/RiskManagementinSportandRecreation to find links to these resources, as well as links to new or updated safety guidelines, or to suggest links that could be added to the Web site. The password for this site is riskmanagementwebsites.

References

American Academy of Orthopaedic Surgeons. 1991. *Athletic training and sports medicine*. Chicago: American Academy of Orthopaedic Surgeons.

American Camping Association. 2003. ACA's position paper on a national criminal background check system. Retrieved from the World Wide Web on May 24, 2005: www.acacamps.org/publicpolicy/bcposition.htm.

American College of Sports Medicine. 1996. Position stand on exercise and fluid replacement. *Medicine and Science in Sports and Exercise* 28: i-vii.

American College of Sports Medicine. 1997. *Health/fitness facility standards and guidelines*. 2d ed. Champaign, IL: Human Kinetics.

American College of Sports Medicine. 2000. *Guidelines for exercise testing and prescription*. 6th ed. Baltimore: Lippincott Williams and Wilkins.

American College of Sports Medicine. *2003-2004 NCAA Sports Medicine Handbook*. Retrieved from the World Wide Web on May 24, 2005: www.ncaa.org/library/sports_sciences/sports_med_handbook/2003-04/index.html.

American Heart Association/American College of Sports Medicine. 1998. Scientific statement: recommendations for cardiovascular screening, staffing and emergency policies at health/fitness facilities. *Circulation* 97: 2283-2293.

American Red Cross. 1995. *Community water safety*. St. Louis: Mosby Lifeline.

American Red Cross. 1997. *Sport safety training handbook*. St. Louis: Mosby Lifeline.

American Red Cross. 2001. *First aid/CPR/AED program: participant's booklet*. St. Louis: Mosby Lifeline.

Andersen, J.C., R.W. Courson, D.M. Kleiner, and T.A. McLoda. 2002. National Athletic Trainers' Association position statement: emergency planning in athletics. *Journal of Athletic Training* 37(1): 99-104.

Appenzeller, H. (ed.). 1998. *Risk management in sport*. Durham, NC: Carolina Academic Press.

Appenzeller, H., and T.L. Seidler. 1998. Emergency action plan: expecting the unexpected. In *Risk management in sport: issues and strategies*, ed. H. Appenzeller, 297-309. Durham, NC: Carolina Academic Press.

Atcovitz v. Gulph Mills Tennis Club, Inc., 766 A.2d 1280 (Sup.Ct. Pa. 2001).

Balady, G.J., B. Chaitman, C. Foster, et al. 2002. American Heart Association/American College of Sports Medicine joint position statement: automated external defibrillators in health/fitness facilities. *Med. Sci. Sports Exerc*. 34(3): 561-564.

Bar-Or, O. 1994. Children's responses to exercise in hot climates: implications for performance and health. *Gatorade Sports Science Exchange* 7(2): 1-6.

Bauman, A. 1995. The epidemiology of heat stroke and associated thermoregulatory disorders. In *Exercise and Thermoregulation*, ed. J.R. Sutton, M.W. Thompson, and M.E. Torode, 203-208. Sydney: University of Sydney.

Becker, L., M. Eisenberg, C. Fahrenbruch, and L. Cobb. 1998. Public locations of cardiac arrest: implications for public access defibrillation. *Circulation* 97: 2106-2109.

Bier v. City of New Philadelphia, 464 N.E.2d 147 (Ohio 1984).

Board v. Earls, 536 U.S. 822 (2002).

Bonanno, D., and N. Dougherty (eds.). 1998. Emergency action plans. In *Safety notebook 3*, 1-3. Reston, VA: American Association for Active Lifestyles and Fitness.

Brown v. Southern Ventures Corporation, 331 So.2d 207 (La. App. 3 Cir. 1976).

Bryant, C.X., and J.A. Peterson. 1998. Becoming heat acclimated. *Fitness Management* 14(8): 50-52.

Byrd v. State, 614 N.Y.S.2d 446, 447 (N.Y.A.D. 1994).

Cal. Civ. Code §1714.21 (2005).

Cal. Health & Safety Code §1797.196 (2005).

Cater, et al. v. City of Cleveland, 83 Ohio St.3d 24; 697 N.E.2d 610 (Ohio 1998).

Centers for Disease Control and Prevention. 1991. Preventing lead poisoning in young children: a statement by the centers for disease control. Retrieved from the World Wide Web on June 20, 2005: http://aepo-xdv-www.epo.cdc.gov/wonder/prevguid/p0000029/p0000029.asp#head001000000000000

Centers for Disease Control and Prevention. 2000. Behavioral risk factor surveillance system. Retrieved from the World Wide Web on May 24, 2005: www.cdc.gov/brfss.

Centers for Disease Control and Prevention. 2002. Nonfatal sports and recreation-related injuries treated in emergency departments – United States, July 2000-June 2001. *Morbidity and Mortality Weekly Report*. August 23, 2002: 51(33), 736-740.

Centers for Disease Control and Prevention. 2003. Web-based injury statistics query and reporting system.

Retrieved from the World Wide Web on May 24, 2005: www.cdc.gov/ncipc/wisqars.

Centers for Disease Control and Prevention. 2004a. Water-related injuries: fact sheet. Retrieved from the World Wide Web on May 24, 2005: www.cdc.gov/ncipc/factsheets/drown.htm.

Centers for Disease Control and Prevention. 2004b. Boating safety. Retrieved from the World Wide Web on May 24, 2005: www.cdc.gov/ncipc/duip/safeboatingweek.htm.

Centers for Disease Control and Prevention. 2004c. Extreme heat: a prevention guide to promote your personal health and safety. Retrieved from the World Wide Web on May 24, 2005: www.bt.cdc.gov/disasters/extremeheat/heat_guide.asp.

Cherington, M. 2001. Lightning injuries in sports: situations to avoid. *Sports Medicine* 31(4): 301-308.

Clement, A. 1998. In *Law in sport and physical activity*. 2d ed. Aurora, OH: Sport and Law Press.

Clement, A. 2003. Legal liability and risk management. In *The complete swimming pool reference*. 2d ed., ed. T. Griffiths, 343-358. Champaign, IL: Sagamore.

Coalition of Americans to Protect Sports. 1991. *Sports injury risk management and the keys to safety*. North Palm Beach, FL: Author.

Connaughton, D.P. 2001. Crisis management. In *Law for Recreation and Sport Managers*. 3d ed., ed. D.J. Cotten, J.T. Wolohan, and T.J. Wilder, 341-351. Dubuque, IA: Kendall/Hunt.

Connaughton, D.P., and J.O. Spengler. 2000. Negligence liability in public swimming pool operations: a review of case law involving supervision. *Journal of Legal Aspects of Sport* 10(3): 154-171.

Consumer Product Safety Commission. 1989. Review of low-level lead toxicology. Memo from B.C. Lee to S.C. Eberle.

Consumer Product Safety Commission. 1990. Revision of the CPSC 0.06% lead in paint standard. Memo from B.C. Lee to S.C. Eberle. Tab C in Briefing Package OS #4367.

Consumer Product Safety Commission. 1992a. Notice of regulatory investigation requesting information concerning limits for lead in paint. Briefing Package OS # 4367.

Consumer Product Safety Commission. 1992b. Regulatory investigation: lead in paint. *Federal Register* 57: 18418.

Consumer Product Safety Commission. 1996. CPSC staff recommendations for identifying and controlling lead paint on public playground equipment. Retrieved from the World Wide Web on May 24, 2005: www.cpsc.gov/cpscpub/pubs/lead/6006.html.

Cooper, M.A., R.L. Holle, and R.E. Lopez. 1999. Recommendations for lightning safety. *Journal of American Medical Association* 282(12): 1132-1133.

Corda v. Brook Valley Enterprises, Inc., 306 S.E 2d 173 (N.C. App. 1983).

Department of Health and Human Services. 2001. *Monitoring the future: national results on adolescent drug use, overview of key findings 2000* (BKD 411).

Department of Health and Human Services and General Services Administration. 2001. Guidelines for public access defibrillation programs in federal facilities. Retrieved from the World Wide Web on May 24, 2005: http://frwebgate.access.gpo.gov/cgi-bin/getdoc.cgi?dbname=2001_register&docid=01-12939-filed.

Department of Housing and Human Development. 1995. Guidelines for the evaluation and control of lead-based paint hazards in housing. Retrieved from the World Wide Web on June 20, 2005: www.hud.gov/offices/lead/guidelines/hudguidelines/index.cfm.

Department of Justice Bureau of Justice Statistics. 1994. *Drugs and Crime Facts* 19.

Department of Labor. 1991. OSHA regulations (standards—29 CFR) bloodborne pathogens—1910.1030. *Federal Register* 56(235), 64175-64182.

DeVivo, M.J., and P. Sekar. 1997. Prevention of spinal cord injuries that occur in swimming pools. *Spinal Cord* 35: 509-515.

Dougherty, N.J. (ed.). 2002. *Principles of safety in physical education and sport*. Reston, VA: National Association for Sport and Physical Education.

Dougherty, N.J., A.S. Goldberger, & L.J. Carpenter. 2002. *Sport, Physical Activity, and the Law*. Champaign, IL: Sagamore.

Dougherty, R.J. 1987. Controversies regarding urine testing. *Journal of Substance Abuse Treatment*, 4(2): 115-117.

Durkin, H. 1998. OSHA standards protect health club staff from bloodborne pathogens. *ACSM's Health & Fitness Journal* (2): 40-41.

Eickhoff-Shemek, J.M. 1996. Opinions of ACSM professional members regarding selected ACSM health/fitness facility standards. Doctoral dissertation, University of Nebraska-Lincoln. *Dissertation Abstracts International* (56): 4699.

Eickhoff-Shemek, J.M., and J.K. Scheer. 1997. Thumbs up or down on facility standards. *ACSM's Health & Fitness Journal*, (1): 21-30.

Ellis and Associates, Inc. 2004. Automatic external defibrillator (AED) policy. Retrieved from the World Wide Web on June 6, 2005:www.jellis.com/news/aed/index.htm.

Environmental Protection Agency. 1996. Lead, requirements for lead-based paint activities in target housing and child-occupied facilities, final rule. *Federal Register* 61: 45778.

Federation of International De Football Association. 1993. *Laws of the Game: Guide for Referees*.

First Overseas Investment Corp. v. Cotton, 491 So.2d 293 (Fla. App. 3 Dist. 1986).

Fitness Products Council. 1999. *Tracking the fitness movement*. North Palm Beach, FL: Sporting Goods Manufacturers Association.

Fulala, P.J., et. al. 1994. An examination of current and proposed drug-testing policies at U.S. colleges and universities. *Journal of American College Health* 42(6): 267-270.

Gabriel, J.L. (1992). *Diving safety: a position paper.* 2d ed. Indianapolis: United States Diving.

Gabrielsen, M.A. (ed.). 1987. *Swimming pools: a guide to their planning, design, and operation.* 4th ed. Champaign, IL: Human Kinetics.

Garner, B.A. (ed.). 2000. *Black's law dictionary.* 7th ed. St. Paul, MN: West Publishing.

Gatorade Sports Science Institute. 2002. 2002 GSSI guidelines on heat safety in football: attacking heat-related death and illness in football players. Retrieved from the World Wide Web on May 24, 2005: http://www.gssiweb.com/reflib/refs/566/attackheatill.cfm.

Gisolfi, C.V. 1996. Preparing your athletes for competition in hot weather. Coaches Corner: Gatorade Sports Science Institute. Retrieved from the World Wide Web on May 24, 2005: http://www.gssiweb.com/reflib/refs/97/d000000020000003c.cfm?pid=38.

Glass, S.C. 1996. Exercise in the heat: physiological consequences, acclimatization and prescription guidelines. *ACSM Certified News* 6(1): 1-3.

Gray, G.R. 1991. Risk management planning: conducting a sport risk assessment to enhance program safety. *Journal of Physical Education, Recreation and Dance* 62: 29-31, 78.

Griffiths, T. 2003. *The complete swimming pool reference.* 2d ed. Champaign, IL: Sagamore.

Hames v. State, 808 S.W.2d 41 (Tenn. 1991).

Herbert, D.L. 1992. *The standards book for exercise programs.* Canton, OH: Professional Reports.

Herbert, D.L. 1997. Legal implications of ACSM's new facility standards and guidelines. *Fitness Management* (13) 20.

Herbert, D.L., and W.G. Herbert. 1993. *Legal aspects of preventive and rehabilitative exercise programs.* 3d ed. Canton, OH: Professional Reports.

Herbert, D.L., W.G. Herbert, and S.M. Collins-Berger. 1988. A trial lawyer's guide to the legal implications of recreational, preventive and rehabilitative exercise program standards of care. *American Journal of Trial Advocacy* 11: 433-456.

Hessert, K. 1998. The 1998 Hessert sports crisis survey. Retrieved from the World Wide Web on June 6, 2005: www.sportsmediachallenge.com/links/1098.html.

Inter-Association Task Force on Exertional Heat Illnesses. 2003. Inter-association task force on exertional heat illnesses consensus statement. Retrieved from the World Wide Web on June 6, 2005: www.the-aps.org/news/consensus.pdf#search='Inter%20Association%20Task%20Heat.

International Health, Racquet and Sportsclub Association. 2003. Automated external defibrillators (AEDs). Retrieved from the World Wide Web on May 24, 2005: http://cms.ihrsa.org/IHRSA/viewPage.cfm?pageId=593.

International Life Saving Federation. 1999. ILSF policy statement no.3: statement on automatic external defibrillation use by lifesavers and lifeguards. Retrieved from the World Wide Web on June 22, 2005: www.ilsf.org/medical/policy_03.htm.

Irick, J.F. 2001. Wrongful death decisions interpreted. *The Indiana Lawyer*, Vol. 4.

Kearns, C. 1990. Drowning and near drowning: the magnitude of the problem in Florida and why it happens. *The Florida EMS Newsletter* October: 1-3. Tallahassee, FL: Office of Emergency Medical Services.

Kids Sports Network. 2004. Criminal background checks. Retrieved from the World Wide Web on May 24, 2005: www.ksnusa.org/cbc.htm.

King v. University of Indianapolis et al., 2002 U.S. Dist. LEXIS 19070.

Kithil, R. 2000. An overview of lightning detection equipment. Retrieved from the World Wide Web on May 24, 2005: www.lightningsafety.com/nlsi_lhm/ewc9.html.

Kleinknecht v. Gettysburg College, 989 F.2d 1360 (1992).

Knochel, J.P. 1975. Dog days and psoriasis: how to kill a football player. *Journal of American Medical Association* 233: 513-515.

Kucharson, M. 2004. Please report to the principal's office, urine trouble: the effect of *Board of Education v. Earls* on America's schoolchildren. *Education Law Reporter* 37: 131.

Locilento v. John A. Coleman Catholic High School, 523 N.Y.S.2d 198 (N.Y.A.D. 3 Dept. 1987).

Maloy, B.P. 2001. Safe environment. In Cotten, D.J., Wolohan, J.T., & Wilde, T J. (Eds.), *Law for recreation and sport managers* (pp. 105-117). Dubuque, IA: Kendall/Hunt.

Maussner v. Atlantic City Country Club, Inc., 691 A.2d 826 (N.J. 1997).

Mawdsley, R., and C. Russo. 2003. Drug testing for school extracurricular activities. *Education Law Reporter* 173: 1.

McGregor, I., and J. MacDonald. 1990. *Risk management manual for sport and recreation organizations.* Corvallis, OR: National Intramural Recreational Sports Association.

Miller v. United States, 597 F.2d 614 (7th Cir. 1979).

Mogabgab v. Orleans Parish School Board, 239 So.2d 456 (La. App. 4th Cir. 1970).

Murray, R., and R. Eichner. 2003. Preventing heat illness: keeping athletes from falling into danger zones. Gatorade Sports Science Institute. Retrieved from the World Wide Web on May 24, 2005: www.gssiweb.com/reflib/refs/570/prevheatill.cfm?pid=38.

Murray, R., R. Eichner, and J. Stofan. 2003. Hyponatremia in athletes. Gatorade Sports Science Institute. Retrieved from the World Wide Web on June 5, 2005: www.gssiweb.com/reflib/refs/604/SSE_88_Content.cfm?pid=38.

Napolitano, F. 1997. What do lawn mower safety and Par-Q have in common? *ACSM's Health & Fitness Journal* 1: 38-39.

National Center for Early Defibrillation. 2004. Understanding medical directions. Retrieved from the World Wide Web on May 24, 2005: www.early-defib.org/03_06_03.html.

National Clearinghouse on Child Abuse and Neglect Information. 2004. What is child abuse and neglect? Retrieved from the World Wide Web on May 24, 2005: nccanch.acf.hhs.gov/pubs/factsheets/whatiscan.cfm.

National Federation of State High School Associations. 1994-95. *National Federation Edition-Soccer Rules Book*.

National Institutes of Health. 1992. Conference on sports injuries in youth: surveillance strategies. NIH publication no. 93-3444. Bethesda, MD: National Institute of Health.

National Lightning Safety Institute. N.d. Lightning safety in NLSI's home town. Retrieved from the World Wide Web on May 24, 2005: www.lightningsafety.com/nlsi_pls/lsvl_plans.html.

National Safe Kids Campaign. 2004. Injury facts: drowning. Retrieved from the World Wide Web on May 24, 2005: www.safekids.org/tier3_cd.cfm?folder_id=540&content_item_id=1032.

National Weather Service. N.d. Heat wave: a major summer killer. Retrieved from the World Wide Web on February 23, 2005: www.nws.noaa.gov/om/brochures/heat_wave.shtml.

Office of National Drug Control Policy. 2005. Prevention. Retrieved from the World Wide Web on March 30, 2005: www.whitehousedrugpolicy.gov/prevent/index.html.

Osinski, A. 1990. The complete aquatic guide. *Parks and Recreation* 25: 36-43.

Peterson, J.A., & B.B. Hronek. 1997. *Risk management for park, recreation, and leisure services* (3rd ed.). Champaign, IL: Sagamore.

Phelan, K.J., J. Khoury, H.J. Kalkwarf, and B.P. Lanphear. 2001. Trends and patterns of playground injuries in United States children and adolescents. *Ambulatory Pediatrics* 1(4): 227-233.

Rabinoff, M.A. 1998. Pounds of prevention. *Athletic Business* 22: 41-47.

Schultz, S.J., S.M. Zinder, and T.C. Valovich. 2001. *Sports medicine handbook*. Indianapolis: National Federation of State High School Associations.

Sobo, G. 1998. Look before you leap: can the emergence of the open and obvious danger defense save diving from troubled waters? *Syracuse Law Review* 49: 175-211.

Soccer Industry Council of America. 1994. *National Soccer Participation Survey*.

Spengler, J.O., and D.P. Connaughton. 2001. Automated external defibrillators in sport and recreation settings: an analysis of immunity provisions in state legislation. *Journal of Legal Aspects of Sport* 11(1): 51-67.

Superville, D. 2003. Survey: few tested for drug dependence. *Waco Tribune Herald* 108.

Thanel, F. 1998. Near drowning: rescuing patients through education as well as treatment. *Post Graduate Medicine* 103: 144-153.

Tinsworth D., and J. McDonald. 2001. *Special study: injuries and deaths associated with children's playground equipment*. Washington: U.S. Consumer Product Safety Commission.

U.S. Public Interest Research Group, The Consumer Federation of America. 2002. *Playing it safe: a fifth nationwide survey of public playgrounds*. Retrieved from the World Wide Web on May 24, 2005: www.consumerfed.org/pdfs/2000factsheet.pdf.

United States Lifesaving Association. 2004. 2000-2004 National lifesaving statistics. Retrieved from the World Wide Web on May 24, 2005: www.usla.org/Statistics/current.asp?Statistics=5.

van der Smissen, B. 1990. *Legal liability and risk management for public and private entities*, volume 2. Cincinnati: W.H. Anderson.

Vernonia School District 47J v. Acton, 515 U.S. 646 (1995).

Walsh, K.M., B. Bennett, M.A. Cooper, R.L. Holle, R. Kithil, and R.E. Lopez. 2000. National Athletic Trainers' Association position statement: lightning safety for athletics and recreation. *Journal of Athletic Training* 35(4): 471-477.

Zeigler, T.A. 1997. *Management of bloodborne infections in sport: a practical guide for sports health care providers and coaches*. Champaign, IL: Human Kinetics.

About the Authors

John O. Spengler, JD, PhD, has both a law degree and a PhD in recreation administration. He has published more than 30 scholarly and practitioner-based journal articles and has written two other texts in the areas of sport, recreation, and law. He has also served as a safety consultant in recreation and sport.

Dr. Spengler is a research fellow with the American Alliance for Health, Physical Education, Recreation and Dance (AAHPERD) and was named the University of Florida College of Health and Human Performance Teacher of the Year. He is currently an associate professor in the department of tourism, recreation and sport management.

Daniel P. Connaughton, EdD, is an associate professor in the college of Health and Human Performance at the University of Florida. He holds four degrees in the fields of sport, recreation, and exercise science. An experienced participant, coach, administrator, and educator of many sports, recreation, and aquatic activities, he has more than 50 publications in scholarly and practitioner-based journals regarding legal, risk management, and safety issues of sport, recreation, and exercise science.

Dr. Connaughton has served as a consultant on safety issues involving sports, recreation, physical education, aquatics, diving, and fitness and health club activities. He also holds several professional certifications, including emergency medical technician, American College of Sports Medicine health/fitness instructor, National Strength and Conditioning Association certified strength and conditioning specialist, certified park

and recreation professional, American Sport Education Program certified coach, certified pool operator, and several American Red Cross aquatic certifications.

Andrew T. Pittman, PhD, is the coordinator of the sport management program at Baylor University in Waco, Texas. He has coauthored a casebook on sport law and authored or coauthored six chapters in a sport law text. He has also written numerous journal articles on risk management and sport law and has presented more than 50 times at international, national, regional, and state conferences primarily in the area of risk management and sport law.

Pittman has held numerous positions in the Sport and Recreation Law Association, among them president, treasurer, and newsletter editor. He is currently the Law Section editor for the *Journal of Physical Education, Recreation & Dance* and is a member of the Sport Management Council of the National Association for Sport and Physical Education. He has received several awards, including the Faculty Achievement Award from Baylor's School of Education in 2003.

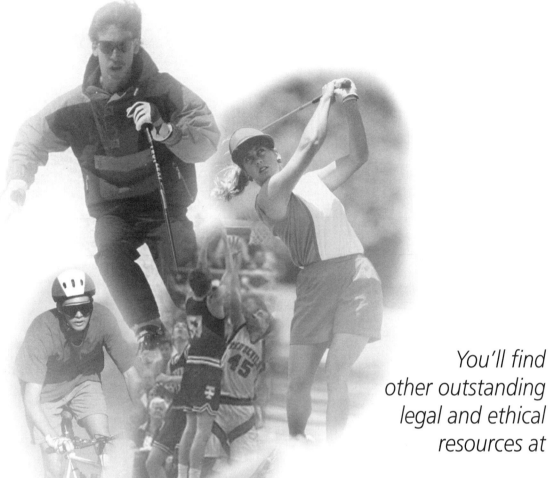